Wingshooter's Guide to

KANSAS

Upland Birds and Waterfowl

TITLES AVAILABLE IN THIS SERIES

Wingshooter's Guide to Arizona

Wingshooter's Guide to Idaho

Wingshooter's Guide to Iowa

Wingshooter's Guide to Montana

Wingshooter's Guide to North Dakota

Wingshooter's Guide to South Dakota

Wingshooter's Guide to

KANSAS

Upland Birds and Waterfowl

Web Parton

Wilderness
Adventures
Press

Gallatin Gateway, Montana

This book was made with an easy opening, lay flat binding.

Published by Wilderness Adventures Press
P.O. Box 627
Gallatin Gateway, MT 59730
800-925-3339
Website: www.wildadv.com
email: books@wildadv.com

10 9 8 7 6 5 4 3 2 1

Printed in the United States of America

Library of Congress Cataloging-in-Publication Data

Parton, William W.
    Wingshooter's guide to Kansas : upland birds and waterfowl / Web Parton
        p.   cm.
    Includes bibliographical references and index.
    ISBN 1-885106-59-9 (alk. paper)
    1. Upland game bird shooting—Kansas—Guidebooks. 2. Waterfowl shooting—Kansas—Guidebooks. 3. Kansas—Guidebooks.   I. Title.
SK323.P375   1998
799.2'4'09781—dc21   98-21692
                                                                                    CIP

Table of Contents

Foreword

At a time when I hoped there would be more time, Gene Hill graciously agreed to write the foreword to this book.

Let me start by saying that as a young person, I read every book with the name "Hill" on it. The name didn't belong to a mere mortal. He wrote about things that were beyond me. I was a ragged kid chasing a ragged setter after topknot quail and cinnamon teal. He talked about woodcock, black ducks, kudu, elk, and elephants. He described double guns with an affection that caused me to try and keep the mud wiped off my 12-gauge pump. He showed me through his words that others shared the undeniable force driving me; there *were* others.

With Gene's passing, I am left with a deep sense of loss: the places he had been and seen, the people he had known, and the things he had done. His was a mind that the world suffered in losing. I will not compound this loss by attempting to replace him on these pages.

The times I spent with him will remain high points of my life. Although he was a man I had looked up to all of my life, he never treated me as anything other than an equal. I was curious about why he had initially chosen to have lunch with me, so I asked him how he felt about people seeking him out—specifically, about the loss of anonymity that comes when a person achieves some measure of notoriety. Gene's comment was, "No good can come of it." Yet, he made time for me.

My wife picked up a little book of Zen sayings, one of those tidy little gift concepts that some writer who needed money and a publisher who knew it was a proven money-maker knocked out. Just the kind of thing I needed in order to procrastinate when I'm sitting at the computer and nothing is coming. One quote by Kierkegaard touched me, "Life can be understood backwards but it must be lived forwards." So, looking backwards, let me tell you a story.

Sometime in early December, several years ago, a friend and I were going south to hunt Mearns' quail. We stopped at a restaurant along the freeway in Tucson to have breakfast. We were finishing our meal and chatting when a gentleman walked up to the register across the room. He was wearing a sports jacket, attire contrary to the uniform of Southern Arizona casual. One of us said, "That looks like Gene Hill." We both studied this person. My friend mentioned that he once saw Gene Hill give a talk and "he really looks like Gene Hill." I said something profound like, "What would Gene Hill be doing here?" As we debated the possibility of a Gene Hill sighting in Tucson, "Gene Hill" paid his bill, walked out the door, got in a car and drove away.

The conversation at our table changed. I made another profound statement like, " I wonder if that was Gene Hill?" My friend said, "It sure looked like Gene Hill." One of us said, "We should have gone up and introduced ourselves and seen if that was Gene Hill." This topic came up sporadically for the next few weeks.

In early spring of the following year, I had a morning appointment in Tucson, which is the better part of an hour's drive from the little town we live in. I don't remember the specifics other than that I was wearing civilian clothes and had some of my bronze dog sculptures with me. By civilian clothes, I mean to say that I was a little more dressed up than normal (no dried dog slobber crust showing). I got home at midday and my first stop was supposed to be at our local convenience store. We had sold the trailer we had lived in before moving into our present home, and the person who bought it worked at this store. Our arrangement was that I picked up the payment on the first of the month.

Short-term memory has never been my strong suit, so my trips to town are organized with a set of objectives listed on a post-it note pad. Two tasks were left undone when I returned home: first, pick up the payment; second, check mail at the post office. My mind being elsewhere, as usual, I drove right by the convenience store. Catching the error as the store flashed by, I tried to stop. However, a car was behind me and by the time this obstacle was gone, I was well past the store. I almost made a U-turn twice, but then decided that I would just backtrack after going to the post office.

The parking lot at the post office was crowded with midday traffic, and I didn't pay much attention as I bopped in to check my box. I pushed through the glass front doors and was taken aback. In front of me, going through some mail at a side counter, stood "Gene Hill." I walked past this apparition to our box, all the while the familiar dialog going through my head, "That sure looks like Gene Hill, that can't be Gene Hill, what would Gene Hill be doing here?" I turned from the inside of the lobby and walked out the doors. "Yes, that could be Gene Hill...I wonder if it is Gene Hill?" I am a little ashamed to admit that I went back in a second time to "double check" the box.

I came back out and sat in the cab of the truck, thinking to myself, "I would sure feel foolish if it wasn't Gene Hill." I screwed up my courage to introduce myself, took a deep breath, grabbed the door handle, and looked out the windshield to see "Gene Hill" walk out of the building, get into a white Mercedes with New Jersey license plates and drive away. Now, here was corroborating evidence: Jersey plates on a car as out of place here as local real estate without cow flops on it. "That was probably Gene Hill," and he was gone. The mantra began anew, "Could that have been Gene Hill?"

The opportunity had passed. I kicked myself, scratched "post office" off the list, and backtracked to the convenience store. As I turned off the road into the parking lot, I was confronted again by the white Mercedes with Jersey plates, now parked in front of the little store. I walked through the door and there, at the magazine display, stood "Gene Hill" holding an open magazine whose title I could clearly read as *Field and Stream*. Now, you don't have to hit me over the head with the obvious. I'll end this story by saying he was Gene Hill.

The person I introduced myself to was gracious and engaging. I brought him out to my truck to show him some sculpture, we talked bird dogs, exchanged phone numbers, and set up a time for lunch.

I offer this as an expression of thanks. Gene was a kind, unpretentious man. Knowing him has made a difference in my life.

Over the next couple of years, I had the profound pleasure of spending time with Gene. He made a point of making sure that I shot a Woodward in the dove field one afternoon; I think his concern was for my soul. He sponsored my membership in the Outdoor Writers Association of America. While having lunch one day, I told him that when our geriatric Chessie passed, I wanted to replace her with a new Chesapeake puppy. He explained to me that there is only one true retriever, and that is a black lab. He questioned if my consorting with Chessies was the sign of a latent personality disorder. I was of the West and Gene was of the World, and knowing him made my world bigger.

He made all our worlds bigger.

I guess you could call this a tribute of sorts, although I don't know what Gene would say about it. I knew him to be human, with no trace of pomposity or ego that seems to be endemic in our species. Gene was honest, direct, and didn't suffer fools. He told wonderful stories. We would be talking about a subject and I would ask his advice. He would say, well you could do this and this and this. I would remind him that he could do these things because he was Gene Hill, and that my options were less varied.

He would remind me that I was wrong.

Acknowledgements

I wish to thank the many people whose help, time, and expertise made the completion of this book possible.

First and foremost, my wife Nicole, who along with living her own busy life tended to dogs, phone calls, keeping money in the debit card account, and an absentee husband. Nicole edited the manuscript and was able to translate it into English, in spite of my assistance. Thanks, love.

Also, Darrell Kincaid, a dear friend of long standing. Darrell is Kansas born and showed me some of the parts he loved. Joann Kincaid, Darrell's wife, graciously opened her home to me and a pack of traveling hounds when it was Kansas-cold outside. She looked out for me when I am sure she had other things to be doing. To both of you: there aren't words to express my appreciation, so "thank you" will have to suffice.

To Don Prentice, who can man a chain gang at ten degrees in a howling wind with a frozen mustache, and still work a shovel with the best of them. As always, thanks Don.

To Bill Tarrant, for his support and introductions.

To Jim Culbertson, a fine hunter who went out of his way to see that I was successful.

Special thanks to Jay Smith and Cliff Russell for dog chores on the home front.

To Chuck and Blanche Johnson, for the opportunity and their trust and patience.

To Julie Phinney and Matthew Phinney, for their editorial skills and efforts in making the project the best it could be.

To the many people I hunted with who made my acclimation possible, in particular: John and Sammy Leonard, Dan Bloom, Ed Anderson, John Sherman, Howard Hawks, Troy Hawks, Chris Hawks, Wes Jones, Jesse Hodges, Mike Lessard, John Kuhry, Clint Menke, Larry Anderson, Jodi Waters, Jay McDorman, Wade Culbertson, Roger Zettl, Richard Burris and Scarlett, Ron Dahlman, Frank Bennett, Tim Heiner, and Carl Coonrod.

To the folks who shared their knowledge and helped me to learn: Randy Rogers, Helen Hands, Ken Giesen, Jerry Cline, Bob Mathews, John Parton, Bev Aldrich, Michael Mitchener, Mr. and Mrs. Lawrence Smith, Marvin Kraft, Richard Harrold, Roger Applegate, Dave Whetstone, and Noreen Walsh.

Also, Rich Wilson of Monument Camera in Tuscon, Arizona.

A special thanks to the personnel of the Kansas Department of Wildlife and Parks, who I found without exception to be competent, knowledgeable professionals always willing to help.

To Wil and Sophie Poissant for their many kindnesses.

And of course, to Aunt Louise: for remembering.

Introduction

Kansas is a big place, a really big place. After a lifetime of reading about Kansas and many hours spent listening to friends, native and otherwise, describe the bounties of Kansas bird hunting, I did have a mental Kansas. What I found the first time I crossed the southwestern border at Elkhart, however, was a panorama grander than my mind's creation.

Kansas rolls in soft, flat folds like an autumn-colored velveteen blanket. The landscape is cut periodically with watercourses lined in hardwoods and pastures. Tall, vertical-sided mountains made of metal and shaped like silos punctuate each small town's horizon. While most towns don't have stoplights, all carry banners that drape their buildings and flutter above the highway, rallying the hometown teams. Each little town looks like the place where a person would want to raise their children.

Kansas is agriculture. Long ribbons of highway divide fields of milo, corn, and prairie. This state has several distinct regions that offer different habitat communities and different hunting opportunities.

The western third of the state is high plains and home to large-scale wheat farming operations, which I heard referred to as "wheat ranching." The Arkansas River runs east to west and partitions the lower third of the state's land mass. This area holds the remaining Sand sage prairie, is the home of scaled quail, and one of the final strongholds of the lesser prairie chicken.

The northcentral shortgrass prairie region transforms into the Flint Hills at its eastern border. This northern tear, which encompasses the lands from the Flint Hills west, has historically been Kansas' premier pheasant area. The Flint Hills region is the largest tract of tallgrass prairie remaining in North America. This grassland is made up of four dominant grass species: big bluestem, little bluestem, Indian grass, and switchgrass. This is the home of the greater prairie chicken.

The eastern third of the state contains the Osage Cuestas, Glaciated, Cherokee Lowlands, and Ozark Plateau regions. In these regions, the grasslands give way to hardwood-covered hills, small agricultural fields, and river bottoms. The edges of these interspersed pastures, fields, and meadows are known for their bobwhite quail.

I undertook this book from the perspective of a Kansas bird-hunting neophyte. Many of the potential readers of this book will be interested specifically because they are coming to Kansas for the first time. Both of us, myself and newly arriving Kansas wingshooters, will have an interest in answers to the same questions. In addition, at approximately the halfway point of my life and for better or worse, I've spent an inordinate amount of time trying to keep within sight the rapidly disappearing rear end of a running bird dog. What I've learned is that there is a lot of carryover experience and knowledge, whether the aforementioned rear end is vanishing into Great Basin sagebrush, Sonoran desert cholla, or Flint Hills tallgrass prairie.

In the 1996/97 season, I made three trips to Kansas during the months of November, December, and January. I covered as much as I could within the available time, about three months of in-state time in all, but as I said at the offset of this introduction: Kansas is a big place. I sweated in a t-shirt under a hot sun chasing chickens. Conversely, I did a frozen impression of a camo-covered, thinsulate stuffed, Michelin tire man lying out in fields for Canadas. In December and January, Kansas can be as cold as it is big. I was fortunate to photograph and collect all of the legal upland bird species, with the exception of woodcock, and I was especially blessed to collect a prime male lesser prairie chicken.

In the process I met many good people, went through 80 rolls of film, and visited some beautiful country. Unfortunately, while I saw most of the regions of the state, much of the looking was done through a truck window at 65 miles an hour. In spite of the long hours, numb fingers, and fast food, the dogs and I had a blast. I bet you will too.

This is a book for bird hunters who share my same tragic obsession. Good luck and good hunting!

Tips on Using This Book

- The state of Kansas is divided between three area codes: (316) covers the southern half of the state, (785) covers the northern half, and the third area code (913) services the Kansas city area.

- Although we have tried to be as accurate as possible, please note that this information is current only for 1998. Ownership of hotels, restaurants, etc., may change, and we cannot guarantee the quality of the services they provide.

- Always check with the Department of Wildlife and Parks for the most current information regarding hunting regulations. Season dates, prices, and regulations may change from year to year.

- For the purpose of organization, the state is broken down into six sections.

- Each of the six sections includes distribution maps for all species of upland birds found in that section. These general distribution maps are only an approximation and may change due to weather conditions, habitat alterations, and farming practices.

- Finding a place to hunt: Kansas has a lot of hunting pressure, especially during the first two or three weeks of pheasant season. Plan your hunt early. We suggest that an interested hunter write or call the local Chamber of Commerce in the area they wish to visit and ask for specific information.

Motel Cost Key
    $ — less than $30 per night
    $$ — between $30 and $50 per night
  $$$ — $50 per night and up

Major Roads and Rivers of Kansas

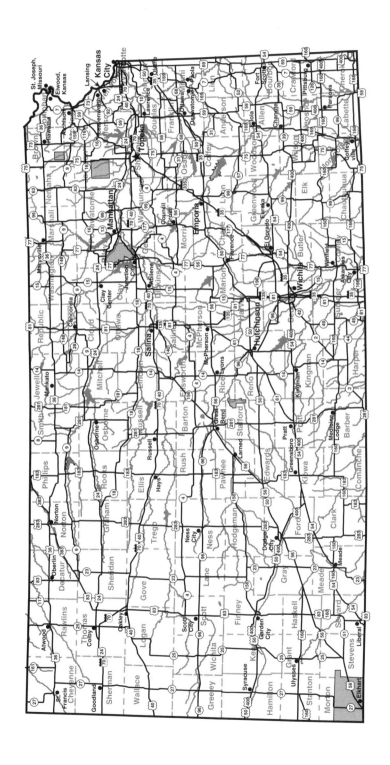

Kansas Facts

82,282 square miles
Ranks 15 in size in the nation
210 miles north to south
400 miles east to west

Population: 2,565,328 (1995 Census)
    Ranks 32 in nation in population
    31 people per square mile
Counties: 105
Time zone: Central

Attractions
    Cimarron National Grassland
    Santa Fe Trail Center
    Flint Hills
    Boot Hill and Frontier Town, Dodge City
    Cowtown Historic Frontier Town, Wichita
    Ft. Scott and Ft. Larned, restored 1800s cavalry forts
    Kansas Cosmosphere and Space Discovery Center, Hutchinson

Name Origin: From the Sioux word meaning "South Wind People"
Nickname: The Sunflower State
Primary Industries: Agriculture, manufacturing, oil, natural gas, minerals, aircraft
    production
Capital: Topeka
Bird: Western meadowlark
State Flower: Native sunflower
Tree: Cottonwood

Author lifts a Kansas ringneck.

Hunting Regulations

Licenses

The following licenses are available through licensing agents throughout the state. Licenses are valid January 1 through December 31. All Kansas hunters, ages 16 to 65, must have a resident hunting license. All nonresident hunters, regardless of age, must purchase a nonresident hunting license. Any person who has not been a legal resident of the state for 60 consecutive days is considered a nonresident.

Hunter Education Certification

"Anyone born in or after July 1, 1957 must successfully complete a certified hunter education course in order to purchase a hunting license or hunt, except on lands they own or operate. Resident hunters under 16 years of age are not required to purchase a hunting license but must carry a Hunter Education Certificate (unless hunting on own land), showing they have completed the course. Anyone under the age of 27 years must carry an approved hunter education card while hunting in Kansas. For duplicate cards or course information, contact the Pratt, state park, or regional offices. Duplicate cards are $5.50."

Current 1997 Fees

Annual hunting license

- Resident: $15.50, over the counter
- Nonresident: $65.50, over the counter
- Nonresident (under 16): $30.50, over the counter

Turkey: Fall

- General: $20.50, over the counter
- Resident Archery: $20.50, over the counter
- Hunt-Own-Land: $10.50, Pratt, regionals, and parks
- Landowner/Tenant: $10.50, over the counter
- Nonresident: $30.50, over the counter
- Application deadlines apply to limited permit drawings. Contact the Kansas Department of Wildlife and Parks for additional information.

Turkey: Spring

- General: $20.50, over the counter
- Hunt-Own-Land: $10.50, Pratt and regionals
- Landowner/Tenant: $10.50, over the counter
- Nonresident: $30.50, over the counter
- Application deadlines apply to limited permit drawings. Contact the Kansas Department of Wildlife and Parks for additional information.

Sandhill Crane Federal Hunting Permit
- $5.50, Pratt Office of Department of Wildlife and Parks
- Kansas sandhill crane hunters are required to have a federal sandhill crane hunting permit in their possession before hunting. To obtain the $5.50 permit, contact the Pratt Office of the Department of Wildlife and Parks.

Waterfowl (Ducks, Geese, and Merganser only)
- State waterfowl stamp : $3.25, over the counter
- 48-hour waterfowl permit: $20.50, over the counter
- Special dark goose units: $5.50, Pratt and regionals
- Federal Waterfowl Stamp: $15.00, U.S.Post Office

Migratory Bird Harvest Info Permits
- Migratory Bird Harvest Info Permits will be required in the fall of 1998. Anyone hunting migratory birds, including waterfowl, coot, dove, sandhill crane, snipe, rail, and woodcock are required to have a HIP stamp affixed to the back of their hunting license.

State Park Fees
- One-day vehicle park permit: $4.00
- Annual motor vehicle park permit: $30.00
  Second- vehicle park permit: $15.00
- 14-day camping park permit: $50.00
- Overnight camping park permit (per night, per unit): $5.00
- Utilities for one hookup: $5.00
  For two hookups: $6.00
  For three hookups: $7.00
- Park permits are available at all state parks, select Wildlife and Parks offices, County Clerks, and some vendors.

For More Information

Office of the Secretary
900 SW Jackson Street, Suite 502
Topeka, KS 66612-1233
785-296-2281

Pratt Operations Office
512 SE 25th Avenue
Pratt, KS 67124-8174
316-672-5911

Region 1 Office
Y.S. 183 Bypass, P.O. Box 338
Hayes, KS 67601-0338
785-628-8614

Region 2 Office
3300 SW 29th
Topeka, KS 66614-2053
913-273-6740

Region 3 Office
808 McArtor Drive
Dodge City, KS 67801-6024
316-227-8609

Region 4 Office
6232 East 29th Street North
Wichita, KS 67220
316-683-8069

Region 5 Office
1500 West 7th Street, Box 777
Chanute, KS 66720-0777
316-431-0380

Kansas City District Office
14629 West 95th
Lenexa, KS 66215
913-894-9113

Emporia Research & Survey Office
1830 Merchant, P.O. Box 1525
Emporia, KS 66801-1525
316-342-0658

Area Offices

Cedar Bluff: 785-726 -3212

Cheney: 316-542 -3664

Cheyenne Bottoms: 316-793 -7730

Clinton: 785-842-8562

Council Grove: 316-767 -5900

Crawford: 316-362-3671

Eisenhower: 785-528-4105

El Dorado: 316-321-7180

Elk City: 316-331 -6295

Finney Game Refuge: 316-276-8886

Glen Elder: 785-545-3345

Hillsdale: 913-783-4507

Kanopolis: 785-546-2565

Lovewell: 785-753-4971

Marais des Cygnes: 913-352-8941

Meade: 316-873-2572

Milford: 785-238-3014

Mined Land: 316-231-3173

Perry: 785-246-3449

Pomona: 785-828-4933

Prairie Dog/Norton: 785-877-2953

Pratt Sandhills: 316-672-5911

Scott: 316-872-2061

Toronto/Fall River: 316- 637-2213

Tuttle Creek: 785-539-7941

Webster: 785-425-6775

Wilson: 785-658-2465

97/98 SEASON DATES

Upland Birds

- Unless otherwise noted, possession limits for upland game birds are twice the daily bag limit on the second day, three times the bag limit on the third day, and four times the bag limit on or after the fourth day.
- Shooting hours: One half-hour before sunrise to sunset.
- Method of take: Legal equipment for taking upland game birds includes shotguns and muzzle-loading shotguns no larger than 10-gauge with shot only, bow and arrow, and falconry.
- Blaze Orange: While the wearing of blaze orange for upland bird hunting is not legally required by the state of Kansas, its use is recommended.
- Illegal Pursuit: No game may be shot at, killed, or pursued from a motor vehicle. It is also illegal to locate or give information concerning the location of game by radio or other mechanical means. No wild game bird (except wild turkeys) may be

shot at or killed unless that bird is in flight (Wild turkeys may be shot on the ground or in flight).

Pheasant
- Season: 2nd Saturday of November–Jan. 31st, annually
- Area Open: Statewide
- Limit: Daily bag limit, 4 cocks
- Note: Pheasants in possession for transportation must retain intact a foot, plumage, or some part that will readily determine sex.

Prairie Chicken (see map)
Early season: Sept. 15th–Oct. 15th, annually
- Limit: Daily bag limit, 2
Regular Season: 1st Saturday of November–Jan. 31st, annually
- Limit: Daily bag limit, 2

Southwest season (Lesser Prairie Chicken): Dec. 1st–Jan. 31st, annually
- Limit: Daily bag limit, 1

Quail (see map)
- Season: 2nd Saturday of November–Jan. 31st, annually (eastern zone, Regions 2, 4, 5); 3rd Saturday of November–Jan. 31st, annually (western zone, Regions 1, 3)
- Area Open: Statewide (in two areas)
- Limit: Daily bag limit, 8

Mourning Dove
- Season: Sept. 1st– Oct. 30th, annually
- Area Open: Statewide
- Limit: Daily bag limit, 15; Possession limit, 30 after first day. State and Federal duck stamp are not required.

Woodcock
- Season: Oct. 17th–Nov. 30th
- Area Open: Statewide
- Limit: Daily bag limit, 3; Possession limit, 6 after the first day. State and Federal duck stamps are not required.

Rail (Virginia and Sora only)
- Season: Sept. 1st–Dec. 16th
- Area Open: Statewide
- Limit: Daily bag limit, 8; Possession limit, 16 after the first day. State and Federal duck stamps are not required.

Common (Wilson's) Snipe
- Season: Sept. 1st–Dec. 16th
- Area Open: Statewide
- Limit: Daily bag limit, 8; Possession limit, 16 after the first day. State and Federal duck stamps are not required.

Waterfowl

- Nontoxic Shot: Kansas requires nontoxic shot, whether on public or private land, for all migratory game bird hunting—except dove. This includes ducks, geese, coots, mergansers, rail, sandhill crane, and snipe. Legal shot includes steel, bismuth, and steel shot coated with copper, nickel, or zinc chromate.
- Nontoxic-Shot-Only Areas: "Nontoxic-shot-only" areas include Cheyenne Bottoms, Isabel Wetlands, Jamestown, Marais Des Cygnes, McPherson Wetlands, Neosho, Texas Lake, Wild Turkey Playa, and Slate Creek Wildlife Areas and Flint Hills, Kirwin, and Quivira National Wildlife Refuges. In these areas, nontoxic shot is the only shotgun load allowed, whether ducks, upland game, or other small game are being hunted. State-managed areas adjoining federal areas may also be affected; check local department offices for details.
- Possession of lead shot: It is illegal to possess toxic shot while hunting waterfowl or hunting in a "Nontoxic-Shot-Only" area. "Possession" means that lead shot cannot be in a hunter's gun, pockets, or within reach while in the process of hunting. Lead or other toxic shot left in a vehicle is not considered "in possession."

Early Teal
- Season: Sept. 13th–21st
- Area Open: Statewide
- Daily bag limit: 4
- Possession limit: 8

Youth Waterfowl Day
- Each duck zone has one day in which hunters 15 and younger may hunt ducks outside of the regular season. Bag limits are the same as regular season. Youth must be accompanied by an adult 18 or older. The adult may not hunt. Both adult and youth must be licensed and possess both State and Federal duck stamps if required.
- High Plains Zone: Sept. 27th
- Low Plains Early Zone: Sept. 27th
- Low Plains late Zone: Oct. 18th

Fall Duck Seasons (see map)
- Low Plains Early Zone: Oct. 4th–Dec. 7th and Dec. 20th–Dec. 28th
- Low Plains Late Zone: Oct. 25th–Dec. 14th, and Dec. 20th–Jan. 11th
- High Plains Zone: Oct. 4th–Jan. 4th, and Jan. 15–Jan. 18th
- Daily Bag Limit: 6 ducks
- A conventional bag limit has been set. The daily bag limit is 6 ducks, which shall include no more than 5 mallards (only 1 can be a hen), one mottled duck, one canvasback, two redheads, two wood ducks, or three pintails. Merganser limit is 5, including no more than 1 hooded merganser.

Coot
- Season: Same as regular duck season
- Area Open: Statewide
- Daily Bag Limit: 15
- Possession Limit: 30

Regular Goose Season (see map)
Dark Geese (Canada and white-fronted)
- Season: Nov. 1st–Jan. 25th
- Area Open: Statewide, except three areas that require permits for dark goose hunting
- Limit: 2 Canada geese or 1 Canada and 1 white-fronted. Possession limit is twice the daily bag limit.

Light Geese (Snow, Blue, and Ross')
- Unit 1 season: Nov. 22nd–March 8th
- Unit 2 season: Oct. 25–Nov. 21 and Dec. 20–March 8th
- Limit: Daily bag limit, 10 geese; Possession limit, 40 on and after the fourth day

Dark Goose, Permit-Only Areas (See map)
- The following 3 areas are open to dark goose (Canada and white-fronted) hunting by permit only. Hunters are limited to one $5.50 permit per unit. Hunters may write for an application to the Kansas Department of Wildlife and Parks, 512 SE 25th Avenue, Pratt, KS 67124, or contact one of the five regional offices.
- Daily bag limit is the same as for regular dark goose season outside these special units.

Marais des Cygnes
- Application period: Through end of season
- Season: Dec. 20th–Jan. 25
- Special shooting hours: one half-hour before sunrise to 1PM
- Permit limit: 6 dark geese
- Carcass tag required: Yes

Flint Hills
- Application period: Through end of season
- Season: Dec. 20th–Jan. 25th
- Permit limit: Same as statewide limits
- Carcass tag required: No

Southeast Unit
- Application Period: Through end of Season
- Season: Dec. 20th–Jan. 25
- Permit Limit: 6 dark geese
- Carcass tag required: Yes

Sandhill Crane (see map, page 90)
- Permits: In addition to a hunting license, a valid federal sandhill crane hunting permit is required to hunt cranes. To obtain the $5.50 permit, contact the Pratt Office of the Department of Wildlife and Parks.
- Shooting Hours: Sunrise to 2PM
- Season and bag limit: The sandhill crane season runs Nov. 1st–Dec. 28th. The daily bag limit is 2 birds, and the possession limit is twice the daily bag limit.
- Nontoxic shot requirement: Nontoxic shot is required for sandhill crane hunting. Lead shot may not be possessed while crane hunting. A duck stamp is not required.
- Area Open: Crane hunting is restricted to the southwest quarter of the state (see map).

Turkey (see map, page 84)
Fall Turkey
- Application Deadline: Firearms, Unit 1 (closed to nonresidents): Aug. 15th. Unit 2 (open to nonresidents): Oct. 18th. Archery: Dec. 30th.
- Firearms Season: Oct. 8th–Oct. 19th
- Archery Season: Oct. 1st–Dec. 2nd, and Dec. 15th–Dec. 31st
- Limit: 1 turkey, either sex

Spring Turkey
- Application Deadline: Tags available over the counter with the exception of a limited permit drawing, with a deadline of Feb. 20th in Unit 1
- Firearms and Archery Season: Apr. 8th–May 17th
- Limit: 1 bearded turkey per tag; second tags may be available

Guides, Outfitters, and Lodges

For those hunters who enjoy the assistance of a professional guide or a commercial hunting operation, there is a host to choose from in Kansas. The state is large and almost exclusively private property. Someone who knows the ground can make the success and enjoyment of a Kansas hunt more readily assured.

This book is broken down into separate geographic areas, and individual guides, outfitters, and commercial shooting operations are listed in those sections. Listing does not constitute an endorsement. It is important to speak directly with a potential guide or shooting preserve operator about your expectations and requirements. Some situations just are not a "fit." Some pheasant hunts are conducted as a large drive with several guns present. A hunter looking for a one or two gun shoot may not have envisioned being involved in driving large fields in a line of guns. Ask those questions.

For statewide information and a list of hunting guides contact:

The Kansas Outfitters Association
1548 17th Road
Washington, KS 66968
(785) 325-2747

Operations Office of the Kansas Wildlife and Parks Department
512 SE 25th Ave.
Pratt, KS 67124-8174
(316) 672-5911

For statewide information on shooting preserves contact:

The Kansas Sport Hunting Association
P.O. Box 174
Tipton, KS 67485
(913) 373-4965

Southwest Quartet

Kansas has a southwestern region with a sky just a little too wide and blue, and a sun whose light is just a touch too bright to be shining down on the central plains. There is a feeling of the West in southwestern Kansas.

For the visiting bird hunter, there are also two Western birds: lesser prairie chickens and scaled quail are found in the grasslands. The other two Kansas mainstays, bobwhite quail and ring-necked pheasants, are also present. Bobs are found in good numbers along the river courses and in the uplands. Ringnecks are found sporadically in small pockets throughout the agricultural areas.

In the extreme southwestern corner of the state lies the town of Elkhart and the Cimarron National Grasslands. This federal grassland comprises one of the largest public hunting areas in the state of Kansas. I had been through and hunted the area earlier in the season, but I was back in early January with two days free before I had to head east to the Flint Hills for greater prairie chickens. It was a narrow window, but I wanted to try for all four species and have a little fun. Leave the camera in the truck and actually go bird hunting instead of taking pictures of someone else doing it.

I pulled into the motel parking lot in the early afternoon and found a sunny sky and a forecast for more of the same for the following two days. I had been snowed on, hailed and sleeted over, and drowned with rain in the earlier two trips and was expecting more of the same for this go around. It was a pleasure to start this new trip on such a pleasant afternoon. The dogs had been traveling for a day and a half and were ready to stretch out on the prairie. I stowed gear in my room and headed out to the Cimarron National Grasslands a few miles west of Elkhart. We had enough of the afternoon left to see about finding some bobwhite quail along the Cimarron River bottom.

The main dirt roads that provide access to the grassland are wide and easily passable, but once a vehicle enters the small side roads, the ride gets a little more exciting. Many of them have long stretches of sand with shoulders that tend to bowl out. With the speed it takes to float over the sand and the rolling back and forth from the hollow shoulders, a driver gets the feeling that he is racing along a luge track.

The drive into the hardwood river bottom was uneventful and a little misleading. The Cimarron is actually dry over most of its course. I would guess that the hardwood channel that lines the riverbed is up to a quarter mile wide in stretches. The trees are interspersed with brushy grass clearings and provide an unbroken line of picturebook quality bobwhite habitat.

I had six dogs with me and each one was doing a passable impersonation of a political candidate on election day morning. I figured I'd run three dogs and go one way for an hour or so, come back, and then swap dogs for a run in the other direction. I had two males and four females with me so I split them and released Jasper, a large white male setter, and two female setters, Emma and Dandy.

I thought the scenting conditions might be a little difficult as the bright sun had given the air a warm edge, but with the afternoon winding down I knew it could only improve.

Worry wasn't necessary because within a hundred yards of the truck, Dandy made an abrupt U-turn and began walking up a scent trail. Emma caught the action and came in on the side. Together, the two dogs slowed and then began catwalking into the wind towards a brushed-in tree line. Dandy froze and then Emma backed. I saw Dandy's tail start to flag and an embarrassed look came across her face. She shifted to move and caught Emma backing to her side. She immediately backed Emma and it degenerated down to an English setter stand off, with each dog suspecting the worst and neither dog willing to be the first one to acknowledge the mistake.

I circled in from the side and gave the edge of the brush line a few swipes with my boot. The dogs tensed and relaxed with each nonproductive swing of my leg. After a half dozen kicks, they stood there limp, ready to be released. I sent them on with a soft whistle and both dogs vanished in a blur.

I pushed through to the far side of the shadowed tree belt and re-entered the sunlight in an open clearing. A hundred yards across the clearing, on the far side of a plum thicket, I spotted an erect white plume that looked a lot like a Jasper tail. Dandy zoomed across the clearing and slid to a halt as she came even with the plume. Emma, working independently of the other two setters, came from the low side and pointed bird scent when she hit the scent stream. The diagnosis was confirmed.

I shut the action on the 20-gauge side-by-side, checked the safety, and then checked to make sure the action was closed again. Like every time in those tense moments before a covey flush, the action was just as closed as when I'd closed it the first time.

Jasper has a rattlesnake tail when he knows he's got birds. On point, he carries his tail very high and the upper quarter has a slight tremor in it. I stepped up to the low thicket and I could see Jasper's head and back where there had just been a tail before. I could clearly see that the tail was shaking.

Then all I saw were birds: brown, blurred projectiles exploding in all directions. I looked for the white throat of a male bird and stabbed the shotgun in his direction. At the same time that the sight plane along the top of the barrels met the bird and the butt stock met my shoulder, the weapon fired. Mr. Bob puffed in a slow roll and slid into the grass. Another quail entered my sight picture, moving in the same direction. The end of the barrels covered the bird and the quail danced sideways from a cloud of feathers, its forward movement stopped just short of a near tree line. The dogs ran for the downed game.

The first bird was a gimme and Dandy found it in short order, a nice plump male. The second bird fell in grass but still had some go in it. Jasper and Emma double-teamed the crippled runner. The bird led them on a short chase that ended out of sight, in the middle of a plum thicket. Apparently Emma won the race because she squirreled out from under the brush with the bird in her mouth.

Dandy brings a bobwhite to hand.

We pushed after singles and found several buried along the tree line. I called the dogs in for water. All three had a good pant going, so rather than push on further away from the truck, we circled back and swapped out dogs.

The new shift was happy to get out of their boxes. I put three generations of our setters on the ground: Rose, white and orange; Concho, tricolor; and Rascal, tricolor. Mother, son, and granddaughter.

We had taken a few birds out of the last covey. Rather than adding additional insult to injury, we left those birds alone. We went in the opposite direction down the river bottom. Finding the last group of birds so close to the truck was too good to happen twice, and so of course, it didn't. We went half a mile before Rose hit some interesting scent. Her tail started cranking tight figure eights and she slowed down to a slow creep and locked up. Her body language didn't go unnoticed, and Concho and Rascal bore in from two different directions. Concho slid into a solid back behind Rose. Rascal, true to her name and age, blurred past both of them and sent the birds packing to Topeka.

I whoaed the two older dogs and got Rascal under control. I picked her up and carried her back to the end of the conga line. I whoaed her also and we had a dress rehearsal of the way it was supposed to have looked. She looked apologetic and unrepentant at the same time, so we discussed it a little further until the point came across. I released the dogs and we went looking for singles.

The first single Rascal found and held. I was able to take the bird and reward her with a retrieve. She followed suit by honoring Rose on a find with just a slight prompting from me. Rascal then backed her father on a pointed double that got away clean.

With the evening approaching, the scenting conditions just kept getting better. Our success rate was regulated by the fact that the cover was getting denser, making it more difficult to get into shooting position. Invariably, if a shooter only has one clear way in for a shot, the quail will oblige by going out the other. Coupled with the diminishing light that allowed birds to disappear into the advancing shadows, we weren't a serious threat to the bobwhite population. However, I did do some serious tree pruning.

It was time to head in. All the dogs had been exercised and we had taken care of one of the four species. We could scratch bobwhite quail off the list.

As promised, the following morning broke bright and clear. I got to the field a little after dawn. I figured to start with pheasants and get out onto the grasslands for scalies and chickens afterwards.

Pheasants are not a common bird in the southwestern part of Kansas, but they are found locally in pockets around agriculture. I drove to some private farmland west of Elkhart that held pheasants. The cover looked good and I opened Concho's box and cut him loose. Concho is a big tricolor male who has always worked heavy cover well. We started off by working a grass swale between two stubble fields. The energetic setter pushed into the deep grass and slowly worked it out. He would dive into the heavy cords of grass and tunnel through and snort, like a pig after truffles. I could tell in short order that he was into birds because the speed of the tunneling and the tempo of the snorting accelerated.

Fifty yards ahead I could see some old machinery and culvert pipes exposed through the thick grass mat. Thirty yards out, a hen pheasant popped out of the metal, then a second, and then a third. Each bird that rose jarred me a little bit further away from calm, until the fourth bird showed. At this point, I had closed the distance to twenty yards. It took me a second to recognize the long tail and bright white neck ring.

I swung on the big bird and fired as he topped out on the rise. The first shot wobbled the bird and the second crumpled him so that he parachuted softly back onto the grass mat that he had just vacated. Concho broke to make the retrieve. I hoped the bird was done and not running. A cripple could go a long way in this type of cover in a hell of a hurry. The rooster had a little bit of go in him, but not enough to get past the setter.

Concho moved into the area of the fall. He dove into the vegetation and the snorting got real loud and the movement got real fast. It ended with a blazing trail of mounded grass and then, complete silence. A second later, Concho's head poked up

Point on the Grasslands.

through the grass with an unamused rooster in his mouth. I whistled him over to me to deliver the bird.

We had our pheasant and we had a little bit of a drive back to the grassland to finish out the hunt. We needed to think about turning around and going back to the truck. However, there appeared to be birds here.

The grass swale ended at a fence that followed the edge of the stubble around to a windbreak of Osage orange. The line of trees traveled a ways, then made a hard bend and looped out to some old rusted machinery parked in a fallow weed field. Opposite of the machinery was another grass draw, dividing a CRP field that came back in the general direction of the truck, more or less. Using bird hunter logic, this would make the straightest line possible (and maybe move a bird or two in the process).

We moved forward, returning to the truck.

The fence line on the edge of the stubble didn't produce any action until we approached the beginning of the windbreak. As Concho was casting through the last bit of stubble, he raised his head into the wind and followed it towards the sand sage on the backside of the Osage orange. He locked up thirty yards off the nearest cover. I walked up, off his far side, and studied the ground for some sign of where the birds were holding. There was mostly dirt, some thin stands of grass, and a few thin low weeds. As close as I looked, there were no birds there, so I took a step.

A single scaled quail blasted out. I pointed the shotgun and blasted up and Concho blasted off. With the trust of an innocent, he was confident something would be fluttering on the ground to carry back. Gratefully, he wasn't disappointed. I reloaded hoping for more singles, but none obliged. After Concho came in with the bird, he sniffed around. There had been more birds there, but they were long gone.

I pulled the freshly killed scalie back out of the game bag and checked the wings and throat feathers. He looked like a juvenile male, a youngster who made a mistake and should have run off before our approach, like his cohorts.

Concho made scent again halfway down the tree line. He was pointing like he had a covey in front of him. I stepped past him expecting scalies and instead flushed 20 bobs. The majority of the covey flushed straight down the tree line and pitched in. We worked singles clear through the weed field and into the CRP. We turned two more hen pheasants in the heavy grass field, and a pair of roosters that may still be running today. We'd had a good morning and it was time to get after prairie birds.

Driving back on the grasslands I made a small detour towards where I had seen a covey of scalies hanging out on an earlier trip. It was midmorning, and the warm sun would have them loafing in the shade on their "roost." The prairie subspecies of scaled quail are different from the type that I hunt in my home state of Arizona. Arizona birds could be anywhere; the prairie birds, however, will use a particular place as their roost site. This might be the enclosure and accompanying brush of a manmade guzzler, or the rusted, bent remnants of one of man's abandoned endeavors. Some coveys adopt a single large staghorn cholla or an old homestead site as their official clubhouse. The prairie is almost exclusively grass so anything more than two feet high sticks out like a lighthouse on the ocean.

A person would reason that this choice of single, isolated roosts would subject the birds to increased predation. But apparently not, as this is precisely the choice that the birds make.

An early drilling site had been left with some metal struts and fencing in a picturesque, heavily grassed valley, and a covey had set up housekeeping. I parked well away from the area so as not to tip the birds to our presence. I put Concho on a lead and we came in slow, low, and quiet. In spite of our clandestine approach,

Thirty-five birds flushed out of range from the grass on the far side of the roost. We marked them down a hundred yards out. I cut Concho loose to see if any birds had hung in. He made a thorough search of the roost site and turned no birds, so we hustled out to where the covey had pitched in.

The landing site held nothing, so we moved forward slowly. Fifty yards further on, a bird bumped wild off of Concho as he quartered in front. Another jumped wild off of me and I turned and fired a two shot parting salute. We were standing in the middle of the covey. I called in Concho and started him working in very close.

Novice scaled quail hunters assume that scaled quail run away, which is only half true. They run away until they stop, and when they stop they hold very tight. Concho knew this from a history with many scalie altercations. The setter held in close and cranked tight. I stood in the middle without moving. It took ten minutes for the first bird to blink. He leaked just enough scent to be detected, but not enough for the dog

Setters working the grasslands for scaled quail.

to point him. Concho started the rooting and snorting stuff and the bird came up. The gun went bang and Concho made a nice retrieve. We took a couple more birds and flew several more over the next thirty minutes. None of them came from a clean point.

We left the quail to regroup and return to their roost. Walking back to the truck I was struck at just what wonderful bird country this was. There was grass as far as a person could see, as far as a dog could run, or a chicken could fly. We had the better part of the afternoon left to find a chicken flock. I loaded the dog back on the truck, got in and headed down the road.

I had taken a good adult lesser male earlier in the season, so I didn't need to take another bird. My wish had already been granted, but a hen to mount along with the male would be a welcome plus. We drove to an area that held chickens that I knew from my earlier time on the Cimarron. Through talking with locals and my limited experience with lessers, I have learned that it is very important for a hunter to know where the chickens are before one starts looking. If that sounds like a catch 22, it is. The grasslands are very big and the country all looks the same to a first-timer. Looking again where one found them the first time will drastically improve one's chance of finding them the second.

I released Emma from her box and picked up the shotgun. I had switched to a full choked, 12-gauge, pump gun and some long-range loads. If an opportunity for a shot presented itself, it would more than likely be at a distance.

It is hard to describe in words the feeling of being in that place. The land and sky mirror each other, and the dog and birds and gun float in between. Grass flows like water in the breeze and reflects the light from the clouds.

I walked as Emma quartered through the grass and sand sage. I knew about where the birds should be, but I had no idea where they would be. We came upon the remains of an early homestead. The foundation, now flush with the ground, had once held a small home's hope in this foreign land. I caught glimpses of colored glass and enamel seeded in the grass. The color of rust melted with the color of the ground. How many prairie chickens were here then? There were pieces of another time spread everywhere, like feathers blown in the wind.

I looked back, after walking another fifty yards, and all visible traces of the homestead were gone. Asleep in the grass, like all the chickens that had been here before.

We did find the chickens. Emma found them after they had been watching us for a hundred yards, or maybe it was a hundred years. They flushed out of range and we watched them fly to the horizon, and that was enough.

It was time to move on.

We loaded up the truck for the trip east. We'd had the distinct pleasure of chasing four fine species of birds in some incredible country. The dogs were going to be crate-bound for another day; it's a long drive across Kansas, but there was more prairie where we were going.

Ring-necked Pheasant

Phasianus colchicus

FIELD FACTS

Local Name

Pheasant, Chinese Pheasant, Ringneck, Big Bird, Long-tailed Bird, Ditch Parrot

Size

Roosters run to 3 feet (36 inches) in body length with the length of the tail accounting for about 22 inches of the measurement. A male's wingspan stretches to 32 inches and adult birds weigh in at up to 4.5 pounds. Females are significantly smaller with an overall length of 26 inches and a wingspan of 28 inches. Hens run 2.5 to 3 pounds total weight.

Identification in Flight

Pheasants make a lot of noise and commotion when they take to wing. Roosters are a riot of bright, vivid color and often cackle as they lift from the ground. The obvious visual reference that distinguishes a cock bird is the metallic green head and white neck ring and the rooster's long flowing tail. Females are an overall brown color at a distance and sport a much shorter tail.

Both sexes initiate flight with rapid wing beats, gain altitude and direction and then coast stiff-winged, pumping their wings only occasionally, until reaching escape cover or out of sight.

Facts

- Pheasants are creatures of agriculture, and are most often found in or around feed fields.
- Only roosters are legal game in Kansas.
- Birds flush with a lot of excitement and noise. It can be difficult to quickly ascertain that the flushing bird is a legal pheasant. Often, at a distance or in diminished light, a rooster pheasant's colorful plumage does not show. Look for a dark body, a broad fan-shaped flowing tail, and a white neck-ring.

Color

The male ring-necked pheasant is a gaudy immigrant addition to the roster of North America's game birds. He rivals the male wood duck as our most metallic, multi-colored citizen.

A rooster's breast, back, and side coverts are varying shades of bronzed gold and brown, laced with patterns of dark darts and light scallops. The scapula feathers at

Pheasant Distribution

Good to Excellent Distribution

Fair to Good Distribution

Locally Good Distribution

Cheyenne, Rawlins, Decatur, Norton, Phillips, Smith, Jewell, Republic, Washington, Marshall, Nemaha, Brown, Doniphan

Sherman, Thomas, Sheridan, Graham, Rooks, Osborne, Mitchell, Cloud, Clay, Riley, Pottawatomie, Jackson, Atchison

Wallace, Logan, Gove, Trego, Ellis, Russell, Lincoln, Ottawa, Saline, Dickinson, Geary, Wabaunsee, Shawnee, Jefferson, Leavenworth, Wyandotte

Greeley, Wichita, Scott, Lane, Ness, Rush, Ellsworth, McPherson, Morris, Chase, Lyon, Osage, Douglas, Johnson

Hamilton, Kearny, Finney, Gray, Hodgeman, Pawnee, Barton, Rice, Marion, Greenwood, Coffey, Franklin, Miami

Stanton, Grant, Haskell, Ford, Edwards, Stafford, Reno, Harvey, Butler, Elk, Woodson, Anderson, Linn, Bourbon

Morton, Stevens, Seward, Meade, Clark, Kiowa, Comanche, Pratt, Kingman, Sedgwick, Sumner, Cowley, Chautauqua, Wilson, Allen, Neosho, Crawford

Barber, Harper, Montgomery, Labette, Cherokee

Kansas' main bird, the ring-necked pheasant.

the base of the wings hang down off the bird's body in bright brown/gold spikes and blend into the blue/green skirt of the upper rump coverts. The bird's long tail is a dark mustard decorated with evenly spaced dark bars running the full length. The pheasant's head is metallic green, sporting well-developed ear tufts (or horns as some have referred to them). The sides of the rooster's face are highlighted with bright red waddles with the texture of velvet.

Hens run to the other extreme, and are a uniform shade of soft, muted brown highlighted with accent bars and darts of dark brown.

Sound and Flight Patterns

Male ringnecks announce their presence in the morning and evening by crowing. The sound carries well and can be best described as a short two-note squawk. I have walked towards the sound of a crowing rooster with the intention of locating the bird and had very little luck in finding a ringneck there when I arrived. The birds, no doubt, were wise to my approach and beat a hasty retreat.

Pheasants often prefer running to flight and use legs as their primary means of escape. When birds are forced into the air, the rooster will at times lead off with a loud unnerving cackle and depart rapidly on strong wings. Once the pheasant gains full speed and an adequate distance from the source of danger, he coasts stiff-winged towards escape cover.

Similar Game Birds

A host of similar large game birds share pheasant habitat. While no other North American game bird carries the bright color patterns and long flowing tail of the adult male ringneck, a female or juvenile male can be very hard to differentiate. Due to the explosive flush and quick departure of a rising bird, hunters must exercise extreme caution before pulling the trigger.

Sharp-tailed grouse, greater and lesser prairie chickens, sage grouse, blue grouse, and ruffed grouse can all be mistakenly identified as a departing hen pheasant or juvenile rooster. The key is to look for the flowing brown tail feathers and the white neck ring of a rooster pheasant. Of the similar grouse listed, all but the sage and sharptails have squared tails that are evident in flight. The sharptails and sages are pointed but do not have the fan-shaped mass of a ringneck. Grouse show white on their bellies and have fully feathered legs while pheasant bodies appear dark at a distance.

Flock or Covey Habits

Pheasants do not live in covey groups, per se, but will at times congregate in impressive numbers, particularly during the winter, on remaining food sources. Sometimes the act of driving birds to a waiting line of blockers will push running birds into a group and, at the flush, give the impression of a large flock of birds taking to wing.

Pheasants live as individuals or in small groups. They tend to be found in close proximity to feed fields and heavy escape cover. During the early part of the season, birds disperse in response to hunting pressure. While a cut corn or green field may look like the place, the birds will more than likely have moved into heavy sections of uncut milo or heavy grass or weeds.

When the opening season madness has ended, the survivors will return to the feed fields and split their time between searching the ground for food and the near horizon for danger.

Reproduction and Life Span

Cocks establish breeding territories in the spring and begin advertising for females with their loud two-note crowing calls. Breeding activity starts in April and runs into August. Adult males vie for dominance and display to impress the females. The winning rooster breeds the hens.

Nests are placed in shallow depressions on the ground in heavy grass cover and lined with grass and feathers. Nine to 10 eggs are laid which take approximately 23 days to hatch. The hens raise the young alone. Chicks leave the nest shortly after birth to follow their mother. The young are capable of short flight within a week and are fully independent at 8 weeks.

Not many wild pheasants survive their first birthday. In captivity, it is possible for a bird to live 8 to 10 years, but a 3-year-old wild ringneck is rare.

Sammy and John Leonard of Topeka enjoying a day afield.

Feeding Habits and Patterns

Pheasants are birds of the croplands. Depending on availability, corn and milo are used heavily. During the winter, the large wheat fields will also hold birds.

At dawn, birds leave the protection of their densely covered roosting areas and move into adjacent feed areas to forage for available seeds and forbs. During some times of the year insects are used heavily, especially by young chicks in their first 6 to 8 weeks of life. Birds are often seen loafing in the sun during midmorning. They retire to roost cover during the middle of the day, and will have another feeding period in the late afternoon. Weather conditions can have a profound impact on their daily routine. In extreme cold, I found the birds feeding much more heavily and often roosting right on the edges of the stubble fields they frequented. They had to keep close to the groceries to keep from freezing to death, and they tucked in close by because they didn't want to expend a lot of energy going back and forth.

Preferred Habitat and Cover

I found pheasants in myriad cover types. The heavily grassed CRP fields are a big draw and hold birds, some more than others. CRP fields surrounding cereal grains such as milo or corn are a real magnet for birds. Pheasants gravitate to strips and edges, hardwood-lined creeks that border feed fields, and uncultivated strips of heavy

Single rooster tops out over a standing sorghum field.

grass and weeds between cultivated fields. We moved a lot of birds out of fallow fields that had been set aside as old vehicle depositories and farm garbage dumps.

Traditional native vegetation such as plum thickets and cattail sloughs hold concentrations of birds and are easily walked by a hunter. Sadly, however, they are few and far between these days in much of the state. With Kansas' partial mosaic of pavement to pavement fields, it was often possible to look at flat ground to the horizon and see nothing but row crops. In these sorts of areas, large winter wheat fields are the birds' refuges. The decline of pheasant populations in western Kansas have been traced to farming practices that mandate a very low stubble height for weed control and the use of herbicides to destroy forbs which are needed by birds attempting to winter over. Additionally, in the spring, chicks need the protein from insects to grow. With the eradication of weeds, insect production is also destroyed and pheasant chicks do not survive.

Hunters should concentrate their efforts on land that has a diversity of covers and edges that have been left uncultivated.

Locating Hunting Areas

Ringnecks are large birds and, of all the game birds of North America, one of the easiest to locate in the wild.

Emma delivers up a rooster.

- Confine your search to agricultural areas. It is possible to find pheasants away from feed fields, but it is unlikely.
- Ask the local farmers, rural mail carrier or propane delivery truck driver. You will be amazed at the information available from many rural feed stores, especially if you buy a bag of dog food or a bale of prairie hay to change dog bedding.
- Once an active feeding field is located, search for adjacent roosting and escape covers.
- Roosters are sometimes vocal in the morning and evening. Listen for them and get a fix on their locations.
- Use binoculars and glass likely edges.
- The birds will take refuge in the worst, most inhospitable cover. Look for wet cattail choked slough, center pivot corners, uncultivated edges and partitions of fields, fallow weed-choked fields, plum thickets, heavy tree belts along water or used as windbreaks, or the one raised mound of earth (too high to plow) in the middle of a hundred-acre stubble field.

Looking for Sign

Feeding pheasants tend to stick out like neon lawn flamingos. Many of my pheasant successes resulted from driving down a road and spotting the dark silhouettes of

Hunters form a skirmish line to drive pheasants in heavy cover.

birds gleaning a field. I pulled over, checked through binoculars to make sure they were pheasants, and then made a mental note to remember the area.

In addition, birds using an area leave distinctive chicken-sized tracks. Like other gallinaceous birds, they take dust baths that leave shallow depressions easily spotted by hunters. Their droppings and loose feathers can also be seen in the areas that birds frequent.

Hunting Methods

The ring-necked pheasant really is America's bird, and because Kansas is the epitome of America, it is Kansas' bird. Forget that the Western Meadowlark has the title of official state bird, we all know who the real heavyweight is. Pheasant hunting is a Kansas tradition.

There are two fall migrations in Kansas. The ducks and geese move from north to south in front of the storms, and pheasant hunters move from the population centers in the east of Kansas to the harvested grain fields of the west. Lines of guns stretch along the edge of those fields and begin pushing birds to blockers stationed at the end of the rows. The strategy is to move the birds to the front until they come up to the blockers and are forced into the air. Typically during a drive, few birds are seen until the last hundred yards, and then Katie bar the door. The blockers generally have the best shooting, and the blocking positions are entrusted to the elder statesmen present

Three German short-haired pointers showing how it's done.

at the hunt. First, because they can generally shoot better; second, the level of exertion is much lower; and last, they can remember when the young whippersnappers walking the line were still in diapers.

Some birds will try to boil out the sides or come back over the tops of the advancing guns. With large fields, gunners will switch back, up and back, until they have traversed the entire distance and in the final sweep towards the blockers, move the pheasants into flight. This all makes for a lot of work.

Within a few days, the surviving birds abandon the hunted fields and lay low in areas such as uncut milo and thick cover along edges and in heavy CRP grass fields. At this point, a hunter must target specific cover and work to move roosters. A rooting dog can get into the deep stuff and push the birds. Little pockets of native cover in a planted field, a long abandoned farm dump at the end of some abandoned fence line, thick cane cover that chokes the shoulder of a farm two track road: these are all the type of places where wily roosters may take refuge. In the first few days, the reason for a pheasant's location was about food, now it's about refuge.

Hunting with Dogs

An experienced dog can be a real asset when hunting pheasants. Birds are generally flushed from the edge of thick cover; if they weren't in the thick stuff to begin with, they run into it at the hunter's approach. A dog that will cover the strips and edges within gun range and root in deep can get a moving runner into the air. A good flush dog is the ticket. Retriever breeds hunted as flush dogs are well adapted to this and, on ringnecks, the pointing breeds are forced into it by default. The Labrador retriever is a popular dog in Kansas.

I have watched running ringnecks out-sprint a pointing dog. If the pheasants don't make the mistake of stopping and holding, they are untouchable. Thinking back on my time in Kansas, I don't know that I killed a pheasant over a clean point with one of my setters. My dogs are out at 50 to 200 yards and the pheasant invariably lit out the other way on the other side of them. In the thick CRP fields, the birds were handicapped, and we killed a few birds in range as they bumped off the dogs.

Severe weather also improves a pheasant's inclination to stay put. There were a few brutally cold mornings that caused the birds to hold, but even those ringnecks jumped wild. It's just that they jumped at 10 yards instead of 25.

I hunted with some close-working German shorthairs who did a good job of working the cover calmly and at easy gun range. It was obvious that they had had ample experience. The GSPs did produce several pointed birds, often hens, while working corn, milo, and CRP; but I think it's fair to say that most of the roosters brought to bag flushed wild from within gun range.

One thing that impressed me was how adept a wounded rooster is at covering ground. A tenacious, no-nonsense retriever who uses ground scent well is worth his weight in recovered pheasants.

Table Preparation

In the annals of wild game cookery, pheasant is the standard that all game birds are judged by. Which is to say, pheasant is very good. Pheasant breast meat is white and leg meat is dark. They run about the size of a medium built frying chicken.

I will confess heresy and admit I generally skin pheasants for the sake of expediency. Most of the pheasants I come by are shot while dog training in the hot weather of Arizona or when I am on the road traveling. For those concerned with presentation, plucking is the only way to go. Most pheasants are hard won and when one is presented at the dinner table, a celebration is in order.

In cool weather, pheasants are best hung, gutted or ungutted (as a person's tastes dictate) for a week or more. In warm climates, it is best to eviscerate the bird before aging it in a cool area or refrigerator. Unless the bird is shot up or chewed up or otherwise suspect, pluck the bird and prepare with the skin on. Damaged birds are best skinned and apportioned as the recipe dictates.

The consummate treatise on preparing a pheasant for the table is in Datus Proper's book *Pheasants of the Mind*, chapter 14, entitled "Flavor."

Shot and Choke Suggestions
- Early season: improved cylinder / modified, heavy loads, 7½ to 6 shot
- Late season: improved cylinder / full, heavy loads, 6 and 5 shot

Lesser Prairie Chicken

Tympanuchus pallidicinctus

FIELD FACTS

Local Name

Pinnated Grouse, Prairie Grouse, Chickens, Wild Chicken, Fool Hen, Prairie Hen

Size

- Males: 16 inches in length; up to 2 pounds in weight; wingspan of about 24.5 inches
- Females: 16 inches in length; up to 1 pound, 11.5 ounces; wingspan of about 24 inches

Identification in Flight

Lesser prairie chickens are indistinguishable from greater prairie chickens in flight. Both species, at a distance, appear a uniform light brown color. They have a strong wing stroke and lift from the ground readily. In flight, they exhibit a short square tail and light colored breast and side coverts.

Birds in flight alternately flap their wings two or three times and then coast. This gives the appearance of the individual birds rising and falling in their line of flight and make a chicken flock readily identifiable even at extended distances.

Facts

- Lesser prairie chickens, like greaters, are grassland residents.
- Birds are associated with healthy stands of sand sage and prairie grasses. They also do well in a mixed grain field/grassland/sand sagebrush habitat. In past decades, large areas of sand sage were destroyed by aerial herbicide spraying to benefit cattle grazers. With an absence of grass, no chickens will be present.
- Lesser prairie chicken populations are currently in severe decline throughout their range.
- The lesser prairie chicken season in Kansas starts December 1 and runs through the end of January.
- Prairie chickens follow a predictable flight path to and from feeding fields, morning and evening.

Color

Like the greater prairie chicken, at a distance, the lesser prairie chicken appears a dull uniform brown. Both sexes are nearly identical, except under close observation. In hand, the pinnated grouse's plumage is an intricate pattern of bronze, black, tan, and brown.

Lesser Prairie Chicken Distribution

Lesser Prairie Chicken Distribution

The pinnated grouse is given its name for the two thin, pointed, pinnate feather groups that run the length of the bird's neck. The feathers are longer on male birds, and bordered with a sharp black line that originates behind the bird's ears. While both lesser and greater prairie chickens are markedly similar, there are subtle color differences. The dark barring on the back and rump is brown on lesser chickens and near black on greaters. Also, lessers carry heavier barring of brown and white on the breast feathers.

In male chickens, the upper service of the tail feathers is a uniform bronze. Barring on the central tail feathers breaks the female's uniform tail color.

Male lesser pinnated grouse have a pronounced yellow comb above the eye and reddish gular sacks.

Sound and Flight Patterns

The sand sage prairie home of Kansas' lesser prairie chicken is measured in vast increments of empty sky. The birds live there in small groups spread over a treeless expanse of grass. A hunter may walk two or three miles between flushes. I found it difficult to locate lessers and harder still to be within gun range when they lifted. Typically, the flock flushes at about 80 to 100 yards. While the prairie appears flat and featureless, there are slight elevations that afford birds a commanding view of an approaching gunner, as well as shallow depressions providing a break from the wind.

Flushed birds leave in one group and aim for the horizon. I did try to follow up a couple of flocks that I marked down a quarter-mile out. The uniform quality of the cover makes it difficult to effectively locate a landing site because once I had moved a couple hundred yards from my marking position, my reference marks were irrelevant.

In flight, prairie chickens have a very distinctive flight pattern. The birds pump their wings two or three times and then glide. They glide to the point of the beginning loss of elevation and then they pump their wings again. Flying chickens seem to float at times and seem unsteady in the air. To the observer on the ground, it gives birds on the wing the appearance of riding bicycles. Their flight cadence is very distinctive and makes identification of chicken flocks, even at extreme distances, very easy.

Lessers, like greater prairie chickens, rely on grain crops during fall and winter as feeding areas. Birds will fly to feed fields both morning and evening. I am told that lessers will also fly into stock tanks at first light in order to water. Traveling lessers use the same flight paths and navigate off of fixed points on the ground. If a hunter patterns feeding birds, it is possible to ambush birds as they fly to or from feeding.

During March and April and to a lesser extent in the fall, lesser prairie chickens gather on their lek sites and engage in mating displays. During their dancing rituals, male birds make a loud booming sound that can be heard from a considerable distance. Also, flushing birds are reported to cackle when they lift into the air. I did not hear this in my limited contact with departing lessers, but I will take the word of others who are more chicken savvy than I. As my wife tells me, there are many things that I don't hear.

Similar Game Birds

While sharptails and prairie chickens are very similar in appearance, the range of lesser prairie chicken and sharptails do not overlap.

Hen ring-necked pheasants and lessers are of a similar size and uniform brown hue, but a hen pheasant trails a long tail in flight, while a chicken's tail is short and square. A lesser's underwing feathers are a white hue; a hen pheasant's underwings are brown. Pheasants rise as singles or staggered small groups, while a flock of lessers rise and leave as a flock. On the wing, pheasants fly with a strong wing beat and then coast stiff-winged to a landing area. Prairie chickens fly with a *flap, flap, flap, glide, flap, flap, flap, glide* flight cadence until out of sight.

Flock or Covey Habits

Prairie chickens are flock birds. Lessers will exhibit a strong territorial fidelity to their lek or booming grounds. While birds will abandon the lek site during the non-breeding times of the year, they will be found somewhere in the general vicinity.

Beginning in March, adult males begin their strutting displays, and the females window shop the dancing males to select an acceptable mate. After breeding, females tend to nest duties and chick rearing, alone. Summer flocks are composed of hens and their broods or bachelor males. During fall and winter, it appears that the sexes may remain segregated. Hunters and area biologists report taking single sex birds from flock rises. Flocks generally number from 3 to 12 birds. Groups of up to 15 birds have been observed.

As I have stated before, lessers exhibit a strong fidelity to their lek site and are often found in close proximity to it. The home range of a group of chickens can include up to a square mile of prairie. Hunters should begin searching for lesser chickens at the lek site and expand their efforts outward to a search circumference of one half-mile.

Reproduction and Life Span

While doing the research for this book, I was shown several lesser prairie chicken lek sites on the Cimarron National Grasslands in the extreme southwestern corner of the state. The only visible characteristics of the lek site were that the grass was shorter, and the leks were situated on a slight rise or elevation allowing displaying males to be more visible. If someone had not pointed out the precise spot to me, my uninitiated eyes would not have been able to discern a difference between the lek and the surrounding grasslands.

A lek's location is determined by its potential for attracting hens. Leks are located in confined areas of prairie grass composed of short grass species such as buffalo grass, or as the result of agricultural activities and/or grazing. The shorter the grass, the more visible the male's dancing displays are to the females.

The same lek sites are used each year with some occasional movement. Depending on habitat conditions, lek sites have been abandoned and activity shifted to as much as a half-mile away. However, such movements are rare. Typically, if a shift

Lesser Prairie Chicken.

occurs, it will only be 100 yards away to an area where shorter grass height facilitates greater visibility for displaying males.

Male chickens attract mates through the broadcasting of a loud booming sound. This booming is produced by the movement of air in the bird's gular sacks that inflate on the side of the bird's neck. This sound can travel across the prairie for a half-mile or more. However, as wind effectively lessens the distance that the sound can be heard, windy conditions tend to discourage booming activity.

After visually locating booming males, the hens approach the edge of a dancing ground and check out the available talent. Males vie against other competing dancers to breed hens as they enter the territories of individual displaying males. Following breeding activity, males share no nesting or rearing duties.

Curious, I asked about the level of predation visited on displaying birds. Apparently, even with birds in such open areas, the impact is minimal. One eyewitness account told of a northern harrier flying over displaying birds, which only caused the birds to flatten down to the ground. Activity resumed immediately after the raptor passed overhead. This same observer related sighting a coyote walking through the middle of an active lek. The displaying male chickens, directly in the path of the advancing canine, flushed at the coyote's approach. As soon as the coyote left the area, however, booming activities resumed. Undoubtedly some predation does occur, but it appears to be minimal.

Prairie chickens are thought to have the potential to live up to 5 or 6 years in the wild.

Feeding Habits and Patterns

Lessers will utilize the same sorts of cultivated food sources as greaters, the big four being sorghum, wheat, corn, and soybeans. Some lesser flocks use no cultivated grains at all and rely strictly on a diet of native plants and insects. In the summer, birds rely heavily on insects for protein and moisture. Grazing issues are a concern because without adequate overstory, bird species cannot survive.

Birds will feed morning and evening. If flocks are feeding on cultivated grains, they fly early into their feed fields, forage, and retire to their home range on the open prairie to loaf midday. Birds will again feed in the late afternoon. I am told that lessers have the same propensity to follow fixed travel paths like their larger cousins. However, my hunting experience has been limited to chasing lessers on open grasslands, and therefore, I have no firsthand knowledge. I did spend one afternoon on a milo stubble field that historically had been a feeding field of lesser prairie chickens, but no birds were spotted.

One other interesting bit of information: I was told by a gentleman who had extensive experience hunting lesser prairie chickens that birds will go to standing water at first light and that hunters waiting in ambush could sometimes collect birds. But again, I have no firsthand knowledge of this.

Preferred Habitat and Cover

Like the greaters, lesser prairie chickens are birds of the open prairie. But unlike their larger cousins, they have not fared as well. The difference is that, where a greater's ideal is 3 parts native grass and 1 part agriculture, a lesser's dependence on unbroken grass is much more critical. Depending on whom you speak with, their ideal mix is something like 1 part agriculture and 7 parts native grass.

The range of the lesser prairie chicken in Kansas is restricted to the high plains and red hills physiographic regions. The high plains lesser prairie chicken habitat is characterized by native grass prairie with interspersed overstory of sand sage. Sand sage seems to have some critical component for lesser prairie chickens, as birds are generally absent from areas without adequate sand sage cover. In other areas throughout lesser chicken range, Shinnery oak replaces sand sage as a low overstory plant.

Locating Hunting Areas

Begin with areas of unbroken grass. Lesser prairie chicken range is limited to the southwestern corner of Kansas.

Ed Anderson of Elkhart hunting the Cimmarron National Grasslands.

- Start by asking someone. It is very difficult for a hunter to locate lessers without the aid of a person who knows of existing populations.
- Locate lek sites and begin hunting in their vicinity.
- Study the lek site for signs of current use like tracks, feathers, or the sighting of actual birds.
- In lieu of locating a lek, try to find feed fields that the chickens are frequenting. Look for milo, corn, or soybeans. Either hunt them on the field, if permission is available, or back trail the birds to their home area and try to secure permission there.

Looking for Sign

Lessers live in such immense stretches of grass that locating them is very difficult. A check of known lek sites for feathers and tracks will tell a hunter if birds are actively using the area, but that presupposes that the hunter already knows where the lek is located.

Watching birds traveling to and from feed fields will also help in pinpointing a flock's home range. Start at a feed field and track the birds backward on their feeding flight. This could take several mornings. Once a general piece of ground is located, another difficulty will be to find the landowner to secure permission to hunt. Kansas is mostly private land, so anywhere the birds go is more than likely going to be private property. See the section on land access for more information.

Hunting Methods

There are basically two methods of hunting lesser prairie chickens. A hunter can walk them up in the open grass, or ambush flocks coming into feed fields. I was fortunate to collect a good adult male lesser in southwestern Kansas during my travels doing the research for this book. I don't have any easy answers for those aspiring to do the same.

I started at a lek site, and using the position of the lek like the hub of a wheel, I walked spokes out across the prairie. I had six dogs with me: five setters and a pointer. I walked a straight line out about a half-mile, walked in an arch over a few hundred yards, or about 10 degrees, and returned in a straight line back to the hub. Upon returning, I changed dogs and started on a new line. Experienced local hunters tell me that lessers are sometimes located directly on the lek site. It took me a day and a half to locate a flock. I estimate that I was a half-mile from the central lek when the birds went up.

Now mind you, there is not much to distinguish one piece of grasslands from another. I was told to concentrate on areas with stands of sand sagebrush remaining. In the area I was hunting, the sand sagebrush had been destroyed through aerial herbicide spraying, from 1979 through 1984, to benefit cattle grazers. The application had not been uniform and swaths were left unsprayed. Little pockets of sand sagebrush remained behind in small depressions and along slopes of low rolls. Ultimately, I found the flock in a shallow sand sagebrush-choked depression about thirty yards in circumference.

By all rights, I should not have taken a bird, but through luck and high winds, I was able to approach the birds and be in position for a shot. I was anticipating chickens because the setter I was running had gotten birdy and false-pointed twice as we approached the area. The wind was absolutely howling so the birds could not hear our approach. The setter was following a scent trail, but in the wind there was no way to pinpoint the location. She swung wide and moved off to the side of me. I pushed through the grass and crested over the lip of the depression, and 4 lessers came up 15 yards in front of me. The limit is 1 bird and I picked the biggest one and folded it 10 feet above the launch pad. Another small group came up and then another. The birds would rise off the ground and hit the wind. They left as though they were rockets. There were about 10 birds, all told.

I was anticipating shots at extreme ranges, so I was carrying a 12-gauge with a full choke barrel. The shotgun was loaded with Federal premium buffered copper 4s. The tertial feathers at the base of the bird's right wing separated from the rest of the bird and scattered with the wind; I assume the wad had plowed through and yanked the feathers. What followed was a Keystone Cops affair of me chasing feathers in the wind, trying to recover as many wing feathers as possible to salvage the bird for an open wing mount. The setter looked at me like I had gone round the bend.

Having found the location of the flock, I was able to return two more times for photographs. I located the birds, quickly, in the same general area. The lesson here is that those who already know where flocks hang out are way ahead of the game. On my follow up, the birds flushed at extreme distances, far out of gun range.

Much of the hunting done for lessers is walk-up hunting. While the population density of lessers is low, and chances for success are marginal, I don't know of a prettier place to take a walk with a bird dog.

While I didn't personally hunt lessers over feed fields, local hunters told me that it could be as productive as when employed on greater prairie chickens. Basically, a hunter scouts for a potential feed field and makes note of when and where lessers fly in to feed. Next, the hunter and maybe a friend or two set up on the field fence line before the designated time and place. The information supplied in the section on greaters applies here.

Hunting with Dogs

In Kansas, there is no early lesser prairie chicken season. By the time the December 1st season opens, the birds of the year have left their brood flocks and are as wild as their parents. This makes the birds difficult to approach.

Contrast the birds' wariness with the fact that lesser prairie chickens live on ground made for running dogs. As I stated earlier, heavy wind made it possible for me and a dog to walk up to a flock of chickens in open grass. Local hunters I spoke with use dogs throughout the season to hunt lessers with some success. I hunted with one gentleman and his German shorthair. I found the dog hunted within gun range in a calm and thorough manner. I could imagine him working into chickens without spooking them, while a pointer running at full throttle 200 yards out would only bump birds.

For the hunter waiting in ambush on a fence line, a retriever is a big plus. A downed bird can be difficult to locate when it pitches into a stubble field or open grass cover. Crippled chickens can leave the area in a hurry. A nonslip retriever who sits calmly with the waiting gunner will be able to mark birds down and make a quick pick-up.

Table Preparation

Lesser and greater prairie chickens share the same culinary qualities and should be handled in the same manner.

Shot and Choke Suggestions
• 7½ to 6 shot, modified/full chokes

Lesser Prairie Chicken Outlook

I was in a used bookstore the other day and came across a very old book on upland bird hunting. The book, *Game Bird Shooting*, was written by Captain Charles Askins in 1931. This book was in pristine condition, in the original dust jacket, and under glass in a display case. This is never a good sign because if a book is under glass, it means it's over my budget. I confirmed the inevitable by looking at the price written on the inside cover of the book. Oh well. I found a chair and went through the table of contents and my eyes stuck on Chapter 1, page 1, on prairie chickens.

Askins opens with a narrative of his early chicken hunting experiences on the Cherokee strip in Oklahoma, before the prairie was broken by plow. This was in the late 1880s. He describes riding out in front of a horse-drawn wagon in the open grass, with two dogs working out front. He recounts flock after flock of birds rising like waves in front of them, swells moving across the face of an open sea. The birds were spread out in a thin line of trees outlining a watercourse. He describes a single flock of 300 turkeys flushing *en masse*. They did their best to fill up the wagon. It must have been something to see.

He goes on to say, "In six years they were all gone, not a bird left east of the Cimarron River... People said the chicken had gone west, migrated through dislike of civilization, of the plow and the reaper. As a matter of fact they were all dead. Had our bob-white quail weighed a pound instead of a short eight ounce, had he, too, been strictly a bird of the open, he surely would have 'gone West' with the chicken," (Askins, 1931, p. 4).

I don't wish to diminish the author's contention that gunning pressure forced the demise of the vast chicken flocks; however, the plow was also there. The intervening years have brought many changes to the formerly unbroken prairie. What now remains bears little resemblance to their former home.

The continued hunting of the lesser prairie chicken is in doubt. Currently hunting of this species is only allowed in two states, Kansas and Texas, though the Lesser is found in small fragmented populations in five states: Kansas, Texas, Oklahoma, New Mexico, and Colorado. The birds have been in real trouble for some time, and numbers have dwindled to varying degrees across the range. In some areas, the impact has been more profound than others. It is important to note that habitat issues, not hunting impact, have been responsible for the declines in population. In Kansas, annual hunting effects are negligible and do not affect population levels. Population reverses have been attributed to a host of possible habitat factors. While some factors seem more likely than others, currently no one agrees on any definitive answers.

A petition was filed in October, 1995, by the Biodiversity Legal Foundation of Boulder, Colorado, to list the Lesser as threatened under the Endangered Species Act. Under the law, once presented with a petition, the Fish and Wildlife Service is legally required to evaluate the species as a candidate for listing and issue an initial finding within 90 days. Due first to a moratorium on listing activities, followed afterwards by budgetary constraints, the Fish and Wildlife Service did not act on the petition within the designated time period. After 14 months of inaction, the Biodiversity Legal Foundation filed suit in December 1996 against the FWS for failure to issue a finding.

According to the law, at the end of the required 90-day period the FWS can choose one of two options: they can determine that the petition does not contain substantial information and dismiss it, or they can confirm that it does contain substantial information and move into a 12-month review process. In July 1997, the FWS found that there was enough substantial information to enter into the 12-month review process. At the time of this writing in April, 1998, the 12-month review process has expired and a final determination is being awaited.

The FWS has three options: 1) Listing is warranted, 2) Listing is warranted but precluded, or 3) Listing is not warranted. If the FWS finds that listing is warranted, states with open hunting seasons on the Lesser will have no choice but to recommend closing the season to their respective game commissions. Consequently, the hunting of lesser prairie chickens will come to an end.

While this process has been ongoing, the five affected state wildlife agencies entrusted with managing their respective lesser prairie chicken populations, other affected agencies, and private individuals and businesses have formed the Lesser Prairie Chicken Interstate Working Group. This has been a proactive effort to develop a regional plan to address habitat issues and reverse population declines within the species at the state management level. This conservation plan, when reviewed by the Fish and Wildlife Service during their deliberations, may have some effect on the choice that the Fish and Wildlife Service ultimately makes.

One hundred years of cohabitation has shown us that the fragmenting of the prairie, and the destruction of the remaining grasslands, ultimately ended the reign of the lesser prairie chickens. However, while my experience with lesser prairie chicken hunting in southwestern Kansas was less productive then the hunting experienced by Captain Askins a century ago, it was certainly no less rewarding.

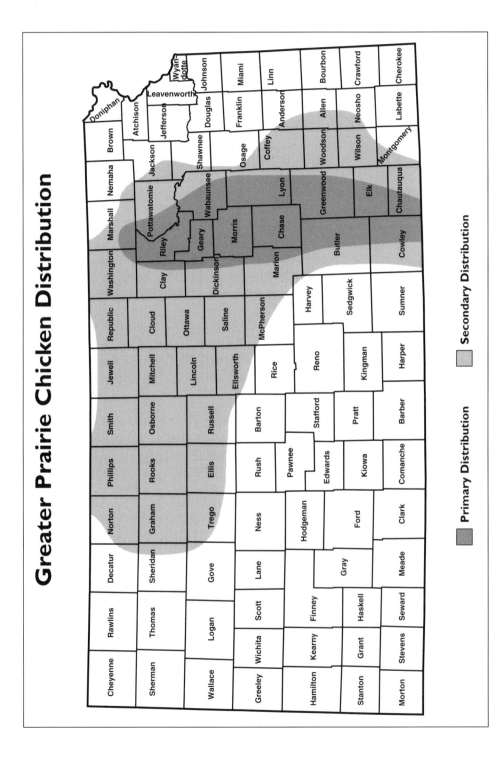

Greater Prairie Chicken Distribution

■ Primary Distribution   ▨ Secondary Distribution

Greater Prairie Chicken

Tympanuchus cupido

FIELD FACTS

Local Name
Pinnated Grouse, Prairie Grouse, Chicken, Wild Chicken, Fool Hen, Prairie Hen

Size
- Males: 18.5 inches in length; up to 2.5 pounds in weight; wingspan of about 27.5 inches
- Females: 18 inches in length; up to 1 pound, 13 ounces; wingspan is 27.5 inches

Identification in Flight
Prairie chickens are a uniform light brown color in flight. They have a strong wing stroke and lift from the ground readily. In flight, they exhibit a short square tail and light-colored breast and side coverts.

Birds in flight alternately flap their wings two or three times and then coast. This gives the appearance of the individual birds rising and falling in their line of flight and make a chicken flock readily identifiable even at extended distances.

Facts
- Prairie chickens are a bird of the grasslands. They will use grain fields. A ratio of three parts grassland to one part agricultural grain is considered ideal. With an absence of grass, no chickens will be present.
- Chickens are currently expanding their range westward in Kansas.
- There are two seasons in Kansas: one in September, and a second running from early November through the end of January.
- Prairie chickens follow a predictable flight path to and from feeding fields and, unless disturbed, can be expected to use the same route on subsequent flights.

Color

When observed from a distance, the prairie chicken appears a dull uniform brown. Males and females are nearly identical in plumage. When observed in hand, the pinnated grouse's plumage is an intricate pattern of bronze, black, tan, and brown.

The pinnated grouse was given its name for the two thin, pointed, pinnate feather groups that run the length of the bird's neck. The feathers are bordered in sharp black and originate from behind the bird's ears. Vertical brown barring covers the bird's breast and side coverts. The back and upper tail coverts are barred in a

A fine pair of greater prairie chickens.

dense pattern of brown with tan and black highlights. In males, the upper service of the tail feathers is a uniform bronze. Barring on the central tail feathers breaks the female's uniform tail color.

Male pinnated grouse have a conspicuous yellow comb above the eye. Below the pinnate feathers, on the side of the neck, male grouse have yellow gular sacks that are used during their March and April courtship displays. The sacks are inflated with air and produce a booming sound. The legs are feathered.

Sound and Flight Patterns

Prairie chickens live in flock groups. While hunting in December and January, I observed flocks of 3 to 40 birds. I am told that flocks occasionally mass in the hundreds. Groups of birds flying into feed fields typically land among earlier arriving birds and form feeding groups of up to 200 birds. The individual flocks fly in from the open prairie from all points of the compass and, at the culmination of feeding, leave the same way. Birds typically forage from 45 minutes to 2 hours.

In flight, prairie chickens have a very distinctive flight pattern. The birds pump their wings two or three times and then glide. They glide to the point of the beginning of loss in elevation and then they pump their wings again. To the observer on the ground, it gives an approaching flock the appearance of riding bicycles. The flight cadence is very distinctive and makes identification of chicken flocks, even at extreme distances, very easy.

Birds that are flushed while hunting will leave the area. Often, with other species of game birds, it is possible to mark the birds in after the initial flush and then approach for another shot. When prairie chickens fly, they fly away.

On the breeding leks in March and April, displaying males make a loud booming sound that can be heard at great distances.

Prairie chickens are reported to cackle when flushed. I will have to take other people's word for it because I couldn't hear anything above the howling wind.

Similar Game Birds

Prairie chickens and sharp-tailed grouse utilize the same grassland habitat. Sharp-tailed grouse disappeared from Kansas in the 1930s. Reintroduction efforts began in 1982 to return sharptails to their historic range in northwestern Kansas. Today, sharp-tailed grouse are only found in Cheyenne and Rawlins Counties in the extreme northwest corner of the state and Ellis, Russell, Osborne, and Rooks Counties in the north central area. In the aforementioned counties, it is possible to encounter both prairie chickens and sharp-tailed grouse in the same area.

- Sharptails and prairie chickens are very similar in appearance. The visual marks to compare when trying to differentiate the two species are:
- Chickens have a short square tail and sharptails have a short pointed tail.
- Sharptails exhibit much more white on their belly and sides when flushing and tend to cackle at the flush.
- In the hand, the chicken's feather pattern is best described as barred while a sharptail's feather pattern can be described as v's and dots.

Flock or Covey Habits

While hunting in Kansas I encountered chickens in groups of 3 to 45. During the early season in September, the young of the year were still traveling in their brood flocks. These flocks might be composed of several hens and their mostly grown off-spring. The birds were found on the prairie feeding on insect protein.

In November and December the birds travel in intact groups while coming into feed fields. Flocks join together on a feed field and, in some instances, number in the hundreds. Typically, a single scout arrives 2 to 3 minutes before the flock and lands in the feeding area. If you want to see the main group, do not shoot at the scout. Unless disturbed, the birds will return to the same area of the field where they fed the

Prairie chickens on the wing as they approach a feed field.

day before. The arriving flock decoys into the landing position chosen by the scout. If earlier arriving flocks are already present, the new flight will land adjacent to them.

They literally use the same landmarks to navigate their feeding flights. A flock of chickens will fly in off the prairie using a fixed landmark like a fence line or defined roll of land. For example, I observed one flock that followed this pattern: at a rusted-out tractor growing into the edge of the prairie, the flock made a 30-degree turn to the west to follow a dirt track; 200 yards along the track, the birds crossed over a dark, railroad-tie fence corner post and angled their flight path north 40 degrees; the birds then cut straight across a disked stubble field and flew into their feed field over the same 2 telephone poles they passed over during the previous 5 days.

Chickens feed both morning and evening, but I found their flight patterns to be more consistent during their morning feeding flights. If 5 flocks were using a feed field, all 5 would show in the morning and maybe only 3 would return in the afternoon. One farmer I spoke with told me that while in the fields at night, he sees chickens feeding by moonlight. This might offer a possible explanation of their afternoon absence.

Their consistency applies to time of arrival, also. I found birds to consistently arrive within the same 30 to 45 minute window as the day before.

While feeding on the ground, the birds were extremely wary and impossible to approach. When glassed through a spotting scope, a few of the feeding birds had their heads up and acted as sentries. No matter how quiet and concealed my approach, the birds would flatten out, run a hundred yards to one side and flush wild. In heavy wind, which covered my approach somewhat, I got as close as 70 yards (which I can advise the reader, through firsthand experience, is not close enough).

Reproduction and Life Span

Prairie chicken society revolves around their courtship sites called *leks*. Adult males go through an elaborate courtship display in an effort to be selected by the attending females. Birds fly into the leks at first light and are active for a couple of hours before dispersing back to the prairie. Another booming period repeats in the afternoon. The male birds assemble on these communal booming grounds beginning in early March. On a calm day, the sound of booming can be heard a mile or more. Booming activity peaks in April but can persist into June. A much-diminished second booming activity period takes place in October, but no breeding occurs.

A lek may have two to forty displaying males with a dozen being the average. Typically the same leks sites are used year after year with some minor variations. Leks are located on high ground or ridgelines. A 1985 Kansas Game and Fish Commission study that surveyed 22 different lek sites concluded that the leks were found on the highest point of land for a quarter-mile. Of the 22 sites, 2 were located on wheat fields and were abandoned when the stubble height exceeded a height of 15–20 inches. The remaining leks were on grasslands in bare or near bare clearings. Hunters should take note because during the hunting season, the flock will be found somewhere in the vicinity of their lek site.

The hen prairie chicken assumes all incubation and parenting duties. Nesting sites require tall grass cover to provide ample grass overstory. Clutches contain 12 to 16 eggs that hatch in 23 days. Most young hatch in late May and early June. Chicks feed heavily on insects. They are capable of limited flight at 2 weeks of age. After 15 weeks of age, young chickens are not readily distinguishable from adults.

Prairie chickens can be expected to survive to 5 or 6 years of age.

Feeding Habits and Patterns

Prairie chickens evolved on the prairie and utilized the native seeds and insects. With the advent of European colonization and the farming of the prairie, the birds readily incorporated cultivated crops into their diet. Initially, close proximity to grain increased chicken populations, but as more and more prairie was converted to agricultural lands, the ratio of grass to crops spelled the end of the chicken's reign.

Today, chickens rely heavily on agricultural fields. During the late fall and winter, depending on the area, cultivated seeds will comprise 50 to 90 percent of a prairie chicken's diet. Chickens feed on sorghum (also known as milo), wheat, corn, soybeans, millet, Korean lespedeza, Japanese brome, and alfalfa. Soybeans are a preferred crop when available. Overall, sorghum is used most heavily.

Chickens rely on the open fields to provide a safety zone around a feeding flock. Fields smaller than 15 acres are precluded from use because they don't provide an adequate approach buffer.

Greater prairie chicken in milo stubble.

In the spring and summer the chickens have an increased reliance on native forbs, grasses, and insects. Seeds of pigweed, lespedeza, coralberry, smartweed, dandelion, ragweed, and bristlegrass are used, among others. Use of insects, particularly grasshoppers and beetles, peaks during the summer.

During the winter, when access to food crops are compromised by snow accumulation, prairie chickens have been observed roosting in cottonwood trees along watercourses and feeding on their buds.

Preferred Habitat and Cover

Prairie chickens are birds of the grasslands. While birds can thrive in a 100-percent native grass environment, they do benefit from adjacent croplands. Grain crops are used heavily, especially during the winter months. A mixture of 75 percent prairie and 25 percent agricultural is considered ideal.

Kansas' prairie chicken range is short grass prairie in the western plains and tall grass prairie in the eastern Flint Hills. These grasslands consist of big and little bluestem, brome, 3-awn, dropseed, sideoats grama, bluegrass, switchgrass, Indian grass, blue and hairy grama, and buffalograss. Healthy prairie grouse populations are indicators of a grassland ecosystem's health.

Much of Kansas' prairie chicken range is rangeland managed for cattle grazing. Grasslands managed with controlled grazing and a prescribed rotational 4-year

Darrell Kincaid surveys his beloved Flint Hills.

burning regime, i.e., burning a quarter of the range area annually, can benefit prairie chickens.

On the other hand, cattle grazing can limit or eliminate prairie chicken habitat. Practices such as year-round grazing and heavy rotational grazing during April, May, and June eliminate necessary grass cover required during the nesting season, resulting in the reduction or elimination of prairie grouse. In addition, the newly expanding practice of annually burning a total area is having a devastating impact on prairie chicken range.

Locating Hunting Areas

Prairie chicken country is open and prospecting hunters should be able to spot potential hunting spots.

- A ratio of three parts grassland to one part feed field is considered an optimum mix in evaluating prairie chicken habitat.
- Birds flying to their feed fields or returning to the grasslands move in the early morning (the first three hours of light) or the late afternoon. Chicken flocks on the wing are very visible and easy to identify because of their unique "flap, flap, flap, coast" wing cadence.
- Depending on the stubble height, birds feeding on the ground can be located through binoculars.

Jesse grabs a downed greater.

- When searching for chickens, use their lek sites as a starting point. Look for feathers and droppings. Birds maintain a high fidelity to these areas and will often be found in the vicinity.
- The average size of a flock's home range is less than a square mile. They may travel less during the summer while feeding on native vegetation and insects, and further distances during the winter as the cold requires that they travel to remaining cultivated grain fields.

Looking for Sign

There are generally telltale traces where birds have been foraging. In milo stubble, I found droppings and feathers present. In a soybean field, which had no stubble height or remaining vegetation to speak of, chicken tracks were clearly evident in the soft soil.

In looking for a lek site, be aware that the birds prefer an area that has very little grass cover. In fact, less than six inches. Some booming grounds are located on the open dirt of a salt lick or cow trail. They are located on high ground with a view of the surrounding area. A lek site will have a total surface area of several thousand square feet.

Morning vigil: Jim Culbertson waits for the next flock coming over.

It will take the assistance of a local who knows the general location of a booming ground to get you into the approximate vicinity. The male birds announce their locations by booming during their courtship dancing in late March and April.

Hunting Methods

There are two seasons for greater prairie chickens in Kansas, with two different ways to hunt them successfully. The early season affords the opportunity to run pointing dogs on birds of the year on the grasslands. The open stretches of prairie are vast and ideal country for big running bird dogs. Brood flocks encountered during the early September season are made up of hens with birds of the year, and like youngsters everywhere, they make foolish mistakes. Dogs are able to approach and hold birds.

By the time the November season rolls around, the foolishness is over. I walked miles of prairie to where I had marked down birds landing after their morning feed flights. I pushed maybe a dozen flocks back into the air. None flushed in range. In a high wind that partially covered my approach, I was able to close the distance to 70–75 yards. I can speak with firsthand knowledge that, with a 12-gauge, that is not close enough. Darrell Kincaid of Topeka has a 10-gauge double gun named "Little Sister" that can reach that far on occasion.

A Kansas trio:
black Lab, model 12,
and greater prairie chicken.

Once, when I approached cautiously under cover of a howling wind, I was able to scratch down a chicken from a flock which had jumped from a stubble field. I tried belly-crawling towards feeding flocks in both stubble and soybeans; the only result was that I got muddy. The only productive methods are to wait in ambush under their flight path into the feed field, or to lay out in the portion of the field where they have been feeding and intercept their landing.

I should have killed birds using both approaches. While lying out in the part of a stubble field where the birds had been feeding the evening before, I had a flock of 35 literally dump in on top of me. I had been scraping to get within some semblance of shotgun range for the preceding two weeks, so I had a full-choked 12-gauge pump gun lying beside me. What I needed was an open choked skeet gun. The birds landed at 10 to 15 yards range. I blew three very small holes into the air, and then watched as the entire flock veered off and flew away.

Something I didn't try but I'm sure would work is using field decoys, along the same lines of setting up for geese in a feed field. Incoming chickens would readily pitch in on top of birds already on the ground feeding. A Kansas friend told me that they have been successful using hen mallard field shells.

Waiting in ambush under the approach path of feed flocks was more productive. If a hunter studies the flight of incoming chicken flocks, he will discover that they tend to follow the same path. If a hunter takes a position under the telephone pole where the chickens entered the field the day before, and the birds were undisturbed, they should follow the same flight path.

Should is the operative word. When I sat alone in ambush, the birds almost always came within one or two poles of the one they had used before. Generally, a single scout would fly in a few minutes before the main group and land in the feeding area. If there was time and I was close, I would adjust my position to get under where the scout had flown. Several times, the main flock was so close behind the scout that they spotted me moving and shifted their approach path to avoid going over the top of me. When I had a second gunner with me, we were able to cover a broader area and improve the odds. Another gunner and I were able to take three birds out of a flock passing between two telephone poles we were concealed behind.

Hunting with Dogs

As I stated before, the early season in September is the time to run pointing dogs on prairie chickens. The prairie country can roll forever and a dog can easily be seen working at 400 yards. Because the cover is so open and the distances so vast, it naturally pulls a dog to stretch out to maximum range.

During the late season, a free running pointer is going to be a liability. Chickens will not hold and an approaching dog is only going to put them into the air, at extreme ranges.

Successful late season hunting involves waiting in ambush for approaching birds. Retrievers are a big help in locating downed birds. Chickens wing-tipped out over stubble fields can be especially difficult to recover. I lost one chicken that ran, and by the time I could return to the vehicle to turn a dog loose, the bird had left the country.

Table Preparation

While some hunters I spoke with expressed a dislike for prairie chicken, I enjoyed it. The meat is dark and flavorful. Prairie chickens are the same size as a ring-necked pheasant and the same table preparation methods apply.

Shot and Choke Suggestions
- Early season: 7½ to 6 shot, improved / modified chokes
- Late season: 5 to 6 shot, full chokes

An American Original

The name 'greater prairie chicken' evokes a powerful image for me. In the years I spent working as a bird taxidermist, I never once mounted one. I never had a physical reference to make this abstract bird tangible. Much of my work was for collectors who made a point of traveling to far-flung places. They returned with examples of local game birds, including spruce grouse, sand grouse, sage grouse, sharptails, ptarmigan, and exotic pheasants which were beyond description. I held in my hands the skins of waterfowl from all parts of the globe. With their skins held up to yellow sunlight illuminating the surface of my workbench, they splintered color into iridescent shades and hues. Each bird had the unique scent of some far away place. I saw many different birds over the years, but no one ever made it back to my shop with a prairie chicken. The bird evaded those who tried.

There were chickens in the London Museum of Natural History, which I visited in the late '70s. They were tattered museum pieces with turn of the century collection dates, further reinforcing their mystique. Finding them there felt a little personal; after all, these were American birds, symbolizing the American experience, the great grassland heart of a continent and the American will to pioneer, struggle, and ultimately conquer. A nation in its infancy. These birds had been abducted and taken across an ocean, left in a glass case to be gawked at by foreigners.

Twenty years later, I came to Kansas to find a prairie chicken. The first chickens I saw lifted off a hillside as Darrell Kincaid, his side-by-side 10-gauge "L'il Sister", and I approached. We were in the northern Flint Hills, a country swept up in rolling expanses of soft tan hills. We had two setters and Darrell's GWP Hattie working the ground in front of us. Hattie was in tight. Darrell calls her his "old man's dog" because she works within gun range and never loses sight of her master. The setters, however, were another story.

The prairie is immense. Setters float on it like white gulls riding the wind currents just above the surface of the ocean. The setters traded in great sweeps and ran to become distant white specks before swinging and returning to the gun.

That morning, we saw ducks lift off the small stock ponds that dotted the drainages. Great Vs of Canada geese traveled the skies above us, their calls rang out on high. In the bottoms, we found coveys of bobwhites exploding in quick flashes of excitement and sound.

The chickens were near a lek site that Darrell knew of. The setters were working off to the opposite side, so when the chickens flushed, they flushed off of us. If the dogs had been in their general vicinity, I'm sure they wouldn't have had any compunction about flushing off of them, either.

The flock jumped at two hundred yards and never missed a beat. They rose up in a scattered group and swept across the hillside, floating with their unique wing cadence: Flap, flap, flap. Glide. Flap, flap, flap. Glide. The birds rounded the hill and were gone. We never saw them again. This sight, however, as fleeting as it was, had made them tangible. There really were prairie chickens!

I traveled to other parts of the state. The dogs and I chased bobwhites, and pheasants that ran and flew. The flashy long-tailed birds did everything right most of the time. A few messed up and came to lie in my hand. While holding the colorful immigrants, I stood in the lowland creeks and marsh edges and flat land stubble fields that provide the ringnecks a home. I marveled at their colorful exuberance, then I raised my eyes and studied the surrounding subtle landscape of prairie grassland hills and sky.

Always, I wondered to myself, "I wonder if there are chickens out there."

I have family living in Kansas. My aunt lives on the prairie, at the midway point of a long stretch of dirt road. The turn-off into her property is punctuated by a large solo standing rock in the shape of a bedded buffalo. She lives alone, having raised a family and survived two husbands. She is surrounded by her land, which is healthy grass dotted with ponds and hedge rows. A river runs at the back of the property.

Her life's work was as a teacher in a rural school, where the job description included helping her students with their lessons as well as, when necessary, using a shotgun for the occasional rattlesnake to make the playground safe for recess. Although she has been retired for many years, she continues to be the local resource for anyone needing information pertaining to the natural world. She keeps the artifacts of a life spent on the prairie as a museum for those who want to understand and learn.

She read me a poem by Stephen Vincent Benet about the spirit of the pioneers who had traveled West. She compared them to our own family, which had arrived in those same wagons, and to the prairie chicken, which was already here when they arrived. This quote from one of his poems, "The weak never started and the cowards died on the way," describes the strength of character required by both pioneers and the prairie chickens to survive in this sometimes harsh land.

My aunt took me to the lek, a small short grass clearing in one of her pastures where the prairie chickens dance their early spring courtship rituals. There was nothing distinct about it, yet this was the spot. She described how the sound of their booming carries over distance. During the spring, they can be heard at her home, a mile away.

She showed me the field where the birds would feed the following morning. The large field lays in the bend of a river. The watercourse is lined with mature trees. One winter in the middle of a severe cold snap, she and her husband drove to the edge of the field to check cattle. She described the flocks of chickens roosting in the frozen, bare winter trees, watching from their perches as they passed by. They were too cold to waste the energy it would require to flee.

The morning after speaking with my aunt, I arrived at the feed field before dawn. It was a large field of several hundred acres and had been planted in multiple strips of different crops. It was cold. A silver patina of frost lay on the soil. I sat on the fence line and watched as the dawn unfolded. At first light, whitetail deer left the field. I got to my feet and slowly walked the perimeter. The river lay below the lip of the field and as I followed the serpentine curves, a beautiful drake common goldeneye flushed from one of the few remaining patches of open water. The majority of the river was locked under an opaque pearl cover of ice. The bright white and black contrasts of the bird's body leapt out of the frozen surroundings, and the metallic green head was luminous in the fresh morning light. I swung the 12-gauge through the bird's body and would have pulled the trigger if there had been steel shot in the gun. With the weapon lowered, I watched fast wing beats disappear down the river.

Further on, I stopped and watched a flock of turkeys feed through a pasture on the other bank of the river. They were gorgeous in the morning light. Every hundred yards, I turned to the field and studied the area for chickens. Well past sunup, when the light was strong and the dawn shadows had vanished, the first flock came. They swept in from a section of prairie to the south. The small group of eight birds circled a portion of the field and then settled into a strip of soybeans. As if on cue, a second, larger flock arrived from the west and was joined in the air by a third flock arriving from the north. All the birds settled in with the others in the soybeans.

Hope springs eternal. I studied those birds for some way to get a shot. I picked a route, circled the field to get in position, and started my sneak. It is hard to imagine how ground can be both frozen and muddy at the same time; yet a quarter of the way out, on my belly crawl, I had accumulated a good coating of frozen soil. It is pointless to chronicle the rest of the grand sneak, because we have all tried them and we all know that they never work. This was no exception. The birds jumped at the extreme edge of shotgun range. I fired three shells from a long hoarded box of Federal Premium, buffered copper 4's. The birds flew away unscathed and i watched the largest flock swing out and fly into a large tract of land that I had permission to hunt.

For the rest of the day I walked that grass. I found bobwhites. I saw a black coyote who was curled up, sleeping in the grass and didn't jump until I got too close for him to abide; he was a sight to behold running in the wind. Silver black fur against gold and tan grass. I had a wonderful afternoon walking the prairie, but I never found a chicken.

The next morning I was at the field, on the fence line waiting for the birds to arrive. They came on schedule, but not over my position on the fence line. I sat with them for an hour and a half, through their feeding, and studied them through a spotting scope. When they left the field, one flock came close, but not close enough.

I abandoned the birds to their solitude. I had disturbed them on their feed field for two mornings, and not wanting them to change their pattern, I elected to move on. I could return later in the season.

The next chickens were near Wichita. A friend had set up an introduction for me to hunt with Jim Culbertson. Jim is a chicken hunter of the old school. His shotgun of choice is the Winchester model 12. Jim was a gracious host and a knowledgeable hunting companion. Jim, in turn, introduced me to another hunter named Larry Anderson. Larry is an excellent hunter and a great guy.

Jim took me to a sorghum stubble field that I both hunted alone and with Jim and Larry over the next four days. The field was large and surrounded on three sides by prairie. Our hunt coincided with some very cold weather that should have forced chickens to feed heavily in order to maintain their body temperature. Feed they did!

The birds came both morning and evening. The morning flights were the largest and the most consistent. During the worst of weather, the thermometer dipped below zero. With the wind chill factored in, it was very cold. The same flocks came daily, and two of them contained between 35 and 45 birds.

I patterned the birds and waited for them under their flight lanes, when they flew into the field to feed. I came close several times, but not close enough for a good shot. After the birds landed, I tried walking them up in the tall stubble. The birds always flushed out of range. I noticed that several flocks were feeding on a piece of high ground, and so one afternoon I laid out in the field in their landing area. It worked perfectly; a large flock of chickens appeared on the horizon and funneled right to me. The whole flock dumped in on top of me. As I had experienced such trouble getting close to birds, I was equipped with a full choke 12-gauge pump gun. I rose up to shoot when the birds were ten and fifteen yards away. Instead of letting the birds leave and gain some distance, I rattled off three quick shots and blew three very small holes in the air around them. The flock flew away unscathed.

After the morning flights left, I followed them out onto the prairie. With some flocks, I was able to get a fix on their general landing area and follow them up. Sometimes I found birds, but never was there a flush quite close enough for 12-gauge shotgun range.

Finally, the break came. Three flocks were consistently feeding in one corner of the stubble field. The birds arrived and entered the field over one of two adjoining telephone poles. Larry Anderson had joined me for the afternoon hunt and he took one pole and I took another. As the birds approached that day, I picked up sight of them out over the prairie. Slowly they came with their fluttery, on again/off again wing beat. Two hundred yards out I knew they were coming over the top of one of us. Luck was with me and they skirted in right over the lines on my pole. I was able to knock down two birds, a beautiful adult male and female. Part of the flock crowded the edge of my pole on Larry's side and he made a beautiful shot on a nice male. Finally, after days of trying, we had three chickens on the ground.

While setting up for photos the following morning, Jim and Larry were holding their guns and waiting for me to finish rigging camera gear. While we were standing out in the open, in plain sight, a flock flew right over the top and both guns were in position to shoot. A gift chicken hit the ground. It seemed a fitting ending, to have tried so hard for so long.

I finally had a chicken in hand! What I was holding was a bird to match any of the other species from around the world that I had mounted in my youth. But this one was an American original, and one I was fortunate and appreciative to add to my hunting experiences.

Bobwhite Quail

Colinus virginianus

FIELD FACTS

Local Name
Bobs, Quail, Birds, Partridge

Size
Bobwhite quail average 10–11 inches in body length, with a wing span running 14 to 16 inches. Birds weigh in around 6 ounces. Females are slightly smaller.

Identification in Flight
Bobwhites generally first rise as a group or covey. On the average, coveys will number 10 to 15 individual birds. The covey flushes with an explosion of sound and movement. Birds can leave in all directions. The wings of a departing bird make a whirring sound which is distinctive to gallinaceous birds and tends to identify the bird even when a visual observation is not possible.

Single birds look dark in flight with short, blurred wings and short, squared fantails. They rapidly move their wings to fly clear of the danger area and then coast stiff-winged to escape to cover. There is some color on the front of the bird, but generally the only observable part of a departing quail is a rapidly disappearing tail section.

Facts
- Bobwhite quail are second only to mourning doves in annual nationwide take. Bobwhites are present statewide in Kansas, with the best populations found in the eastern half of the state.
- Bobwhites can sustain an annual mortality of 70 to 85 percent of their population.
- A mixed diverse habitat is key to healthy bobwhite quail populations.

Color

The bobwhite quail is colored in an exquisite mix of subtle browns, reds, golds, and grays. Both sexes have cream-colored breasts broken with graduating, dark, v-shaped bars. The light breast color blends into russet side coverts accented with cream darts outlined in black. The back of the birds is a grey base color grizzled with russet, silver, gold, and black. The tarsal and scapular feathers lie in a striking pattern of grey, russet, and black outlined in gold. The tail is grey.

Bobwhite Distribution

Good to Excellent Distribution

Fair to Good Distribution

Locally Good Distribution

Mr. and Mrs. Bob.

The male bird has a face masked in black and white, with a russet cap. The female mask is similar with the exception that the facial pattern is zoned in gold instead of white.

Sound and Flight Patterns

The bobwhite quail is so named for the three-note call that unattached males whistle to attract interested, unattached hens. The call 'bob-white' has a sharp clear snap to it and, once heard, is readily recognizable.

Flushed birds lift quickly on blurred wings. The flush is loud and startling, and even when expected, it is unexpected. After years of exposure it still catches me by surprise. Coveys typically jump in unison, fly a short distance, and then pitch into available escape cover and hold. Open space birds may fly further distances at the flush, because their available escape covers are more widely spread geographically. Some of the coveys we flushed flew out into heavy grass CRP fields which made finding a single quail very difficult. Birds located for a second flush were invariably pointed in heavy cover or very near it. Retreating birds escape into very heavy cover and make the possibility of a third relocation unlikely.

Similar Game Birds

Quail are small in comparison to the state's other game bird species. The only other quail found in Kansas are scaled quail. Bobwhites and scalies are the same general size and share range in the extreme southwestern corner of the state. To be specific, they are found in the counties of Morton, Stevens, Seward, Meade, Clark, Stanton, Grant, Hamilton, Kearny, Finney, Wichita, and Wallace.

On the ground, the differences between species are clearly evident. Scaled quail are an overall grey in color to the brown and white hues of a bobwhite. Scaled quail sport an erect white crest on the top of their heads, while male bobs carry white on their throats and in a line across their eyes. Bobwhites tend to become more secretive upon a hunter's approach, holding tight and seldom seen until they flush. Scalies, on the other hand, are often seen running like hell in the other direction at a hunter's arrival.

Even to an experienced eye, it is difficult to differentiate between the two species while in flight. The best clue to identity is found in the location the birds flush from. Bobs are usually found in brush and along edge cover, often flushing through trees. Scalies are more prone to be in open grass away from cover. The truth is, however, sometimes the wrong bird will appear from the right cover. Scalies will sometimes loft at a covey flush.

With experience, it becomes possible to discern the difference. I have done a fair amount of controlled shooting of released bobwhite quail while dog training and most of the time I know what I'm shooting at.

The good news is that bobwhite and scaled quail are both legal game during the quail season, and as they can be taken in an aggregate limit, any concern about illegality is unwarranted.

Hungarian partridge is another species that can be confused with bobwhites. On the ground, both birds share a similar profile. A Hun has a grey body and a russet face mask and belly. Both are covey birds and tend to flush with a lot of commotion. Departing, both types of birds appear dark. Huns, however, are twice the size of a bobwhite, and this difference alone makes identification self-evident. Huns have a very limited distribution in Kansas and currently are (possibly) present only in Marshall, Nemaha, Brown, Pottawatome, Jackson, and Atchison counties.

Flock or Covey Habits

Bobwhite quail are covey birds. They live in covey groups of up to a couple dozen birds, with the average number falling in the range of 12 to 15 birds. Kansas birds are found across a range of different types of habitat, and home range size varies according to the quality of that habitat. In some of the better areas that we hunted in Kansas, we moved a covey every 200 to 300 yards in the edge cover surrounding feed fields.

Hattie delivers a bobwhite to hand.

Typically, birds start feeding early morning after roosting on the ground in a tight circle in low vegetation. Roosting quail lie with their heads facing out and tails pointed inward, like the spokes on a bicycle wheel. This conserves the bird's body heat and allows birds to survive during times of extreme cold. Additionally, when a roosting covey is threatened they can leave in a hurry, heading towards every point on the compass.

The foraging birds move as one unit and rely on others in the covey in their communal effort to locate food sources and evade predators. Birds stay coveyed until breeding pairs start forming in early spring. The coveys disband and pairs start nesting duties in early April. Chicks are raised by both parents and move as a group until coveys reform in the late summer and the cycle begins anew.

Reproduction and Life Span

Pairing begins in early spring with previously mated birds reuniting. Unattached males announce their availability by whistling the distinctive 'bob-white' call in an effort to attract an available female. Nests are constructed on the ground and filled with plant material. A grass cover is used to protect the nest from discovery. Both sexes participate in nest construction. The clutch of 14 eggs, on average, is incubated

Concho nails a single bobwhite in heavy cover.

by the female. Male birds undertake the nest duties if a hen is lost. Eggs hatch in 23 days. By the end of summer, the youngsters are full-sized and the covey groups have reformed.

Bobwhites are a prey species, and as such their annual mortality is very high. Written accounts place the span of annual mortality at 70 to 85 percent of the population. Such a figure is hard to quantify, but it is safe to assume that most bobwhite quail do not live to see their second birthday. In captivity, birds have a potential lifespan of 4 to 5 years.

Feeding Habits and Patterns

Bobwhites eat a varied diet with plant material comprising about 70 percent of the diet in the summer to over 90 percent in the winter. Quail rely heavily on various weed species, and they eat seeds, leaves, stems, and flowers (depending on the plant). When available, cultivated grains such as corn, sorghum, and wheat are eaten. During the summer months, insect protein and the moisture they contain are important in the birds' diet. This is especially so for growing chicks who require ample protein to reach adult size.

Quail feed morning and evening, spending the middle of the day in lofting cover. Daily movement patterns can change according to weather conditions. During times of approaching inclement weather, wildlife species will extend their feeding activity to ingest additional energy, needed to maintain their metabolism and body heat.

Perfect point in perfect quail cover.

Preferred Habitat and Cover

Three types of cover are necessary to sustain a quail population: escape, feed, and nesting. Areas that intersperse these three types of ground hold the most birds. Bobwhite quail like clutter: tangles of weeds and grass, tresses, and brush for escape cover. Feed areas of agricultural cereal grains or native plants provide their food supply. Thirdly, thick ground cover allows birds a place to nest and successfully rear their young.

Birds will use what is available and the density of birds will diminish in proportion to the degree that their home range provides these cover requirements. During the era of the small family farm, quail was available in abundance because much of the land was left untilled and free to grow grasses and forbs. With modern clean farming practices, the tractor runs from road shoulder to road shoulder, and herbicides control weed growth in between. Once a person keys in on what quail require, it is not difficult to look a place over and have a good idea if birds should be present and where to look.

In Kansas, bobwhite quail population densities correlate to the severity of the preceeding winter. If deep snows blanket the ground for several days, area quail will be decimated.

Locating Hunting Areas

Bobwhite quail are found statewide in Kansas. Locating suitable cover is the key to locating quail.

- Ask the landowner or farmer where quail coveys are.
- Bobwhites are found along the edges, in the transitional areas between feed and escape cover.
- Much of the state is cut by small creeks and river courses lined by hardwood trees. Birds love this escape cover, especially if there are adjacent agriculture or CRP grass fields.
- Fallow weed fields can be used heavily by birds. The value of such an area to birds is increased substantially when combined with abandoned farm machinery or junk piles.

Looking For Sign

The most visible indicators of birds I come across while walking likely country are covey rings. Bobwhites nest on the ground, in a tight circle, with their tails facing inward. When they depart in the morning, the birds leave a doughnut-sized ring of feces. The white and black droppings contrast with the ground and are easy to spot, even at several yards. Bobwhites tend to return to the same place to roost, so several rings can be found in a small area. When you see them, you know that the covey's around somewhere.

Quail also use dusting bowls: small depressions, up to a foot in diameter, in open dirt areas. The 'bowls' are disturbed powdery soil where the birds wallow in the dust and cleanse their feathers. Under close observation, tracks and loose feathers are generally evident in the finely textured soil.

Hunting Methods

If a person is going to talk about bobwhite quail hunting, it may be prudent to acknowledge that in the last hundred years more bobwhites have been successfully 'hunted' by farm kids in bib overalls using .22 shots than ever fell to expensive double guns. Few things are deadlier than a rural youngster with a single shot .22 rifle. So, after bowing to the real experts, quail can be hunted in two ways: with or without dogs. Let's start without.

Bobwhites are often taken while hunting Kansas' other upland game birds. Hunters working fields and edge cover for pheasant or grasslands for chickens are going to move quail. Coveys have a restricted home range and locals who know the area can tell you within a couple hundred yards where a covey's going to be found. It's a pretty straightforward affair: work a known or likely looking area thoroughly until something pops. Think in terms of a shot: try to position yourself to push birds to flush where a shot would be possible. Two hunters working together are more productive than one because, with two positions covered, at least one person is generally in position for a shot.

Dogs add another dimension to quail hunting. They will do the searching and indicate by pointing or flushing the birds for a shot. With a little experience, a hunter

Tense moments before the covey goes up.

will learn to read an area and know about where birds should be. The dogs will do the rest by running the edges. Quail will fan out into feed fields from adjacent heavy escape and roosting cover. A hunter/dog team walking the edges of that cover can often cut the trail of feeding birds.

Hunting with Dogs

A person can't talk about bird hunting without talking about bird dogs; the two are synonymous. Otherwise, it's like a country song without a truck in it! The dialog about bird hunting will ramble on about hard-slamming pointers and light-footed setters, burning up cover and turning covey after covey. So, let's start there.

Bobwhite quail can be and are hunted alone, without a dog, but that renders the exercise mostly an act of procurement. It is not bird hunting. The classic quail hunting dog breeds are pointers and setters. Of the setters there are three breeds: English, Gordon, and Red. These days the versatile breeds are also well represented in the bird fields, including German short-haired pointers, German wire-haired pointers, Pudelpointers, Griffons, Weimaraners, Vizslas, and Brittanies. The majority of America's bird dog history and culture developed in the south on bobwhite quail.

Kansas is classic bird dog country with vast expanses of flat to rolling ground and the agriculture needed to raise impressive numbers of birds. Pointing breeds work by running over a lot of country, in broad, casting arcs until they encounter bird scent. The dogs then freeze into a rigid stance and indicate game by 'pointing.' This allows

In Kansas, the Labrador is King. Larry Anderson's Shaq delivers a bobwhite.

the following guns to approach and flush the holding birds within easy shooting range. Now, we are talking about a perfect world in which dogs always hold and birds are always there to flush. Rather than scare off any new would-be bird dog owners, I won't elaborate. To those readers out there who understand, I'll remind you that we choose our own misery.

The retrieving breeds are also pressed into upland bird hunting duties. Labs, Goldens, and Chessies are hunted in close and allowed to flush birds, hopefully within gun range. Retrieving breeds generally hunt in a tight pattern and work well for the gun. A competent hunting retriever can consistently produce birds. If a retriever has also been trained to hup at the flush or shot, so much the better. There is the obvious benefit of having a retriever specialist on hand when a cripple hits the ground which will take some digging to find.

The flushing breeds—springers, cockers, and boykins (to name the most well-known)—are pheasant hunting specialists who do well on heavy cover bobwhites. I encountered a few overgrown CRP fields where my pointing dogs were outmatched, but a flushing dog would have torn up. Flushing breeds work best in precisely the impossibly thick stuff that birds escape to when they are trying to avoid a hunting dog. As long as a bird stays on the ground, running ahead of an approaching hunter, they are safe. The birds will flat leave the county, unseen, with the hunter wondering how a bird could move so fast. A spaniel will work the trail of a running bird until the bird has nowhere to go but up. With a running covey, this may be the only way that a hunter will get a shot.

Table Preparation

Quail are excellent eating! My only complaint is that they were designed too small and it takes a mess of them to make a feed. They can be taken care of quickly and skinned or breasted out, or a bird can be plucked for a more formal presentation.

Breasting involves twisting off both wings. A pair of game shears is unnecessary; the procedure can be done unaided with just a pair of bare hands. Pull the neck and head back over the bird's spine and pull them off. Rip and peel the skin down over the front of the bird's breast, until a thumbnail can be worked up under the bird's breast at the point of the sternum. Lever the breast up and away from the rest of the body. Be careful not to be cut by the broken wing bones. A person can save the legs at this point and discard the rest. No gutting is necessary; everything stays intact in the body cavity.

Skinning is a similar process with the exception that once the wings and neck are pulled from the body, a pair of game shears are used to make a cut straight up the back of the bird. The cut should start at the base of the neck and travel to the bird's tail button. The point of the shears can then be used to cut around the bird's rectum. With the shears, detach both legs where the feathers stop and then peel the bird's skin completely off. Spread the bird's body at the back as if opening a clam. Use the shears to scoop out the offal and the meat is ready to be rinsed and stored.

It is a lot of work, but plucked quail make the prettiest presentation. If convenient, the majority of a bird's feathers can be plucked, in the field, immediately after being taken. Once the body is allowed to cool, the skin tears much more readily and makes the process more tedious than it has to be. I leave the wing and tail feathers intact unless the shooting is slow and I don't expect another flush any time soon. Get the body feathers off and use a knife with a gut hook to pull the offal. Leave the bird to cool in your game bag and finish the job after returning from the field. Once a bird is plucked, I flash singe the surface of the skin with a propane touch to remove any remnants of feathers. The meat is then ready to be washed, patted dry with a paper towel, and stored.

Shot and Choke Suggestions

Quail shooting is a close range proposition and I have found that in most instances, the more open the chokes, the more birds will hit the ground.
- Skeet / improved cylinder 7½ shot

Scaled Quail Distribution

Primary Distribution

Secondary Distribution

Scaled Quail

Callipepla squamata

FIELD FACTS

Local Name
Scalie, Cotton Top, Cotton Top Quail, Blues, Blue Quail, Runners

Size
Scaled quail run 10 to 11.5 inches in length and average 7 ounces total weight.

Identification in Flight
Flushing scaled quail offer no conspicuous markings. The top of their backs and wings are a solid-colored, medium blue-grey. They have a buff white breast and head crest. The breast is marked with a heavy scaled pattern. The side coverts are highlighted with white darts. In flight, their wings make a 'whirring' sound.

Facts
- Scaled quail cover is most often characterized by open grassland and sand sage.
- The most common strategy initially used by scaled quail to avoid hunters is to run. After one or two flushes, the singles will often hold.
- Early in the season, hunt around water sources to locate bird populations.
- Scalies roost on the ground in open grass.

Color
Male and female scaled quail are indistinguishable from each other at a distance. Both are a basic blue-grey overall. Upon close examination, the throat feathers on a male are a solid cream color, while the hens are cream with fine dark streaks. Both sexes' breasts are cream-white overlaid with a dark scaled pattern. The scaled quail sports a distinctive cream-white head crest that is easy to spot on birds when they are running on the ground in front of a hunter. The crest's color glows in a way similar to rabbit ears backlit by the sun.

Sound and Flight Patterns
Scaled quail are vocal, but not to the same degree of other quail species. The 'chuc-ker, chuc-ker, chuc-ker' covey call can be used by the hunter to aid in locating birds, but this call and other scaled quail vocalizations are extremely ventriloquial and thus make it difficult to locate the birds.

Male (left) and female (right) scaled quail are distinguished by the pure cream-colored throat of the mail and the slightly barred throat of the female.

Unlike bobwhites, which hug cover during flight, the scaled quail tend to loft when they flush. Their wings give off the characteristic quail 'whirring' sound when flushing.

Similar Game Birds

Scaled quail resemble bobwhite quail. Their respective ranges overlap throughout Kansas' scaled quail range. The bobwhite is brown overall and carries a black and white face-mask capped with russet and black. This contrasts with the scalie's overall grey appearance and erect white head crest.

Flock or Covey Habits

Scalies are runners. They will hold for a hunter, but it might take a flush or two to get them in the mood. Scaled quail who have received some hunting pressure will at times forego a covey flush altogether. Upon a hunter's approach, they just spread out and hold as singles. A hunter and dog may walk through a spread and holding covey, unaware they are surrounded by birds. When one or two birds bump wild, the hunter assumes they are just isolated individuals. I have learned that when a bird jumps, I need to call the dogs in and have them search the immediate area thoroughly; usually there is a covey somewhere. The search may take several minutes and

Scalies are handsome birds; here, a hunter displays a fine brace.

only produce two or three contacts, but many hunts are made up of these repeated short contacts.

Coveys may number from 15 to 60 individuals, the average being about 30. Bird numbers are tied to seasonal conditions. Foraging quail cover 25 to 100 acres in a day; the average home range is under one square mile. I see scaled quail coveys in the same general areas season after season.

In early spring, coveys disband and males take up breeding territories. Cocks climb elevated perches and issue a 'caw' call. The young are raised by both parents. Coveys are reassembled by October.

Reproduction and Life Span

Breeding activity begins in late February and culminates in April and May. Males occupy a breeding territory and, from an elevated perch, broadcast a 'squawk' call which is returned by adjacent males. Territories are defended from other males.

Nests are on the ground in dense cover. Scaled quail clutches contain 9 to 16 eggs, and like other species, chicks can fly within a few days of hatching.

Depending on summer rains, nesting can be deferred to late summer.

The life span of the scaled quail is thought to be as long as 5 years in the wild, but most birds probably don't reach 2 years of age.

Feeding Habits and Patterns

Birds begin their day roosting in the open grass. Coveys tend to claim a particular point of geography such as a guzzler, an abandoned metal structure, or a lone cholla cactus for the center of their roosting area. This gives the hunter a place to begin looking. Birds forage out from their roost. Scaled quail habitat has a mostly uniform appearance and it is difficult to visually separate a 'feeding area' from any other. These birds' feeding activities peak in the morning and evening. Midday, birds often return to their roosting 'structure' and use it as a loafing area.

Scalies are birds of the open grass. They feed extensively on the green forbs that grow at ground level among the prairie grasses. They utilize various fruits, leaves, and seeds. Scaled quail eat a higher percentage of insects than other species of quail. It is reported that scalies will use sorghum fields where available.

Preferred Habitat and Cover

Open country and undisturbed grasslands interspersed with sandsage, Soaptree yucca, and stag or buckhorn cholla are the characteristics of Kansas scaled quail cover. As stated earlier, these birds will rally around a coveying point such as a lone cholla, an abandoned manmade site, or a guzzler.

Not a lot of scientific research is available on scaled quail. Most of the available studies were done in New Mexico, Colorado, and Oklahoma which all have terrain substantially different from the southwestern corner of Kansas. Therefore, any conclusions drawn from those findings should be taken within that context. However, it is safe to say that scaled quail rely heavily on forbs, the green carpet of weeds which grow in open areas between stands of native grasses. Weed growth starts in early spring, seeds, and then blows away by the end of summer. Birds utilize the leaves and seeds of the different plants as they become available. Weeds and grasses produce insects which are important food sources during the spring and summer. Quail chicks especially rely on the protein and moisture that insects provide. When fall temperatures decline, insect availability soon ends.

Coming into fall, scaled quail utilize the seeds of grasses, weeds, shrubs, and trees. Kansas scaled quail populations exhibit a strong preference for grass interspersed with stands of sand sage. It may be that the brushy sand sage plants are important as overstory alone, or there may be an additional food component. Scaled quail will utilize fruit from cactus plants such as prickly pear when available. It is reported that scaled quail will sometimes forage on cultivated grain crops.

Locating Hunting Areas

Scaled quail are found in southwestern Kansas. They can be found in stands of unbroken prairie grass and sand sage. While hunting, I once located a covey adjacent

Lone cholla cactus are used by scaled quail as "roosts."

to an agricultural area. Whether or not they were using that as a feeding area, I can not say. I encountered them at midday on the edge of a grass field.

- For scaled quail, the most common form of scouting is to drive the back roads and look for quail. Check possible coveying points (lone cholla plants, abandoned manmade structures, guzzler enclosures, etc.).
- Birds will sometimes call both morning and evening.
- If possible, scout during the spring pairing season when the males are 'caw' calling to attract females. That will tell you where scalies are present and give you a general area to return to during the hunting season.
- Early in the season, concentrate on areas around water sources.

Looking for Sign

Scaled and bobwhite quail live in such close proximity that it is difficult to differentiate the origin species of any quail sign located. Tracks found in sandy soil and dusting areas can indicate the presence of either or both birds. Dusting birds sometimes leave feathers in their dust baths which could identify a scaled quail's presence. Listening for calling birds can pinpoint coveys.

The most visible indicators are the doughnut-sized rings of white and black feces left after birds depart a roost in the morning. The ring's color contrasts with the ground and is easily spotted, even from a distance of several yards.

Hunting Methods

Typical scaled quail country is wide open. Coveys will usually flush wild out of range. Flushed birds will usually run when they land. If the hunter can mark flushing coveys down and follow up quickly, it is possible to find singles. Once a single is located, the hunter needs to slow down and work the immediate area thoroughly; there are probably other birds present. A good rule of thumb to remember is that the birds will seem to run about a third as far as you think they have. I make it a point to double back and work the ground I previously covered. Dogs will often turn up birds on their second go-around. Check the 'sides' of the path you followed when chasing the covey. These birds will peel off in ones and twos and hold.

Another rule of thumb concerning coveys is that the hunter can expect to locate only about a third as many of the scalie singles as he would of bobwhite singles. On some days, the singles will come fairly easy; on other days, one or two will be an accomplishment.

Scalies sometimes loft when they flush. They rocket up 10 feet above the grass and level off before they put any distance between themselves and the gunner. A shooter anticipating this can take advantage of some nice open shots.

Hunting with Dogs

I have seen some very good dog work on scaled quail. While scalies are difficult, they can be worked successfully by dogs.

Scaled quail will respond to an approaching dog or hunter by running. The birds will run until they decide to hold. An experienced dog learns to hunt close and slow when singles are present and to push hard when the birds are running and not going to hold. Like billiard balls exploding in a fast break, a covey that flushes in all directions will be much more likely to hold as singles.

Open grass calls for a big running dog who can locate coveys at a distance. What a man can walk in an hour, a dog can run in ten minutes. On the open prairie, the view is unrestricted. It is possible to watch a dog running at 500 yards out. A hunter learns to trust that the dog will hold the coveys he can and bust the ones he can't.

Table Preparation

Scaled quail are slightly larger than bobwhites, but they still take a half-dozen to feed two people. Birds should be cleaned promptly and cooled in an ice chest (see the bobwhite quail section on table preparation for cleaning suggestions). Because of the large multi-species bags common in Kansas, most local hunters will breast quail at the end of a hunt. Scaled quail are as delectable as they are hard-earned.

Shot and Choke Suggestions

- Improved cylinder/modified 7½ first shot, 6 shot back-up (the larger shot helps reduce lost cripples).

Mourning Dove

Zenaida macroura

FIELD FACTS

Local Name

Dove, Common Dove

Size

Mourning doves run 11 to 13 inches in length. They weigh in at an average weight of 5 ounces. Their wing span is 17 to 19 inches wide.

Identification in Flight

In flight, mourning doves appear as medium-sized, fast moving, pigeon shaped birds. They are grey overall with a buff colored breast. Their tails come to a conspicuous sharp-pointed end with a pronounced white 'v' on the dark underside. Mourning dove's wings make a rhythmic whistling sound in flight.

Facts

- The daily bag limit for mourning doves is 15 per day.
- Mourning doves are found statewide.
- Mourning doves are very prolific and have a very high reproductive potential.
- In summer, doves drink approximately 7% of their body weight in water each day.
- Dove hunting should be considered an early season proposition. Cold weather pushes the birds south to warmer climates.

Color

Males and females look nearly identical in appearance. Their overall plumage is a grayish brown which softens to a light tawny brown on their chest and belly. The bottom tips of the tail feathers are highlighted with white. On close inspection, the bird has small black ear marks and several small black spots on the scapulars and upper wing coverts. The top of the dove's head is capped with a blue-grey crown, and the unfeathered skin around the eye is powder blue. The sides of the nape of the neck shimmer with a translucent purple iridescence. Legs and feet are red.

Sound and Flight Pattern

In flight, mourning doves are swift and direct, resorting to acrobatics only when eluding predators or gunfire. Their wings make a distinctive whistling sound. On opening day, birds will fly at tree-top level. Hunted doves respond to shooting pressure by flying at 30 to 40 yards of elevation or higher.

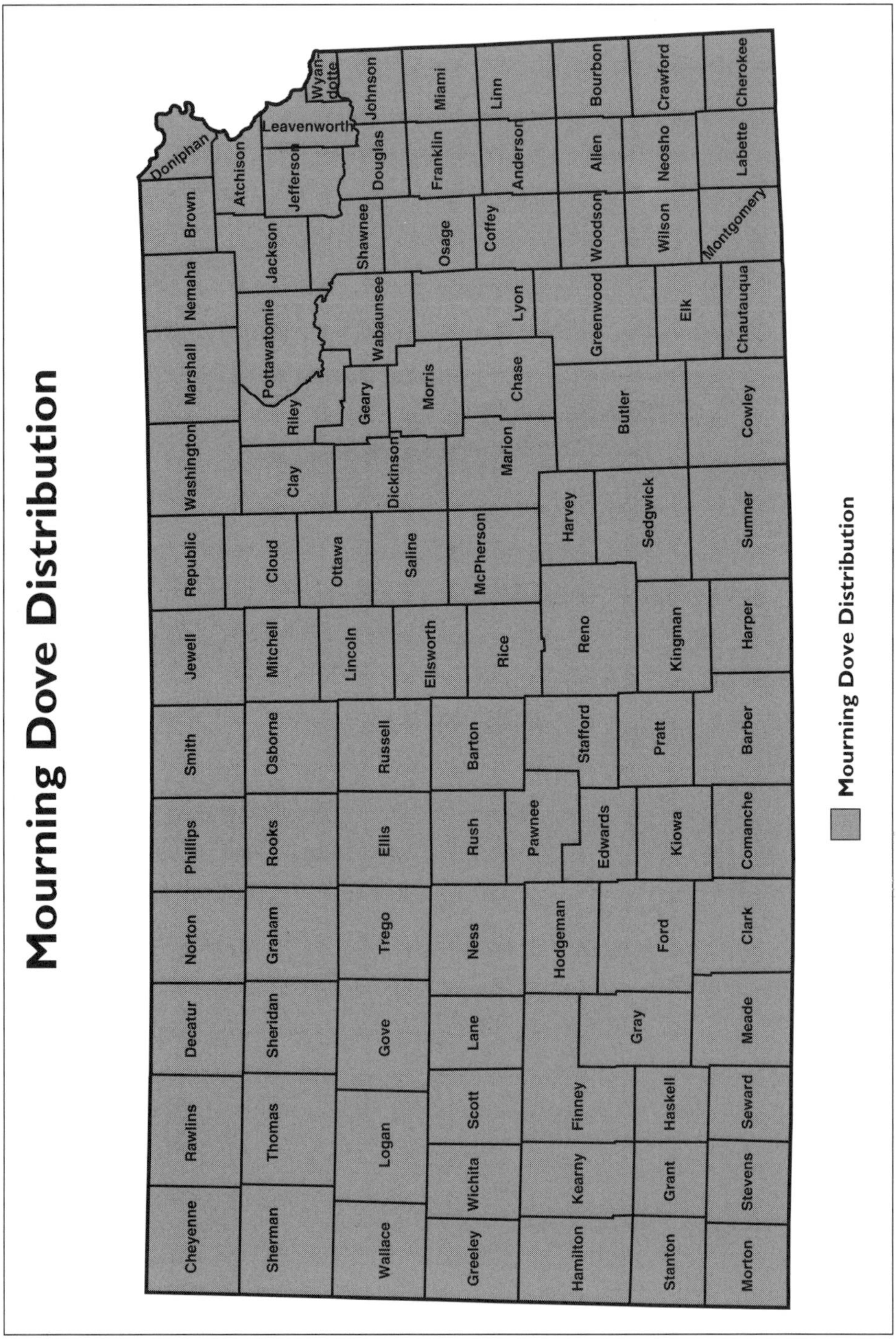
Mourning Dove Distribution
Cheyenne
Rawlins
Decatur
Norton
Phillips
Smith
Jewell
Republic
Washington
Marshall
Nemaha
Brown
Doniphan
Sherman
Thomas
Sheridan
Graham
Rooks
Osborne
Mitchell
Cloud
Clay
Riley
Pottawatomie
Jackson
Atchison
Jefferson
Leavenworth
Wyan-dotte
Wallace
Logan
Gove
Trego
Ellis
Russell
Lincoln
Ottawa
Dickinson
Geary
Wabaunsee
Shawnee
Douglas
Johnson
Greeley
Wichita
Scott
Lane
Ness
Rush
Barton
Ellsworth
Saline
Morris
Lyon
Osage
Franklin
Miami
Hamilton
Kearny
Finney
Hodgeman
Pawnee
Stafford
Rice
McPherson
Marion
Chase
Coffey
Anderson
Linn
Stanton
Grant
Haskell
Gray
Ford
Edwards
Reno
Harvey
Butler
Greenwood
Woodson
Allen
Bourbon
Kiowa
Pratt
Kingman
Sedgwick
Elk
Wilson
Neosho
Crawford
Morton
Stevens
Seward
Meade
Clark
Comanche
Barber
Harper
Sumner
Cowley
Chautauqua
Montgomery
Labette
Cherokee
Mourning Dove Distribution

Mourning doves are America's bird.

Birds fly in the morning and evening. They begin their morning feeding flight at full light, typically 10 minutes after sunrise. They are active for about two hours and then return to their midday roosts by around 10 AM. Hunters might shoot an active feeding area for the first half of the morning and then relocate, intercepting birds as they return to their roosting areas. In hot weather, doves need water daily and will fly long distances to get it. Birds coming to water in the mornings do so only after having fed. Hunters waiting in ambush on water tanks should not expect to see incoming birds until midmorning.

Similar Game Birds

American kestrels are occasionally mistaken for mourning doves. In flight, kestrels lack the strong downstroke of a flying dove. Kestrels also have a heavier head and shoulder, and a rounded tail.

There are two species of small doves (Inca doves and ground doves) which are also sometimes mistaken for the larger mourning dove. These other doves have a silver cast to their bodies and their wings flash russet in flight. These smaller doves are half the size of a mourning dove and they fly close to the ground. An observant shooter shouldn't have any problem discerning the difference.

In appropriate range, white-winged doves are sometimes confused with mourning doves. The differences are readily apparent in flight. White-wings have a broad, white line on their upper wing. They fly later in the morning, are larger, fly slower, and have a slower wing beat. A white-wing's tail is square while a mourning dove's comes to a sharp point. White-wings are considered a vagrant species in Kansas, with only four sightings on record.

Flock or Covey Habits

Mourning doves congregate in large numbers to exploit a food source. Rather than moving in one large flock, feeding doves come in sporadic singles and small groups. Once the birds have massed for feeding, large flocks can lift up and swing over a field in response to an overhead raptor or as a prelude to their return flight to their roosting areas. By studying the birds' approaches as they enter the field, the hunter can position himself under their flight pattern. It will generally remain consistent as long as the birds use the field.

Flying birds follow watercourses and tree lines. If a hunter plans his shots, he can drop birds on open ground as they fly into feed areas. Dead birds are easily recovered when lying in the open. Without a dog, as many as half the birds dropped in heavy cover can be lost.

When the dove season opens on September 1st, many of the resident birds have already begun their migration south. September hunters will notice a significant reduction in the mourning dove population after the first few days of the season. A Kansas hunter will find that the further west he travels, the more he will encounter greater numbers of birds which stay for a longer period of time. The southwestern corner of the state holds doves the longest.

Reproduction and Life Span

I see mourning doves nesting everywhere: little random assemblies of twigs that don't look as if they could make it through a 10 mph breeze stuck on the side of the eves at the post office, in short trees at the shopping mall parking lot, wedged into the bracing of a dilapidated windmill tower on a remote prairie water tank. To say mourning doves are prolific is an understatement. In some areas of North America, doves have been observed nesting every month of the year. Kansas doves begin nesting in April or May. American gunners take more mourning doves per season than any other game bird species.

Courtship activities begin in early spring when pairs perform grand swooping courtship flights. Males can be heard broadcasting their soft cooing courtship call. Breeding activities peak in April and May.

Mourning doves return to their hatching areas to breed and raise their young. Nearly 95 percent of returned dove bands are recovered within one degree of their original banding site.

Two white eggs are laid and incubation duties are shared by both parents. Fledglings appear in 14 to 15 days. Squabs grow very rapidly and are ready to leave the nest in 12 to 14 days. Then a new clutch of eggs is laid and incubation begins anew. On the average, mourning doves bring off multiple nests per season, with 7 being the record. Mourning doves are thought to live as long as 6 or 7 years in the wild.

Trapper delivers a mourning dove to hand.

Feeding Habits and Patterns

Mourning doves feed both early and late on small seeds they glean from the ground. Once a food source is located, birds will continually return until forced by hunting pressure or weather to move elsewhere. Birds work fallow agricultural fields for weed seeds and congregate on sources of grain such as cattle feed lots and dairies. The preferred food for doves is sunflowers. Sunflower fields are not common, however, and unless planted early are not mature enough to provide a reliable food source. Therefore, grain fields are used most heavily for feed by mourning doves. Throughout Kansas, milo is not cut until after the dove hunting season (some years, however, southeastern Kansas is an exception to this rule). Birds will feed on standing milo; wheat stubble is also used heavily. Successful dove hunting requires prospecting for shootable feed fields. Scout early, locate several fields, and then monitor them before the opening to see which will afford the best shooting.

Preferred Habitat and Cover

Mourning doves are found statewide and utilize all available habitats to a greater or lesser extent. Their preferred habitat includes agricultural areas which provide them

*Dr. John Sherman
of Covington, Kentucky,
with a limit of mourning doves.*

their preferred food sources and roosting areas. Preferred roosting sites are made up of long multiple rows of dense, heavily leafed, shelter belt trees. As all of Kansas holds some farming, concentrations of birds can be found in all parts of the state.

Locating Hunting Areas

Opening day of early dove season is a popular event in Kansas. Dove hot spots are found throughout the state. Historically, birds are found in the same general areas year after year. Ask around and you'll end up with a general direction to a productive area. After locating an area, here are some tips to pinpoint a spot:

- Look for water. Birds follow watercourses, specifically the heavy tree lines bordering water and edge covers.
- Watch for doves congregating on power lines midmorning and late afternoon.
- Look for likely agricultural and weed fields, and during shooting hours, hunter's vehicles grouped around those fields. Remember to obtain permission before entering private lands.
- Cattle feedlots and dairies attract birds that glean waste grain.
- In western Kansas, look for birds using windmills and stock tanks.

*Chesapeake Bay retriever
guards her birds.*

Looking For Sign

Large flocks of feeding doves are easy to spot. Drive rural roads and follow trading doves. Watch for concentrations of birds on power lines near agricultural fields from 8 to 9:30 AM and again in the late afternoon. Use binoculars and glasses for doves feeding on the ground or boiling above the vegetation in likely looking fields. Sitting on a tank before the opener will tell you if dove are watering there.

Hunting Methods

Dove hunting means pass shooting. It's all pretty straightforward: find a spot with ample birds, study how the birds travel, get underneath their flight pattern, and ambush them as they trade back and forth. A hunter can embellish this with a dove call and decoys set up on a high wire or silhouetted on a dead tree.

The September 1st dove opener brings to an end the long night of darkness and despair that befell wingshooters when the bird season ended the previous January. In 1995, Kansas hunters harvested 1,100,000 mourning doves! Opening day dove is a social event complete with shooting stools and ice chests. There are ample birds and heat radiating down from the summer sun, both of which make for a short early morning shoot. Dove fields can accommodate enough guns to keep the birds moving, leaving a volunteer or two at the end of the shoot to count up the empty hulls in the bird bucket and compute your bird to shell ratio. The first couple of days the shooting's pretty easy.

A few days into the season, however, the birds begin flying higher. There is also a noticeable reduction in the number of birds flying and the remaining hunters are concentrated into those areas where the doves are working the best. The opening day dove hordes have been replaced by a sporadic trickle, and a limit is much harder to scratch down. However, if a hunter is able to locate a good, out of the way field or fly-way and the weather holds, the hunting can continue for several weeks.

Hunting with Dogs

Retrievers will get a real workout on a dove shoot. With the daily bag at 15 birds per day, a dog retrieving for two or three guns has got some nonstop fetching to do. All breeds are used. Many versatile and pointing breed quail dogs serve double duty.

As it is the season's first hurrah, dogs generally aren't in good enough physical shape to handle an extensive workout. In addition, early September days in Kansas can reach 100 degrees or more. Dogs will need plenty of water. If at all possible, I hunt beside a water source such as a canal or tank. A dog who can get into water and swim will stay cool.

If I'm field shooting, I carry a 3-gallon, covered bucket full of water that I set on the ground beside me and leave available at all times for the dogs. The loose feathers that build up on a frothing dog's mouth while retrieving doves can cause some retrievers to swear off doves. The water bucket cools them down and helps keep their mouth free of feathers. Also, this water is readily available for the hunter to soak down his dog's belly periodically, helping to lower body temperature.

A short tie-out cable or Jaeger lead is a handy way to control a slipping, nonslip retriever. The sheer numbers of birds overhead and constant shooting can temporarily derail a steady young dog's resolve. Rather than add frustration to what is supposed to be an enjoyable outing for both of you, cable a runner to a fence post, truck bumper, tree trunk, or what have you. Release him when there is something to fetch.

Table Preparation

Dove meat is dark and similar to duck. It has provided the main course for many a beginning of the season feast. Hunters carry ice chests for cooling out cleaned birds, and breast out doves by twisting off the head and wing and pushing their thumbs up under the bird's sternum. One good pull and the breast rips free. Remember, federal law requires that one fully feathered wing remain attached for identification.

Shot and Choke Suggestions

- Low fliers: skeet / improved cylinder 8, 7½ lead shot
- High fliers: modified / full 7½, 6 lead shot

Wild Turkey

Meleagris gallopavo

FIELD FACTS

Local Name
Turkey, Wild Turkey, Tom, Gobbler

Size
Male 30–36 inches; female 21–25 inches; 5-foot wing span

Identification in flight
On the wing, turkeys look huge. Their body and tail are a dark, iridescent, bronze-brown. Primary flight feathers are light grey with black barring. Turkey tails are square. The heads of adult male turkeys are colored with vivid shades of white, red, and powder blue. The overall impression made is that of a large dark shape sailing through the sky.

Turkeys take wing with a thunderous commotion. Once airborne, they flap their wings for a distance and then coast out of sight on stiff wings. I'm always taken aback when I flush a group of turkeys: how could something so big leave so quickly?

Facts
- Turkeys are found statewide, with the greatest populations being found in the eastern half of the state.
- Birds are found where there are trees available for roosting.
- Both spring and fall hunts are offered.
- Only bearded birds are legally taken during the spring season.
- Any turkeys are legal game during the fall season.

Color

A turkey ghosting through the shadows looks dark and nondescript until the sunlight hits it. Then the dark brown feathers of the chest and back shimmer with a purple iridescence. Most of the birds in Kansas are a hybrid between Rio Grande and Eastern strain bloodlines. These crosses can carry the light blonde accent color of the Rio Grandes, or the dark chocolate coloring of the Eastern, or any color range in between. These birds have tan to chocolate edges highlighting the ends of their rump coverts. They also have a wide blonde to chocolate terminal band running along the edge of their large, square tail.

There are small isolated pockets of pure strain Eastern subspecies turkeys along the Missouri border. This subspecies is the color of dark chocolate frosting .

Turkey Distribution

Turkey Distribution

In the southwestern and southcentral part of the state, the birds are pure Rio Grande blood. Rio Grande turkeys have the light, blondish-gold accent colors. The heads of hens and poults are partially feathered and dark. Gobbler's heads are arrayed in a striking blend of white, blue, and red. Turkey flight feathers are light grey with dark grey accent bands.

Sound and Flight Pattern

The image of a strutting tom turkey is an American icon. The Thanksgiving trilogy of Pilgrim, blunderbuss, and fantailed turkey are learned by every school-aged child in the country. Ask any child what sound a turkey makes and they will tell you. In reality, however, turkey vocalizations are extensive and thus better addressed as the subject of an entire book, rather than through the few short paragraphs dictated by the format of this book.

It is important for one intending to kill a turkey to learn how to use a turkey call. I am not a good turkey caller, but I have spent some time chasing elk with a diaphragm and bugle tube. The same type of diaphragm is used for calling turkeys.

When I first started bugling elk, the state-of-the-art calls were awful-sounding whistles. When diaphragm calls first hit the market, they sounded good but were difficult to master. Initially, cassette tape instruction was a student's only (and limited) guide. Once videotapes were developed, however, they became the teaching aid which allowed the masses to learn how to work bull elk into a bugle.

No amount of quotation-marked, bird vocalization pronunciations I could write for you would bring a strutting gobbler within shotgun range. If I wanted to become deadly with a turkey call, I would buy several different types of turkey calls, check out every turkey hunting/calling video available, and practice like hell to get proficient. Then I would go into the woods and spend a lot of time with the real thing.

A turkey's escape pattern is to wheel and run. These birds often do not fly, but instead run for the cover of dense trees. However, for such a large bird, turkeys can take to the wing easily; when caught in the open, they will take flight in order to reach heavy cover quickly. Their flight is more in line with a diving duck which runs and becomes airborne, as opposed to a puddler which springs straight into flight.

Similar Game Birds

Turkeys stand alone in stature and appearance when compared to Kansas' other birds. It is unlikely that a turkey could be confused with any other type of bird.

Flock or Covey Habits

In Kansas, turkeys are hunted during both the spring and fall seasons. Hunters patterning birds will see different flock patterns depending on the time of year.

In the fall, hens with poults do not associate with gobblers. Most turkey flocks encountered in the field consist of a hen with partially grown birds of the year or a communal grouping of two or more hens with young. These maternal flocks are very active as the young poults search out the food energy they need to grow. Hens and chicks work the open edges of grass and grain fields along tree lines, feeding on insects and greens. As a result, they are the most exposed and most commonly seen turkey flock during the fall.

In the winter, turkeys combine into large flocks sometimes numbering 200 to 300 birds. These are groupings which have accumulated from fairly extensive areas of range. Commonly, pure strain Easterns are on the low side, numbering from 25 to 30 individuals. Rio Grandes, on the other hand, are more gregarious and frequently number from 75 to 100 birds.

Groups of 'jakes', young first-year males, are seen feeding separately from the females. Adult male bachelor groups, on the other hand, are more secretive during the fall and tend to stick to heavier cover. The adult males become very difficult to find.

During the spring mating season, gobblers actively seek out the company of hens. Males stake out strutting territories and do their best to attract hens. At this time of year, both males and females are found in common areas. They spend the night roosting in trees, and fly down at first light. If a hunter can locate an evening roosting site, he can put himself in a good position to intercept a gobbler at first light the following morning.

Reproduction and Life Span

Starting at the end of March, running through April, and (depending upon the weather) continuing into early May, mating activities are undertaken. There appears to be a north/south gradient, with birds in the south starting and concluding mating activities a few days to a week earlier than the birds in the north. There doesn't appear to be a corresponding east/west gradient.

Adult gobblers engage in elaborate strutting displays where they slowly step, stiff-legged and tail fanned, with all their body feathers fluffed out and wingtips quivering. Gobblers attract and hold harems of hens through strutting and calling. Males vigorously defend their strutting ground from other males.

After mating, hens construct nests in dense low grass and lay 8 to 15 eggs. Eggs hatch in 26 to 28 days. Chicks arrive from late May through early June. Males take no part in the hatching or rearing of the young. Poults are reared by the hens and stay in maternal flocks through the fall.

In the wild, the average life span of a turkey is 8 years of age, although turkeys are capable of reaching 12 years of age or more.

Feeding Habits and Patterns

Turkeys feed in a loose flock formation. The birds tend to sweep into an area and move fairly quickly as they feed. The birds which I have seen feeding are wary and perpetually moving. The flock has many eyes, and one warning 'pert' can freeze every bird stone-still or send them exploding for cover. They often work the edges of fields and openings in tree belts so that, if needed, escape cover is just a few steps away.

During the strutting period, turkeys feed primarily on green vegetation. They can be seen foraging in green wheat fields and on green forbs growing in grass fields. Hens with chicks concentrate their feeding efforts in open clearings and along water where they feed on greens and insects. Poults rely heavily on insects during their first

5 to 6 weeks of life. The protein provided by bugs is essential for the chicks' early development.

As summer progresses into fall, turkeys shift over to waste agricultural crops. In years when they are available, turkeys will feed heavily on wild berry and mast crops. During this time, turkeys abandon the fields and confine their activities to the wooded belts, making them more difficult to locate.

Preferred Habitat and Cover

Several components are required for turkeys to survive in an area. The primary requirement is appropriate roosting cover. Turkeys retire at night to the safety of high limbs in mature trees. The trees must be dense enough to provide them protection. Typically, good roosting sites are provided by the trees growing along watercourses, in dense wind breaks, or in the forests found in the eastern third of Kansas.

Additionally, adjacent agricultural fields provide the birds with a ready supply of food as a buffer against years with poor mast production. In particular, winter wheat fields are sought out by turkeys because they provide both surplus grain and greens.

Locating Hunting Areas

Turkeys are found statewide, with the eastern third of the state having the broadest distribution.
1. Start with maps of the areas you are interested in hunting.
2. Using the maps, concentrate on water courses and river bottoms that contain roosting trees.
3. Make note of the high ground that follows hills and permanent watercourses.
4. Go to the areas you noted and start at the water sources. Look for tracks and droppings of birds coming in to drink. Confirm that birds are in fact in the area.
5. When sufficient signs of turkey use have been located, look for roosting sites. Walk the mature stands of roosting trees and dead snags early and late and listen for birds. Try to elicit gobbles from males by owl hoots, howling, yelling, crow calling, etc. Try to get the turkeys to betray their positions.
6. The night before the hunt, be sure the birds are still in the area and, if possible, pinpoint their evening roosting site. Be in place before first light the following morning and call to the birds as they come off the roost.

Looking for Sign

Turkeys have a large and distinctive track which, because of its size, can't be mistaken for another type of bird. They also leave large droppings that are hard to confuse with any other bird's and are indicative of gender. The male's droppings are a long semi-straight segment that is rounded on the thickest end and pulled to a thin sharp point on the other; hen droppings are smaller and deposited in tight coils. The color of the droppings is olive with white frosting on the end.

Begin searching the edges of watering areas and look for tracks in the mud at the water line. Search for droppings and feathers. Walk the edges of possible feeding areas and again, look for droppings and feathers.

Listen for turkey vocalizations. Even the sound of a turkey flying onto, or out of, a roosting tree is very distinctive and during the still time of day can be heard from a long ways off.

Hunting Methods

Turkey hunting is broken down into two seasons: spring and fall. During the fall hunt, the most productive method is to still-hunt through likely turkey habitat and try to ambush flocks. Most of the birds encountered will be groups of hens and poults. If a good shot is not available, or if a hunter is interested in only taking called birds, a person can flush the group and then set up and recall the birds with a 'kee, kee, run' call series. After the flock breaks up, pick out a good concealment spot and wait silently for a few minutes and then begin calling.

In spring hunting, gobblers are the only legal bird. The first trick is to be in an area that contains birds. Finding likely country was covered earlier in this section. Once a hunter knows he is working an area that is holding turkeys, he needs to locate their roosting sites. It is counterproductive to go exploring during the season. This will more than likely scare birds and should have been done during preseason scouting. Instead, try to get the toms to gobble from their roosts and let you know where they are. There are many tricks people use to try to elicit a gobble; an owl hooter, crow call, coyote howl, siren, and loud shrieking yell are some of the ones I've heard of. In the old days, a simple gobble from a turkey call used to work.

Once a tom responds, work into the bird and set up an ambush. Two people work better than one. Have the gunner out front and the caller in the rear. That way, as the bird works in, he will have to walk past the shooter's position on his way to the caller. Some hunters have had good success using hen decoys or hen and jake decoys. The caller needs to know just the right words to say, and the shooter should hold for the base of the neck.

Field Preparations

Birds should be eviscerated immediately after being taken and allowed to cool. A turkey that has been plucked makes the best presentation for the table, but birds can be skinned and/or boned out, according to an individual's personal preference.

Shot and Choke Suggestions

The stories of shot-dead turkeys getting up and running are legendary—arrow shot birds, especially. Legal weapons are 20-, 12-, and 10-gauge shotguns and archery gear. Shotgunners express a broad range of opinions regarding the kind of load that is most effective on a turkey. Let me offer you a consensus of what I've heard.
- Close range, called birds: 10 & 12 gauge, full choke, shooting 3- and 3½-inch, 4 or 6 shot.
- Longer range, still-hunted birds: 10 & 12 gauge, full choke, 3- and 3½-inch, 4, 2 or BB shot.

Sandhill Crane

Grus canadensis

FIELD FACTS

Local Name
Crane, Sandhill, Sandhill Crane

Size
34 to 48 inches in length with wingspans of up to 7 feet. Greater sandhill cranes weigh in at 10.8 to 14.8 pounds; lesser sandhills at 5.4 to 8.2 pounds.

Identification in Flight
Sandhill cranes are huge and impressive in flight and, once seen, not easily mistaken or forgotten. Overall, cranes are colored grey and have a very large wingspan which darkens on the outside primary feathers. Cranes have long necks, and their heads carry a red cap from the eyes forward and a white chin. In flight, a crane's long stilt legs trail straight behind and readily distinguish them from a juvenile swan. While flying, birds are very vocal, announcing their continuous 'pu th th th th th th th th th th th ut.'

Facts
- The open sandhill crane hunting areas are in the southwestern and south-central part of Kansas.
- Kansas crane hunters are required to have a federal sandhill crane hunting permit in their possession, in addition to the state hunting license.
- Kansas crane hunters are required to use nontoxic shot.
- Shooting hours for cranes are sunrise to 2 PM.
- Cranes feed principally in cultivated grain fields.
- Cranes prefer wide shallow water, sand bars, and mud flats as roosting areas.
- Cranes are thought to mate for life.

Colors
Kansas has a huntable population of both Lesser and Greater sandhill cranes. Canadian subspecies are also present in Kansas. Hunters' bag samplings the first weekend of November have shown that Greaters make up 24 to 45 percent of the birds taken. While adults of both subspecies are predominantly grey, the Lesser is nearly half the size and darker overall than the Greater. Cranes may have a varying degree of yellow/rust-stained breast feathers and tertials. They have a white chin, and the skullcap is bright red on adult birds and rust brown on juveniles. Crane eyes

Sandhill Crane Distribution

Legal Sandhill Crane Hunting Area

Other Sandhill Crane Distribution

are straw-colored, and their long stilt legs are black. Seen from below while flying, the outside edges of the bottom of the bird's primary wing feathers are darker grey than the rest of the bird. Juveniles are a mottled brown.

Sound and Flight Pattern

Sandhills begin leaving their roost area shortly after first light. Hunters waiting in the surrounding fields will hear the cranes calling, working themselves up to begin their morning feeding flights. Occasionally, small groups of birds will temporarily take wing and boil up only to settle back in.

When the birds begin to leave in earnest, long strings of cranes form in ragged lines and head out to their feeding areas. Departing birds travel in large groups of 15 to 40 or more.

The call of the sandhills is very distinctive and heard as a floating lilt above the wind when the birds are mere specks on the horizon. Their 'pu th th th th th th ut' call is an easy call to mimic with the human voice, and with a little practice a hunter can mouth-call to prospecting flocks. The birds call with a rising and falling pitch which I'm sure means something to the cranes, but what it means eludes me. Cranes have a myriad of other vocalizations consisting of croaks and pertts, to long trills that they use to communicate from overhead to birds on the ground.

By midmorning, flocks have fed and begin returning to the safety of the roost to loaf. By 10:30 AM, a day's crane hunting is generally considered over.

Similar Game Birds

Sandhill crane hunts are closely monitored because of their visual similarities and close association with whooping cranes, a federally listed, endangered species. Adult whoopers are white and easy to distinguish from sandhills. Juvenile whoopers still carry white on the belly and chest, but are mottled overall and more difficult to differentiate. Whooping cranes winter on the gulf coast and along the Rio Grande River in New Mexico.

Annually, up to 20 whoopers travel through the state during their migration south, and they can be present in Kansas from late October through mid-November. One year, a couple of whoopers camped out at Cheyenne Bottoms until the beginning of December. Quivira National Wildlife Refuge and Cheyenne Bottoms Wildlife Area are the centers of crane activity, and Quivira National Wildlife Refuge is considered to be a critical habitat for whooping cranes. As a result, the entire refuge is closed to all crane hunting. However, most of Kansas' sandhill crane hunting takes place on the private lands surrounding the refuge. When whoopers are present at Cheyenne Bottoms, only the portion of the wildlife area or 'pool' that the birds are actively using is closed to hunting. In addition to this closure, the pass shooting zone on the southern edge of the wildlife area is also closed to the hunting of sandhill cranes and snow geese when whoopers are present.

Kansas' first crane season was held in 1994. Initially, the Fish and Wildlife Service imposed crane hunting area closures whenever migrating whoopers passed through.

Cliff and Morgan Russell wait for the cranes to arrive

In 1995, all of Stafford county, where Quivira Refuge is located, was closed to crane hunting in order to prevent a whooper from being mistaken for a sandhill and accidentally taken. Since that time, the restrictions have been loosened, and while refuge lands are still closed for cranes, the surrounding private lands are open to hunting.

Great Blue herons are sometimes identified as sandhills by novice hunters. Herons are much smaller, multicolored, and fly with their necks tucked in. Juvenile swans are the right size but carry some white, have longer necks, and don't trail long stilt legs.

As a result of the crane's large size, long neck, and long trailing stilt legs, they are seldom confused with any other type of birds.

Flock or Covey Habits

As mentioned earlier, cranes travel in flocks of several to dozens on their daily feeding flights. Birds use communal roosting areas where up to thousands of birds congregate to spend the night on shallow water pans, mud flats, and wide river sand bars. The principal roosting area for Kansas birds is Quivira National Wildlife Refuge in Stafford County and Cheyenne Bottoms Wildlife Area in Barton County. Quivira has held up to 90,000 cranes, while Cheyenne Bottom's flock has numbered up to 30,000.

Sandhill cranes begin leaving shortly after sunrise to forage. They return to the safety of the roost by midmorning to loaf through the afternoon. Although cranes do feed in the evening, hunting hours are only authorized from sunrise to 2:00 PM, thereby eliminating an afternoon hunt.

Reproduction and Life Span

Lesser sandhills breed in the far north, in Alaska and Canada. The Greater's population breeds in the intermountain west and Canada. By mid-spring, crane populations have left the state and begun their northward migration to their nesting areas. Cranes have a strong allegiance to these areas and return annually. Sandhills are not given to nesting in new areas and will continue to use less than ideal nesting sites rather than abandon historic use areas. Some mated pairs have been seen to literally use the same nest year after year.

Cranes are sexually mature by their fourth year. Cranes mate for life. Mate selection begins on the wintering grounds and escalates through the spring migration. They engage in elaborate strutting displays and courtship dancing. Sandhills construct a raised mound of vegetation as a nesting platform and stake out a nesting territory of 40 to 90 acres which they defend vigorously. Two eggs are laid, of which one generally survives. Both parents incubate the eggs, and chicks appear in 28 to 32 days.

Young sandhills rely almost entirely on insects for food. Within 3 months, youngsters are flying with their parents to feed in grain fields. By the end of August, sandhills have begun their migration southward.

The life span of a sandhill crane in the wild is thought to be 12 to 15 years.

Feeding Habits and Patterns

The sandhill crane's food of choice is corn. Kansas is an important agricultural area with corn, as well as other crops, grown under center pivot irrigation.

Cranes using Quivira Refuge concentrate their foraging forays on corn and milo stubble and winter wheat fields. Cranes in Cheyenne Bottoms focus on winter wheat and milo stubble.

Preferred Habitat and Cover

Sandhill cranes have specific habitat requirements which, when absent, preclude use of an area. Foremost, cranes need a large shallow water area such as a pan, mud flat, or sand bar as a nonviolated roosting site. Second, they need nearby agricultural fields for feeding, preferably corn. Finally, birds seek out midday loafing areas such as fallow and dirt fields.

Locating Hunting Areas

The secret to successful field hunting is knowing which field the birds are going to feed in before the fact. Then be there early and set up a convincing decoy spread that allows you to control where the birds will land in the field. Finally, shoot straight so that your efforts don't go for naught. Crane hunting is increasing in popularity in Kansas, and as that interest grows, more and more of the good fields adjacent to Quivira and the Bottoms will be leased.

Crane hunters need to arrive in the hunting area a day or more before their hunt begins. This is so they can be there the preceding dawn to follow the birds out from the roost and locate the particular field they are using. It is best to locate several fields so that a hunter has alternatives should a problem develop, such as showing up on opening morning and finding another group already setting up, or not getting permission to hunt in that field. It is not always possible to locate more than one or two fields in a morning scouting run, so a hunter might consider budgeting several days.

Looking for Sign

The most productive means of locating feeding fields is to physically see the cranes in the field; then you know how many and where. Take binoculars and a good map to mark promising fields. Ask local farmers where they are seeing birds. They know which fields are planted in corn and who owns them. The real search sometimes comes after a hot field is located and you need to find the owner to obtain permission to hunt.

Hunting Methods

Kansas' first crane season was authorized in 1994. Interest has grown steadily since that time, culminating with 375 crane hunters taking 950 birds during the 1996–97 season.

Sandhill cranes are most successfully hunted in feeding fields over decoys. Unlike ducks and geese, where the more decoys used the better, cranes respond well to smaller groups of decoys. Hunters will have good success with spreads from 4 to 12. There is only one commercially-made, full-body crane decoy currently on the market, a standing alert sentry bird. A hunter needs a spread composed of mostly head down feeders. Therefore, out of necessity, crane hunters make their own decoys.

Silhouettes are popular and easy to make. I have seen birds work to simple cardboard cutouts held up by wooden stakes, as well as much more elaborate wood/goose shell composites. Some hunters fabricate standing full-bodied decoys that look very convincing. As with any decoying, some days anything works and other days nothing does.

Blind construction is very important. Cranes respond best to spreads placed in the open middle of a field away from anything that could conceal a hunter. Some types of cover lend themselves to easy concealment, such as corn stubble, the edge of standing corn, or a tumbleweed field. Lying out in the ruts caused by center pivot wheels or covering up against the wheels also works well. Large obtrusive blinds made of vegetation not native to the field should be avoided. Shallow pits dug with the owner's permission can be deadly on birds.

Flagging trading flocks works very well on cranes and can turn wavering groups. Kites should work very well also, although on the several hunts on which I've taken them, I've never had enough wind to keep them airborne. Calling to overhead groups helps to convince wary birds that all is as it seems. A hunter may choose to voice call; Sure Shot game calls of Groves, Texas, is also currently marketing a call (Crane 1175) that sounds pretty good.

Cranes coming into a decoy set up may not buy it completely and will land off the decoys and well out of range. Any new birds approaching the spread will invariably shun the confederates and land off with the real birds. The temptation is to leave

*Handmade, full-bodied
crane decoys bring in the birds.*

the blind and put the real birds back into the air, thereby removing any competition. However, if a hunter waits it out until the down birds leave, they or later arriving birds will often swing over the decoys for a look see and offer a shot.

Hunting Dogs

The downside to using a retriever on cranes is the potential for injury to the dog. On the flat, open fields where hunting takes place, a dog really isn't necessary anyways. I have taken my Chessie on crane hunts, just to take her, and know for certain that her movements have flared incomers and cost us birds. I suppose I felt protected by the belief that she was far too mean to be damaged by a mere mortal crane.

I had a Red setter who was a regular on crow shoots when I was young. We killed a ton of crows and I couldn't begin to guess how many she retrieved in her career. A crow has the same sharp, pointed-type beak as a crane. Early on, she came in from a retrieve with a beak buried half way up her nostrils, a half per side, and a very agitated crow pinching and twisting the hell out of her nose. From that point on, if she came

Sadie, the Chessie, guards the pile at the end of a sandhill hunt.

upon a downed crow and it was still alive, she would stand over it and bark, but she would not pick it up.

I have heard stories from other hunters of how good an account crippled cranes gave of themselves when they walked out to dispatch the wounded birds. The ones that were crippled stood their ground and didn't back down. I would think that a dog, without the capacity to stand back and fire a finishing shot, could easily end up losing an eye.

Field Preparations

To my mind, a plucked crane minus the long legs, looks and tastes very similar to a Canada goose and can be field-handled in the same way. Some hunters clean birds by removing the leg and breast meat and preparing dishes accordingly.

Shot and Choke Suggestions

Sandhills have a reputation for being pretty tough customers. The secret to killing cranes clean (as with any large bird) is to wait until the birds are close enough before you pull the trigger. I have seen birds smacked hard at 35 and 40 yards that wobbled all over but didn't fold. The birds locked their wings and started gliding. Some were recovered and some weren't. Out of a 12-gauge, close enough means not more than 25 yards coming at you. Those who shoot 10-gauges, myself included, swear by them.

Kansas crane hunters are required to use nontoxic shot. My experiences crane hunting have only reinforced my contention that cranes are part kevlar. A hunter willing to forego shooting until decoying cranes are within 20 yards can take birds with steel out of a 12-gauge. Otherwise, I would advise crane hunters to use a 10-gauge shooting bismuth.

- Close range: 12-gauge, 3 or 3½; full choke, lead and bismuth shot, 2s and BBs; modified choke, steel shot, BBs, Ts and TTs
- Past 20 yards: 10-gauge, 3½; modified or full choke, bismuth shot, BBs

Sharp-tailed Grouse

Pedioecetes phasianellus

NOT LEGAL GAME IN KANSAS

Local Name

Sharptails, Pintails, Prairie Grouse, Grouse, Little Chickens, Chickens

Facts

Sharptails were originally native to Kansas. They were wobbled by the breakup of the prairie into farm and ranch lands during the later part of the 1800s. Then, populations were further decimated by the advent of poor grazing management around the turn of the century. Finally, the drought of the 1930s hit, and it spelled the birds' final demise. Sharp-tailed grouse retreated to north of the Platte River in Nebraska.

Beginning in 1982, reintroduction efforts were initiated by the Kansas Department of Wildlife and Parks to return sharptails to their former range in Rawlins County in northwestern Kansas. Additional releases have continued in the north central counties of Rooks, Ellis, and Osborne. Populations have taken hold and there is evidence that sharptails have spread to adjoining counties.

Much of this early sharptail reintroduction work was pioneered by Randy Rogers, wildlife research biologist for the Kansas Wildlife & Parks Department. The problem, which doomed earlier release efforts in other states, was that the prairie grouse social structure centers around a communal lek or breeding ground. Previously, released birds had scattered to the wind and disappeared, specifically because the birds had no communal breeding ground in which to establish a home territory.

Rogers found that by creating an artificial lek, equipped with displaying sharptail decoys and an audio system broadcasting the sound of displaying males, released birds would begin displaying upon release and bond to the release site.

Currently, sharptails are not legal game in Kansas. Down the line, it is hoped that they will be listed as a lawful game species. Rogers states that if the birds are still present in two decades, he will declare it a success.

Gray Partridge

Perdix perdix

NOT LEGAL GAME IN KANSAS

Local Name
Hungarian partridge, Huns, European Partridge

Facts
Huns have recently crossed the border into Kansas. The bird's range has been slowly extending south through eastern Nebraska for the past 15 years. Rare sporadic sightings of Huns in the extreme northeastern corner of Kansas were first detected in 1995. Randy Rogers, the upland bird research biologist for the Kansas Department of Wildlife and Parks, tells me that they are present in very small numbers. He didn't know if their range would spread appreciably, but he did not anticipate a population buildup. His comment was that it would be a "fluke" for a hunter to see Huns in the field.

Huns appear to be double the size of a bobwhite. An adult partridge runs 12–13 inches in length and a pound in weight, while a bobwhite trails at 9.5–10.6 inches and 9 ounces. Flushing Huns are grey in color with a russet face patch, tail feathers, and body accents. They also have a russet horseshoe identification patch on their belly. Some white is present. They live in covey groups and have a similar body profile to a very large quail.

I mention this possibility for the benefit of some lucky shooter who steps past a locked-up dog and has a covey of the largest bobwhites on record lift up and roar away. Hungarian partridge are not considered game in Kansas and their take is illegal. Counties of concern are Marshall, Nemaha, Brown, Pottawatome, Jackson, and Atchison.

I spent some time in the area hunting bobwhites and pheasant. It is a region of small to medium-sized farms spread throughout beautiful rolling, soft, low hills and drainages. The area is considered one of the better quail areas in Kansas.

Ruffed Grouse

Bonasa umbellus

NOT LEGAL GAME IN KANSAS

Local Names

Ruffs, Partridge, Grouse, Wood Grouse, Mountain Grouse

Facts

Ruffed grouse are present in the northeastern corner of Kansas. Populations are extremely small and fragmented. Grouse numbers are such that the Department of Wildlife and Parks publishes a mail-in postcard form requesting members of the public to report any ruffed grouse sightings. Sightings in suitable habitat, principally forested areas adjacent to water, are occasionally reported. In the years 1994–95, 29 observation forms were mailed in.

Ruffed grouse became expatriated from Kansas when their hardwood habitat became fragmented through agricultural land-use patterns. Starting in 1981, a reintroduction effort was initiated to bring ruffed grouse back to Kansas. For a seven year period, from 1983 through 1989, grouse were live-trapped in Wisconsin and transplanted on 9 release sites in northeastern and southeastern Kansas. An additional effort was initiated on Fort Riley (near Junction City) by U.S. Army personnel. Forty-nine grouse were captured on the military post in the fall of 1991.

From the persistent reports of grouse observations, it is apparent that the birds released in the northeast have survived and reproduced. The southeastern reintroductions, however, appear to have failed. Of the 29 observation reports in the 1994–95 reporting period, 16 were 10 or more miles away from the nearest release site. This can be interpreted to indicate that birds have relocated or expanded their range. As it stands, ruffed grouse may persist in small numbers, but it is unlikely that populations will ever grow large enough to sustain any hunting pressure.

Woodcock

Scolopax minor

Local Names

Timberdoddle, Wood Snipe, Bog Sucker

Facts

Woodcock are legal game in Kansas with a season that, during the 1997–98 season, ran from October 17th through November 30th. The daily bag is 3 per day; possession limit is 6. However, this open season should not lead a hunter to think that Kansas would be the place to hunt woodcock.

In reality, woodcock are bordering on the extreme western edge of their range in eastern Kansas and therefore, rarely seen. *Birds in Kansas, Volume 1*, labels them as 'an uncommon transient in the eastern and central part of the state and rare in the west.' The majority of woodcock sightings occur in the eastern third of Kansas. Forty-three of Kansas' 105 counties have recorded woodcock sightings, with most birds being seen from April through November. The majority of fall migrants first appear in late August and continue into November.

Birds are found in association with eastern forests and wetlands. The woodcock's long bill evolved for probing in soft soil to gather earthworms, their principle food. Interested Kansas hunters should confine their hunting to areas of suitable habitat along the state's eastern boundary.

The Dabblers

General Characteristics

Puddle ducks are a common sight while traveling in Kansas. They utilize a broad range of habitat types, from small farm ponds and flooded fields to large refuge marshes. Males are brightly colored with ornate plumage patterns. Hens are drab colored and inconspicuous in comparison. Dabbling duck types range from small green-winged teals to large mallard ducks. Their legs are well centered on their bodies so that they walk efficiently. Species such as mallards and widgeon sometimes forage by gleaning grass and waste grains from open fields. Puddlers live on shallow water and feed by tipping up and harvesting aquatic plants and insects.

Floating on the water, puddlers exhibit a high tail and long body. Their neck appears long in relationship to their body. They are strong fliers and tend to congregate in large groups.

Species and Identification

Mallard

- **Males:** Metallic green neck and head, bill is bright yellow with a black nail. Male mallards show a conspicuous white neck-ring which transitions into a solid chestnut-brown breast. The belly, side coverts, and scapular feathers are pearl grey. The back and rump coverts are metallic black. The tail feathers are white. The rump coverts form into two black feathers that curl up in a circle above the bird's tail. These birds are large and have orange legs and feet. Their eyes are brown.
- **Females:** Mottled brown neck and head, dark cap and accent line across eye, bill is mottled orange with a dark nail. Hens are mottled brown overall. Back coverts are darker, while belly feathers are lighter. These birds are large and have orange legs and feet. Their eyes are brown.
- **Wing:** Upper wing is olive, tertials are grey, edged with chestnut brown. Wing speculum is metallic blue that fades to black at its edges. A thin white highlight edges the black.

Mottled Duck

- **Males:** Mottled brown neck and head, dark cap and accent line across eye, bill is olive green with a dark nail. Male mottled ducks are mottled brown overall. Their brown base color is a midway hue between the colors of a hen mallard and that of a black duck. Back coverts are darker, and belly feathers are lighter. These birds are large and have orange legs and feet. Their eyes are brown.
- **Females:** Mottled brown neck and head, dark cap and accent line across eye, bill is mottled orange with a dark nail. Hens are similar to males.
- **Wing:** Similar to a mallard's wing, with the exception that a mottled duck's wing speculum has no white highlight at the top of the metallic blue speculum.

Gadwall are often seen in the early season bag of Kansas duck hunters.

Black Duck

- **Males:** Medium-brown neck and head, dark cap and accent line across eye, bill is yellow with a dark nail. Male black ducks are mottled burnt-cork brown overall. Their brown base color is a rich chocolate hue. These birds are large and have muted orange legs and feet. Their eyes are brown.
- **Females:** Medium-brown neck and head, dark cap and accent line across eye, bill is mottled olive with a dark nail. Hens are similar to males.
- **Wing:** Similar to a mallard's wing, darker overall, metallic purple speculum which fades to black at the top and bottom, slight white highlight edges the black at the bottom of the speculum.

Gadwall

- **Males:** Mottled grey neck and crested head, light grey checks, dark highlight across the eye, bill is solid black. Male gadwalls are a medium-grey overall with an intricate black vermiculation that covers the breast, side coverts, and scapular feathers. The scapulars are pointed and highlighted with a muted orange. The belly is white. The back and rump coverts are a deep velvety black. The tail feathers are grey. These birds are large and have orange legs and feet. Their eyes are brown.
- **Females:** Mottled brown neck and head, dark cap and accent line across eye, bill is mottled orange with a dark nail. Hens are a mottled brown. Back coverts are darker, belly feathers fade to white. These birds are large and have orange legs and feet. Their eyes are brown.

Male American widgeon.

- **Wing:** Upper wing is grey with rust-red middle wing coverts. The red fades to a black and white wing speculum. This is the only North American species of puddle duck that carries red, white, and black on its wing.

Widgeon
- **Males:** Light cream neck and head heavily flecked with black, crown of head is solid white, an extensive solid metallic green zone extends from the back of the eye to blend at the base of the neck, bill is powder blue with a black nail and highlights. The breast, side coverts, and scapular feathers are plum colored and etched with fine black vermiculation. The back and upper rump coverts are patterned in grey and white. The pin-shaped tail feathers and its surrounding coverts are black. The belly is white. These birds are medium-sized and have grey legs and feet. Their eyes are brown.
- **Females:** Light cream neck and head lightly flecked with black, bill is powder blue with a black nail and highlights. The breast and side coverts are light plum. Scapular feathers, and back and upper rump coverts are mottled in plum and olive-grey. The belly is white. These birds are medium-sized and have grey legs and feet. Their eyes are brown.

- **Wing:** Upper wing has an extensive white field above the speculum that flashes white in flight. Primaries are grey. The tertials are pointed and flowing in shape, colored grey, and edged with silver. Wing speculum is metallic green. A black band separates the speculum from the white upper wing coverts.

Northern Pintail
- **Males:** Solid brown head with long white neck. When held in the right light an iridescent purple sheen is visible on the side of the head behind the eye. The bill is solid black with a powder blue accent that runs the length of the sides of the bill. Male pintails are a medium-grey overall with an intricate black vermiculation that covers the side coverts and scapular feathers. The scapulars are pointed and flowing, and highlighted with silver-grey. The breast and belly is white. The back and rump coverts are a deep velvety black. The long pin-shaped tail feathers are black. The remaining tail feathers are silver-grey. These birds are large and have grey legs and feet. Their eyes are brown.
- **Females:** Mottled brown neck and head, bill is mottled blue-grey with a dark nail. Hens are a mottled brown. Back coverts are darker, belly feathers fade to white. These birds are large and have grey legs and feet. Their eyes are brown.
- **Wing:** Upper wing surface is grey. A mustard accent line highlights the edges of the upper wing coverts directly above the violet green wing speculum. Tertials are silver and black.

Green-winged Teal
- **Males:** Brown neck and head, head crests in a brown crown, a solid metallic green zone extends from around the eyes to blend into a well-developed black mane on the back of the neck. Bill is black. The breast is cream-colored and accented with small black polka dots. A sharp white chevron comes off the shoulder and separates the breast and side coverts. The side coverts and scapular feathers are light grey and etched with fine black vermiculation. The tertials, which are pointed and flowing, are grey and tinted with a mustard-yellow hue. The back and upper rump coverts are patterned in grey and white darts which mirror the pattern of the tertial feathers. The tail feathers are medium-grey and separated from the side coverts by a triangular zone of mustard-tinged buff colored feathers. The belly is white. These birds are very small and have grey legs and feet. Their eyes are brown.
- **Females:** Mottled brown neck and head, dark cap and accent line across eye, bill is mottled blue grey with a dark nail. Hens are a mottled brown. Back coverts are darker, belly feathers fade to white. These birds are very small and have grey legs and feet. Their eyes are brown.
- **Wing:** Upper wing surface is grey. A mustard accent line highlights the edges of the upper wing coverts directly above the speculum. The speculum is composed of two zones of color: the upper half, against the body, is metallic green; the lower half, toward the wing tips, is black. Tertials are flowing and grey.

Greenwings are America's most common teal.

Blue-winged Teal

- **Males:** Solid blue head and neck with a pronounced white crescent on the side of the face in front of the eye. The crown of the bird blends to black. When held in the right light, an iridescent purple sheen is visible on the side of the head behind the eye. The bill is solid black. Male blue-winged teals are buff colored overall, with an intricate field of black polka dots that cover the breast, side coverts, and belly feathers. The black scapulars are pointed and flowing, and highlighted with powder blue and mustard accents. The back and rump coverts are black with slightly visible mustard chevrons. The dark tail feathers are also highlighted with mustard. A pronounced white zone is visible between the side coverts and tail. These birds are small and have yellow legs and feet. Their eyes are brown.
- **Females:** Mottled brown neck and head, dark cap and accent line across eye, throat is white, bill is mottled blue-grey with a dark nail. Hens are a mottled brown. Back coverts are darker, belly feathers fade to white. These birds are small and have yellow legs and feet. Their eyes are brown.
- **Wing:** Upper wing surface is powder blue. Primary flight feathers are olive-grey. A white accent line highlights the edges of the upper wing coverts directly above the violet-green wing speculum. Tertials are black and accented with powder blue and mustard chevrons.

Cinnamon Teal

- **Males:** Cinnamon-red head and neck. The crown of the bird head blends to black. The bill is solid black. Male cinnamon teal are cinnamon-red overall. The black scapulars are pointed and flowing, and highlighted with powder blue and mustard accents. The back and rump coverts are black, with slightly visible mustard chevrons. The dark tail feathers are also highlighted with mustard. Powder blue from the upper wings may be visible below the tertials. These birds are small and have yellow legs and feet. Their eyes are orange.
- **Females:** Mottled brown neck and head, dark cap and accent line across eye, throat is white, bill is mottled blue-grey with a dark nail. Hens are a mottled brown. Back coverts are darker, belly feathers fade to white. These birds are small and have yellow legs and feet. Their eyes are brown.
- **Wing:** Upper wing surface is powder blue. Primary flight feathers are olive-grey. A white accent line highlights the edges of the upper wing coverts directly above the violet-green wing speculum. Tertials are black and accented with powder blue and mustard chevrons.

Northern Shoveler

- **Males:** Metallic green neck and head, bill is solid black and spoon shaped. Male shoveler has white breast and scapular feathers. The side coverts and belly are chestnut brown. Powder blue from the upper wings may be visible below the scapulars and tertials. The back and rump coverts are metallic black. The tail feathers are white. These birds are medium-sized and have orange legs and feet. Their eyes are yellow.
- **Females:** Mottled brown neck and head, dark cap and accent line across eye, bill is mottled olive green and orange with a dark nail. Hens are mottled brown overall. Back coverts are darker, and belly feathers are lighter. Powder blue from the upper wings may be visible below the scapulars and tertials. These birds are medium-sized and have orange legs and feet. Their eyes are orange.
- **Wing:** Upper wing surface is powder blue. Primary flight feathers are olive grey. A white accent line highlights the edges of the upper wing coverts directly above the violet-green wing speculum and the secondary flight feathers below the speculum. Tertials are black and flowing with powder blue and white accent chevrons.

Wood Duck

- **Males:** Metallic blue and green neck, crested head, white throat with two white curved bars that run behind the eye and at the back of the head crest. In addition, thin white piping accents the side of the drake's head crest. Bill is bright yellow, red, white, and black with a black nail. Male wood ducks, at a distance, are dark in appearance and resemble mud hens. At hand, they have a metallic blue and green head, neck, back, and tail. Their breast is chestnut brown and decorated with small white triangles. The belly is white. Side coverts are straw yellow and etched with a fine black vermiculation. The ends of the side coverts sweep over

Male spoonbills are very colorful birds.

the metallic purple and blue scapulars and are decorated with black and white accents. A metallic, plum-colored zone separates the side coverts from the tail. The rump coverts and tail feathers are metallic black. Birds are medium-sized and have yellow legs and feet. Their eyes are red.

- **Females:** Grey neck and crested head, dark cap, white throat, and pronounced white eye patch. Bill is dark and mottled with a dark nail. Hen's bodies are mottled brown overall. Back and rump coverts and tail feathers are darker. Some blue and violet iridescence is present on the bird's scapulars. Belly feathers are white. These birds are medium-sized and have yellow legs and feet. Their eyes are brown.

- **Wing:** Upper wing surface is grey brown and decorated with multiple hues of iridescent colors. Wing speculum is metallic blue through the secondary flight feathers and zoned in metallic colors of violet, black, purple, and blue at the tertials. The primary flight feathers are tipped with metallic blue and carry leading edges frosted in white.

Migration

Large numbers of puddle ducks travel through Kansas during their southward migration to their wintering grounds along the gulf coasts of Louisiana, Texas, Mexico, and beyond. Some of the first migrants of the season are the blue-winged teal. Kansas has an early teal season in mid-September, allowing hunters a chance at these birds before they head for their wintering grounds in South America. Other species soon follow, and, depending on the weather, the migration peaks in mid- to late November.

Some birds hold throughout the season and can be found wherever ice-free water is available. Once the freeze occurs, however, the shooting is mostly restricted to the ample numbers of greenheads that winter through in Kansas. Wintering birds rely on available waste grain, such as corn and sorghum, for sustenance.

Habits and Habitat

As their name implies, puddle ducks prefer shallow water. They are at home anywhere they have food, water, and adequate protection from disturbance. Birds congregate along main river drainages and use isolated stretches of the main river and inflow creeks for loafing and feeding areas. Water impoundments, both small and large, also provide critical habitat for puddle ducks. In the western part of the state, where water is not abundant, birds utilize small farm and stock ponds as layover stops on their trips south.

Kansas has many large-scale reservoirs and birds will use the many coves, river/creek deltas, and bays that a large body of water provides. Traveling waterfowl will return year after year to wetland staging areas like Cheyenne Bottoms State Wildlife Area and Quivira National Wildlife Refuge. The Kansas Department of Wildlife and Parks and the Federal Fish and Wildlife Service manage these refuge locations to benefit waterfowl populations.

Puddle ducks leave their nighttime roosting areas at first light, and travel to feed. Morning flights can last until midmorning depending upon numbers of birds present and the weather. Before incoming storms, ducks will feed much more actively and heavily, in anticipation of being denied access to food sources during the storm.

During midday, birds return to the marshes and open water to loaf. Ducks will leave to feed again from late afternoon to dusk, depending on the moon and the amount of disturbance they have experienced in the area. During a full moon, birds may feed by moonlight.

Hunting the Dabblers

There are a lot of ways to shoot a duck. Waterfowling is really an American tradition, and the methods that developed in North America are as broad and diverse as the continent is big.

Pass shooting is the simplest type of duck hunting and requires the least amount of equipment. With a shotgun, camouflage clothing, and something to carry dead birds in, a hunter is set to go. With a minimum amount of study, the flight times and travel lanes of trading ducks can be patterned. A hunter can wait in ambush in a likely spot and take birds as they pass overhead. Birds will tend to follow water courses and familiar flight lanes year after year. Weather plays an important part in determining when and how high the birds will fly. Factors such as wind, fog, incoming storms, and extreme cold can all influence the height that the birds fly at, and how active they will be during their feeding flights. Once an area is figured out, a hunter can return repeatedly to the same places and take birds.

Another approach is to use duck decoys to lure the birds to the gun. This is where traditional waterfowling begins. The first prerequisite is to set up where the ducks want to be. The biggest and best decoy spread on the marsh won't be able to compete with a dozen blocks floating in just the right spot. So, it behooves the prospecting duck hunter to find that spot. Like most other types of hunting, scouting is the key. It may take several trips to figure a place out. Over a period of time, conditions change and last month's spot may also change. A hunter needs to watch what the birds are doing and shift his location accordingly.

Decoys are the next part of the equation. In most situations, the more the better. The quality of decoys is also important. It is a tradeoff because the truth is that one or two gunners can only do so much work, and the only certainty involved in waterfowling is that it is going to be a lot of wet, finger numbing, mud slurping, backbreaking, hard work.

Modern plastic waterfowl decoys are a vast improvement over the wooden decoys of old. Not to diminish the wooden decoy as a piece of sculpture or negate the joy of shooting over a stool of hand carved wooden birds, but as a matter of practicality, plastic beats wood hands down. Plastic is nearly indestructible. In addition, plastic decoys are a fraction of the cost of wood counterfeits, even when they are made at home. Finally, on the issue of weight, a hunter only has to make two predawn trips out to the duck blind with two dozen blocks slung in a burlap bag over his shoulder, one full of wooden birds and the other full of plastic, to know what he will be carrying out on the next hunt.

The hunter's next concern is where to hide once the decoys are spread. Ducks have keen eyesight, making concealment of utmost importance. A permanent blind offers the most in amenities and comfort, but its one major drawback is that it can't be moved to where the birds are currently working. If a hunter knows an area well, and birds consistently use a particular place, then a permanent blind may be in order. There are commercially manufactured steel and fiberglass blinds on the market that are dug into the ground and buried. These are generally large and built to accommodate multiple shooters. These blinds are generally equipped with covers and propane heaters. They are most often seen in use on commercial shooting operations because of the considerable expense involved with their purchase, installation, and operation.

A private individual with access to a farm junkyard and the ability to operate a welding torch and back hoe will be able to find and put together something that will suffice. Things like rusted-off steel water tanks, steel feed bins, cement culverts and septic tanks can all make serviceable sunken blinds.

Wood can also be used, both above and below ground, to construct a permanent blind. Plywood, 2X4s, a shovel, some hand tools, nails, and a chain saw can create a

A Kansas river blind.

serviceable pit blind. The box can take the shape of a piano box and conceal the shooter in a seated position, or the shape of a coffin and be dug in to hide a laying out hunter. While it is easier to forego burying a blind, if at all possible I would recommend getting as much of the shooter's body below ground as possible. It will much improve the blind's effectiveness.

Incorporating natural wood and vegetation to conceal the blind will make it invisible to trading birds. Blinds can be constructed entirely of materials found on-site. A frame of found natural wood, wired together with rusted baling wire to prevent shine, and embellished with camouflage netting and natural vegetation, can be deadly in the right spot. Remember that the bird's perspective is from above. What you see from the side doesn't matter. It's that shiny face peering up from the dark hole in the bushes that is going to flare the incoming birds.

The other concealment option is the use of a duck boat. There are literally dozens of different duck boat designs that have developed regionally throughout North America. The advantages with a boat are that it is mobile and will float all your gear (as opposed to carrying your gear on your back). The disadvantage is that in order for a duck boat to be effective as a blind, it needs to be small. This restricts the amount of gear it can carry. Some big decoy spread outfits haul gear in a large tender boat and tow smaller craft behind to use as blinds.

A hunter interested in using a duck boat should look at what is being used on the water that he is interested in hunting. Different water, such as a cattail marsh compared to a large water reservoir, will require different hull designs. There are several books that list different types of duck boat designs, if a hunter is interested in constructing his own boat. In addition, there are several commercial outfits now producing old boat designs in modern fiberglass. These companies are also producing modern designs that are both large enough for multiple guns and covered over to maximize their concealment.

The most inexpensive way to get a serviceable boat is to modify an existing hull by either decking it over or by constructing a portable blind to be carried in the boat to a hunting area and set up on site. Two books that explore this topic in much greater depth are *(Getting the most out of) Modern Water Fowling*, John O. Cartier, St. Martin's Press, New York, 1974; and *Successful Waterfowling*, Zack Taylor, Crown Publishers, Inc., New York, 1974.

There are a host of other goodies that the serious duck hunter can't do without, calls being one of the most coveted and most often abused. I have about two dozen assorted calls, if you combine the duck and goose models together. There is a bewildering array of calls offered, and all claim to be the final answer to the waterfowler's dreams.

I remember, as a kid, going to hunt Tule Lake Refuge in the Klamath basin on the California/Oregon border. The hunting was great and the concentrations of waterfowl were a sight to behold, but the highlight of the trip was going to Tule Lake Hardware to look at their selection of calls. As you can imagine, the store, being the only sporting goods outlet in this waterfowl mecca, was solid waterfowl hunting merchandise. The centerpiece of the store, for me, was a large, lighted, revolving jewelry display case— one of the types with suspended trays that move in a circuit when a button is pushed. It seemed, at the time, that every call known to man was available in that case. Every trip to Tule added one or two new calls to my collection, and I would leave the store with the absolute conviction that the "answer" was somewhere in that case. These days I'm not as easy to convince, but there isn't any harm in stopping to look, is there?

If I'm hunting puddle ducks, I use two mallard calls. One has a lower tone and more volume and blows a better highball and lonesome hen call. The other is slightly higher pitched and gives a better feeding chuckle. They both have nylon reeds. In addition, I have a pair of very old handmade calls I bought years ago at an estate sale. They have metal reeds, and I will use one of them if I am hunting sheltered water and I will be mostly feed chuckling. I don't know if the particular models I use would be of use to another hunter because everybody blows a call differently. My theory is that it has to do with the shape of the inside of a person's mouth, much like one brand of perfume will smell differently on two different people.

One brand I can recommend is a pintail/wigeon/teal whistle called a wingsetter. I bought it over twenty years ago and wouldn't try to hunt puddlers without it. Perhaps the greatest testament I can offer is that in this amount of time and use, I haven't lost it. I still see the whistle offered in the call catalogs. It is a molded, olive-green, two-barreled whistle with a kazoo slide in one barrel that adjusts to change the pitch. The call can sound like a single bird or a small flock.

One word to those who want to learn how to blow a duck call: it can't be learned through the written word. The best course of instruction is to find someone who can blow a duck call and ask for help. Then, practice using audio and video tapes, and the real thing down at your local kiddy park duck pond.

A waterfowler needs a "possibles" bag. It can be a day pack or shoulder-strap model, in a drab color or camouflage pattern. Inside there should be things like extra shells, calls, chokes, hat, gloves, sunglasses, chapstick, bug repellent, sunscreen, binoculars, camera, and lunch.

A duck hunter's feet will always end up in water, even when he doesn't intend to do any wading. A hunter has three choices: chest waders, hip waders, or rubber boots. A hunter needs to look at the type of hunting he will be doing and make the appropriate choice.

Table Preparations

Puddle ducks primarily eat plant matter and make excellent table fare. The meat is dark and best not overcooked. Birds may be skinned and breasted out, or plucked for a more formal presentation.

Gun and Shot Suggestions

- **Gauge:** 12, 10
- **Choke:** Improved cylinder / modified for double guns, modified for single barrels.
- **Shot:** For large ducks use nontoxic shot in waterfowl loads of No. 2 or 1. Second barrel or third shot backup shell loaded with BB shot. For early teal, use nontoxic shot in waterfowl loads of No. 4.

The Divers

General Characteristics

In contrast to puddle ducks, diving ducks have evolved for life on open water. Their bodies are shorter and more streamlined, with short tails and legs set further back on their bodies to facilitate swimming. Accordingly, they walk with greater difficulty than a puddle duck. Also, unlike puddle ducks which upend and extend their necks to feed on aquatic plants, divers often swim to great depths to harvest plants or feed on small fish and aquatic animals and insects.

Male diving ducks are colored in solid patterns of either grey and black or white and black. Depending on the species, their head color can be either red, purple, or green. A diving duck's profile on the water shows a low tail at or near the water line, making them easily recognized as divers even from great distances.

Divers tend to loft in large rafts or pods, and at midday can be seen sleeping out in the middle of open water.

Species and Identification

Canvasback
- **Males:** Solid red neck and head with a black bill. Canvasbacks have a triangular head shape and thick long neck. This bird's back and side coverts are pearl white in a mature male, and light grey in an immature bird of the year. The rump coverts are black and the short tail feathers are colored a silver-grey. Canvasbacks are large and have large grey paddle feet. Their eyes are red.
- **Females:** Soft brown neck and head fading to light brown on the cheeks, the bill is black. A Can is a soft, mottled brown overall, with highlights of pearl-grey on the bird's back and side coverts. These birds are large and have large grey paddle feet. Their eyes are brown.

Redheads
- **Males:** Solid red neck and head with a blue grey bill, with a black bill tip and nail. Male redheads are a silver-grey color overall, with some dark feathers highlighting their rump coverts. These birds are large and have large grey paddle feet. Their eyes are orange-yellow.
- **Females:** Soft brown neck and head darkening to a medium-brown crown. Their bill is blue-grey with a black bill tip and nail. The hen's side coverts are the same brown as her neck and head. The back and upper rump coverts are a darker olive hue. These birds are large and have large grey paddle feet. Their eyes are brown.

A ring-necked drake is a handsome bird.

Lesser Scaup (Nickname: Bluebill)
- **Males:** Solid dark neck and crested head appearing black at a distance and metallic purple in hand. Bill is blue-grey with a black nail. The male bluebill has a black breast and upper rump coverts. The bird's side coverts are white. The bird's scapulars are also white, but etched with unbroken black vermiculation. These birds are medium-sized and have large grey paddle feet. Their eyes are yellow.
- **Females:** Solid brown neck and crested head with a white crescent in front of the eye. Bill is mottled in medium blue-grey and dark blue-grey, nail is black. The hens are mottled brown overall, with some white showing on the side coverts and belly. These birds are medium-sized and have large grey paddle feet. Their eyes are yellow.

Ring-necked Duck (Nickname: Ringbill)
- **Males:** Solid dark neck and crested head appearing black at a distance and metallic purple in hand. Bill is a medium blue-grey with a white band and black tip and nail. The male ringneck has a black breast, back, and rump. The bird's side coverts are white at the shoulder, fading to a silver grey. These birds are medium-sized and have large grey paddle feet. Their eyes are orange-yellow.
- **Females:** Solid brown neck and crested head with a slight white crescent behind the bill and a white ring around the eye. Bill is mottled in medium blue-grey with a white band and dark nail. Hens are mottled brown overall, with light brown side coverts and belly. These birds are medium-sized and have large grey paddle feet. Their eyes are brown.

Common goldeneyes are often seen on the rivers of Kansas.

Common Goldeneye
- **Males:** Solid metallic green neck and crested head with a white spot in front of the eye and a solid black bill. Goldeneyes have a triangular head shape and a short, thick neck. The bird's breast, belly and side coverts are a brilliant white with delicate black striping showing at the top of the side coverts. The back, rump, and tail coverts are black. These birds are large and have orange legs and feet. Their eyes are yellow.
- **Females:** Medium brown neck and crested head. Bill is dark blue-grey with a black nail. The hen's side coverts are mottled grey and white, with the belly turning to solid white. The back and upper rump coverts are also mottled grey with light grey highlights. These birds are large and have orange legs and feet. Their eyes are yellow.

Bufflehead
- **Males:** Solid-colored dark neck and large crested head appearing black at a distance and metallic blue-green in hand. These birds have a white zone that quarters in a pie-shaped wedge, with the point originating at the eye and expanding to the back of the head. Bill is blue-grey with a dark tip and nail. The male bufflehead has a white breast and side coverts. Delicate black lines etch the outer edges of the bird's side coverts. The bird's belly is in shades from white to grey. Birds are small-sized and have large pink paddle feet. Their eyes are dark brown.
- **Females:** Grey neck and crested head with a white crescent behind the eye. Bill is mottled in light to medium blue-grey. Hens are mottled grey overall, with a light

A male ruddy duck in breeding plumage.

colored breast and light grey side coverts and belly. These birds are small-sized and have grey paddle feet. Their eyes are brown.

Ruddy Duck

- **Males:** Mottled grey neck, crested head with black crown and white cheeks. Bill is blue-grey with a dark nail. The male Ruddy has a mottled olive-brown breast, back, and rump. The belly and underside of the bird's rump is light olive-grey. Ruddys are classified as stiff-tailed ducks because of their straight, erect, feathered tails. These birds are small-sized and have large grey paddle feet. Their eyes are brown.
- **Females:** Mottled olive-brown neck and crested head with dark crown and slight white feather highlights on cheek. Bill is mottled olive-brown with a dark nail. The female Ruddy has a mottled olive-brown breast, back, and rump. The belly and underside of the bird's rump is light olive-grey. Ruddy's are classified as stiff-tailed ducks because of their straight, erect, feathered tails. These birds are small-sized and have large grey paddle feet. Their eyes are brown.

Hooded Merganser

- **Males:** Solid black neck and crested head with a white crescent radiating from the eye to the back of the crest, and a solid black merganser saw-bill. Hooded mergansers have a pronounced triangular head shape and a short, thick neck. The bird's belly and breast are a brilliant white. Heavy black striping accents the transition to the bird's light sienna side coverts. In addition, the side coverts are covered with a delicate black vermiculation. The tertial feathers are white, edged with black, and hang in striking darts off the back of the bird. The back, rump, and tail coverts are black. These birds are small and have yellow legs and feet. Their eyes are yellow.

- **Females:** Solid black neck and crested head with a white crescent radiating from the eye to the back of the crest, and a solid black merganser saw-bill. Hooded mergansers have a pronounced triangular head shape and a short, thick neck. The bird's belly and breast are a brilliant white. Heavy black striping accents the transition to the bird's light sienna side coverts. In addition, the side coverts are covered with a delicate black vermiculation. The tertial feathers are white, edged with black, and hang in striking darts off the back of the bird. The back, rump, and tail coverts are black. These birds are small and have yellow legs and feet. Their eyes are yellow.

Common Merganser

- **Males:** Solid metallic green neck and head, and a red merganser saw-bill with dark accents and nail. Male common mergansers are quite striking because of their size and sharply contrasting black and white color pattern. The bird's belly and breast are a brilliant cream white. The back is solid black. Rump and tail coverts are medium-grey with dark-grey accents The tertial feathers are white, edged with delicate black accent lines that highlight the rump of the bird. These birds are extra-large and very stout. They have red legs and feet. Their eyes are red.
- **Females:** Solid, rust-colored neck and crested head with a small white chin patch, and an orangish-red merganser saw-bill. The bill is mottled on top and has a dark nail. Hen common mergansers have a pronounced triangular crested head shape and a thick neck. The bird's belly and breast are white. The rest of the bird is a uniform mottled medium-grey. These birds are large and stout and have orangish-red legs and feet. Their eyes are brown.

Migration

The majority of diving ducks which migrate through Kansas start in mid-October and continue through the end of November. Common mergansers and American goldeneyes are found on open water and frequent flowing, ice-free rivers. The flocks of divers that traverse Kansas nest in the pothole region of the Dakotas and the Canadian prairie provinces. The birds follow migration routes that run north to south and winter along the gulf coast of Texas and Louisiana and the east coast of Mexico.

Habits and Habitat

Diving ducks are birds of open, deep water impoundments. They raft on open water for the protection it offers and to dive for food. Divers tend to congregate in large flocks, and the groups of ducks observed loafing midday, in big rafts on big water, are generally made up of diving duck species.

John and Sammy Leonard, father and son duck hunting team of Topeka.

Hunting the Divers

Occasionally, divers are taken as coincidental birds while hunting puddle ducks: a small group of canvasbacks or redheads roar around the outside of a spread of mallard decoys floating on a cattail marsh; a lone drake goldeneye or buf-flehead bombs a sandbar decoy spread in the middle of a large river channel. One quick overhead pass, some quick shooting, and hopefully a splash. Most divers are killed in this way.

Those hunters wishing to concentrate solely on diver species need to use special-ized hunting methods and equipment. As divers use big open water, the first problem is: where does the gunner hide? There is a rich history of specialized water craft which evolved for open water gunning of divers. East coast market gunners, of the late 1800's, shot out of sink boxes. They were commercial operations that used pickup boats to recover down birds and large tender ships as living quarters.

Today, the blind of choice for open water hunting is a layout boat. These are small pumpkin seed-shaped boats made in one- and two-man configurations. The boats are painted a neutral grey to match the color of reflected water. The gunwales are at the waterline so that when the weight of a gunner and his gear are put into the boat, the gunwales sink below the water and the boat has no shadow line. The craft appears as an inconspicuous grey bump on the water. A layout boat is anchored from one end, like a decoy, so it can swing with the wind. A stiff canvas collar protects the

Wade Culbertson and his black Lab watching for birds.

inside of the boat from taking on any water, even in heavy chop. While they may sound dangerous to someone who has never logged any time in one, they are actually very seaworthy. I have been on saltwater bays, Brant hunting, in heavy seas and high winds. At times, the swells and wind were too severe to allow me to hit an incoming bird or even get picked up from the layout boat by the tender boat. During one of those ocean bay hunts, I was stuck in the layout boat for an extra 2 hours because severe weather conditions precluded my removal. During those times, I floated like a cork in an agitating washing machine and remained dry.

Large spreads of diving duck decoys are used in conjunction with a layout boat. Often 100 or more decoys are rigged with long lines and multiple gang rigs for this sort of deep water gunning.

The other type of effective craft for open water is a scull boat. These, too, are specialized craft developed during the market hunting era. Unlike the layout boat designs, however, this boat's seaworthiness get real dicey with every minimal wind. At the first sign of any incoming chop, a scull boat needs to head for shore.

Scull boats are dagger-shaped and run to around 16 feet in length (with the two-man models). The boat I have is 14 feet, 4 inches, and has 13.5 inches of foot space between the bottom of the deck and the top of the hull. There are two styles of scull boats. One was developed on Merrymeeting Bay, Maine, and is hunted with the point of its bow above water, hidden by a screen of brush that is dropped forward just before the flush. These "brush boats" are anchored upwind of a decoy spread and drift down on the decoys after birds land in the spread. They are more seaworthy but not as effective as the second style of boat.

The second style of scull boat is hunted with a low sled containing about 120 pounds of weight that is slid forward towards the front of the boat before a scull begins. With this weight forward, the point of the bow is submerged under water and the bow's shadow line disappears. The boat is propelled by a single oar, worked in a slow figure eight motion, through the back of the transom. The hunters, lying flat in the boat, and the movements of the sculling oar, are both invisible to any floating waterfowl. This is an aggressive style of hunting as opposed to passively sitting in a decoy spread waiting for trading birds to appear. Much like stalking a big game animal, rafts of resting birds are glassed at a distance and if conditions allow, a "scull" is begun.

For those without access to these specialized hunting boats, a v hull design runabout can be used with some modifications to hunt open water. Two books that explore this topic in much more depth are: *(Getting the most out of) Modern Water Fowling*, John O. Cartier, St. Martin's Press, New York, 1974; and *Successful Waterfowling*, Zack Taylor, Crown Publishers, Inc., New York, 1974.

Table Preparations

Some species of divers, such as goldeneyes, ruddy ducks, buffleheads, and mergansers eat a high percentage of animal matter which can adversely affect the flavor of the meat. Redheads, ringnecks and canvasbacks feed primarily on aquatic plants and make fine table fare. Palatability can be gauged at the time of cleaning by the degree of fish odor the meat carries. Birds that carry a strong odor are probably best marinated or prepared in such a way as to offset any strong flavor.

Gun and Shot Suggestions

- **Gauge:** 12, 10
- **Choke:** Improved cylinder/modified for double guns, modified for single barrels.
- **Shot:** Nontoxic shot in waterfowl loads of No. 2 or 1. Second barrel or third shot backup shell loaded with BB shot.

The Geese

General Characteristics

Wild geese are one of this continent's great success stories. Maybe too great, in the case of the central flyway's lesser snow goose population. Highflying chevrons of migrating geese are a common sight in Kansas during the fall and spring. All goose species are very gregarious and will congregate on their staging and wintering areas in large numbers. These birds are very vocal and are often heard before they are seen. They feed communally and are drawn to fields where birds are already on the ground and feeding.

Flocks are made up of family groups, and the big bird at the front of the 'V' is the oldest and wisest, ever alert to danger. Lead birds control where the flock goes and when they land. They do their best to keep every bird in the flock healthy.

Geese are large birds and do not take to the air as readily as a puddle duck will. They require a bit of a running jump to gain the air. Their legs are centered on their bodies, and they can walk easily. They forage by gleaning grains and green feed from agricultural fields. Unlike most puddler species, which require ever-diminishing wetlands to provide their food needs, geese have adapted to using cultivated fields and, as a result, have an unlimited supply of food available.

While geese do not require water to feed, they do need undisturbed areas in which to loaf midday and roost at night. A critical habitat requirement is either a refuge area that geese can retire and remain unmolested or large pieces of open water where they can raft in the middle, away from repeated disturbance.

Species and Identification

Canada Goose (Honker)

On its black neck and head, a honker carries a pronounced white chin strap that covers the side of the face, behind the eye, and extends down and around the bird's throat. Canada's are olive-grey to chocolate-brown overall, depending on the subspecies (there are 11 different subspecies). These birds are darker on the back and scapulars, while the breast and belly are lighter. Their lower belly and under tail coverts are white; the rump is black with a thin white zone above the tail; and the tail feathers are black.

Snow Goose

- **White Phase:** Solid white neck and head, some birds carry mustard-colored, iron oxide-stained flecking on the sides of the face and breast; the bill is reddish-pink with a black grinning patch and a white nail. The bird's entire body is solid white, and the wings are also all white, with the exception of black primary feathers and grey primary coverts. The legs and feet are reddish-pink.

Black Labrador and Canada goose.

- **Juvenile:** Mottled light silver-grey and white neck and head, some birds carry mustard-colored, iron oxide-stained flecking on the sides of the face and breast, bill is grayish-brown. The bird's entire body is mottled light silver-grey and white. The back is darker, while the breast and belly fade to white. The wings are mottled light silver-grey, with the exception of faded black primary feathers and grey primary coverts. The legs and feet are greyish-brown.
- **Blue Phase:** Solid white upper neck and head, some birds carry mustard-colored, iron oxide-stained flecking on the sides of the face and breast, lower neck is olive-grey, bill is reddish-pink with a black grinning patch and white nail. The bird's body is primarily olive-grey, while the belly blends to white. However, the belly's color conversion is variable—some birds have solid white bellies, while others are more olive-grey than white. The wings (excluding the primary feathers and primary coverts) are blue-grey with silver-grey highlights. The greater coverts and greater tertial coverts are pointed and flowing and highlighted in silver-grey and blue-grey. Primary and secondary flight feathers are black, and primary coverts are grey. The legs and feet are reddish-pink.
- **Juvenile:** Solid brownish-grey neck and head, white chin spot, bill is a purple-hued greyish-brown. The bird's entire body is solid brownish-grey. The back is darker, while the breast and belly fades to a lighter hue. The wings are mottled blue-grey and highlighted with silver-grey, with the exception of black primary and secondary flight feathers and grey primary coverts. The legs and feet are a purple-hued greyish-brown.

Ross' Goose

The Ross' goose is much smaller than a snow goose. Solid white neck and head; some birds carry mustard-colored, iron oxide-stained flecking on the sides of the face and breast; the bill is pink with a white nail; light purplish pink, rough warting appears behind and below the nostrils. The bird's entire body is solid white. The wings are also all white, with the exception of black primary feathers and grey primary coverts. The legs and feet are pink.

- **Juvenile:** Mottled light silver-grey and white neck and head; some birds carry mustard-colored, iron oxide-stained flecking on the sides of the face and breast; the bill is a pink-hued greyish-brown. The bird's entire body is mottled light silver-grey and white. The back is darker, with the breast and belly fading to white. The wings are mottled light silver-grey, with the exception of faded black primary feathers and grey primary coverts. The legs and feet are a pink-hued greyish-brown.

Greater White-Fronted Goose (Specklebelly)

Neck and head are solid olive-brown, with the exception of a white highlight on the front of the bird's cheek and forehead; the bill is reddish-pink with a white nail. The bird's body is primarily olive-brown, with the breast a lighter hue of olive-brown. The tips, of the side covert feathers and individual scapular feathers, are frosted with a lighter colored hue. The belly blends to white with black accent bars interspersed across the breast. Black accent bars are variable, with some birds showing no black at all, while others show all black. Their tail feathers are olive-brown and edged in white, and their wings are olive-brown. The greater coverts and greater tertial coverts are highlighted with lightly frosted light grey edges. The primary and secondary flight feathers are black. The primary coverts are olive-grey. The legs and feet are orange.

- **Juvenile:** Solid olive-brown neck and head, white chin spot, bill is a yellow-hued greyish-brown. The bird's entire body is solid brownish-grey. The tips, of the side covert feathers and individual scapular feathers, are frosted with a lighter colored hue. The back is darker, while the breast and belly fades to a lighter hue. The tail feathers are olive-brown and edged in white, and the wings are olive-brown. The greater coverts and greater tertial coverts are highlighted with lightly frosted light grey edges. The primary and secondary flight feathers are black. The primary coverts are a faded olive-grey. The legs and feet are straw yellow.

Migration

White-fronted geese are the first to begin traveling through Kansas on their annual journey south to wintering areas along the coasts of Texas and Louisiana. Migration activity for white-fronted geese peaks from mid-October through early November.

Snow geese start arriving in early November and follow a migration corridor that leads through eastern Kansas and western Missouri. Snow geese tend to meander during their migration flights and will stop and stall, according to their own whims and the weather. There are tens of thousands of snows using different public areas in the eastern edge of the state, but the harvest has never been high. With the new

Geese moving overhead.

liberalized bag and season dates being offered, it remains to be seen if a new tradition of February and March snow goose hunting will take hold. It is interesting to note that snows heading south in the fall tend to travel along the state's eastern border, but during their migration north, they will cross the state on a much broader travel lane. As a result, snows are seen further west into central Kansas on their return migration.

Canada geese begin entering Kansas in October. Their population numbers peak in late December and early January, with total numbers being variable, depending on the year. Kansas is a central flyway state, and the central flyway has been characterized as a boom or bust proposition.

The first Canadas to arrive are the smaller subspecies birds, with their shorter bill length and high-pitched call. These small birds will remain in the state for a time before moving further south. Historically, the small birds have wintered in Oklahoma and along the gulf coasts of Texas and Louisiana. Recently, however, 600,000-plus birds have started short-stopping in the Texas panhandle.

Some small Canadas will stay in Kansas throughout the winter, but by mid-November and into December, the vast majority of Canada geese in Kansas is the large subspecies birds that winter within the state boundaries and present through the end of the gunning season.

Resident flocks of Canada geese in the state began with restoration efforts in 1980. There are no official population estimates on these resident flocks, but there are geese present wherever suitable habitat is available. When I queried about the percentage of these birds being Giant Canadas (*Branta canadensis maxima*), I was told that, in reality, all the resident flocks in the flyway, from North Dakota south to Oklahoma, resulted from multiple introduction efforts. Much of the original seed stock was a genetic mix. Transplant stock from North Dakota were the offspring of a transplant program that originated during the '60s and '70s. North Dakota had selected birds that were large-boned and exhibited the physical traits of the *maxima* subspecies. Kansas also transplanted Canadas from Illinois that were 2 or 3 pounds lighter in weight. Along with these geese, Colorado birds of varying sizes were thrown into the mix. In addition, crippled geese recovered within the state augmented the ranks of the transplanted birds. As a result, there are no pure-strain resident birds available. Some resident birds may reach the 11- to 12-pound mark, but most birds peak out at 9 to 10 pounds.

Currently, there is no September, early season, resident goose hunt. These types of hunts are generally the result of large populations of resident nuisance geese. While the state is not there yet, areas like Kansas City and Wichita have large resident flocks and may at some point need the relief that sort of hunt would offer.

Habits and Habitat

Geese use a mixture of habitats. They are neither of the water nor of the land, and that is what accounts for their population successes. The North American continent has undergone dramatic changes over the last century and a half, and according to how you look at it, most of the changes have not boded well for the native wildlife. Some of our goose species are an exception to this. Duck species have floundered because of the draining of wetlands. Geese, on the other hand, feed on cultivated grains, and the conversion of our nation's wildlands to agriculture has provided the birds with an unlimited food supply.

Geese do require water in the forms of large open water and marsh roosting and loafing sites. Geese stop at these predetermined staging areas during their seasonal migrations. Many of these sites are national wildlife refuges and state wildlife areas managed specifically for visiting waterfowl. Management programs include planting crops for the benefit of waterfowl and containing the birds on the refuge property, off of adjacent private farm fields. Large concentrations of feeding birds can inflict economic damage onto surrounding farms. Additionally, on the refuges and wildlife areas, minimum water levels are maintained to provide secure daytime loafing and nighttime roosting areas—areas that are secure from disturbance. The one thing required to hold birds is some place of refuge, closed to public entry, where birds know that they will not be disturbed.

Laying out for Canadas.

Hunting Geese

Goose hunting is generally a cold temperature proposition, requiring an inordinate amount of decoys and gear. The work begins long before dawn, with numb fingers and clouds of frost frozen into your face mask, but there isn't much in the world of hunting that compares to the sight and sound of a sky full of geese falling on top of you.

While geese can be hunted successfully on both land and water, most geese are killed over land. Goose hunting generally means field shooting. Hunters conceal themselves in the middle of feed fields, dry stubble fields of corn or sorghum or green winter wheat. Concealment can take the form of an elaborate pit blind, or be as simple as laying out flat on the ground wearing camouflage clothing or tan Carhartts. In the case of snow geese, hunters lie out in white jumpsuits among the white decoys. Hunters often will cover up with burlap cloth or light chicken wire screens woven with corn stalks. When using the largest-sized goose shells, a decoy can cover half a shooter's body and make a very effective hide.

Picking the right field to hunt is important, and here scouting is vital. Often geese are spotted feeding in a field by watching where morning feed flights land. If trespass permission can be obtained, the hunt is on. Arrive the next morning, several hours before light, and budget enough time to be completely set up a half-hour before sunrise. Sometimes the birds start arriving very early, and if everything is not perfect the opportunity will be lost. Remember that geese remember: once they get stung coming into a field, it will be very hard to fool them there again. As you are working a field that birds are actively feeding in, they should not be particularly wary as they

Flagging for Canadas.

approach. Try to set up in the same spot where the birds were feeding previously. If everything checks out visually on their approach, they should lock up and drop into an opening in the decoy spread. Lay out the spread, so that the birds will land in the most advantageous position for a shot.

For refuge hunters or those prospecting on unscouted ground, sometimes all you can do is set up in a likely looking field and hope for the best. If birds are trading above, there is always the chance to pull birds down to your spread. Calling can be very important in convincing reluctant birds. The new goose flutes on the market are a little pricey, but they sound good and fool birds. The most effective style of calling is double clucking, where instead of sounding like a single goose, the call is blown to sound like an entire flock.

Sometimes juvenile birds will mess up and pull other birds down to a decoy spread with them. Flagging can be very effective in pulling birds from great distances. My experience with both geese and cranes is that flagging will get them to close the gap to 150 yards. Then they start looking for a sign. Stop flagging when they are a couple hundred yards out and lay low. Try some low feeding clucks and don't do anything flamboyant. Less calling is better than more and on some mornings, no calling is best of all. If the flock swings and flares, and it looks like you have nothing left to lose, then get on the call and make some noise. Maybe you can change their minds.

With decoys, the rule is the more decoys the better. For Canada geese a minimum would be 2 or 3 dozen, with 8 or 12 dozen being better. With snow geese, the sky is the limit. Three or four hunters, working together, can only put out so many birds, so gauge what you can afford in both time and money.

Most of the time, the bigger the size of the decoy the better. The exception would be with a population of birds that have been hunted hard. Decoy-shy geese tend to avoid oversized decoys or large decoy spreads. A small spread of life-sized decoys, possibly interspersed with mallard field shells and good calling, will sometimes dupe them. The best thing for wary birds is a taxidermy mount.

Make sure that you are wearing a face mask or face make-up, so a shining face doesn't flare incomers. Let the birds work; they may circle a time or two just to check things out before they commit. The risk is that the flock will take one swing and leave. If the spread isn't right, that is precisely what they will do. If birds are flaring on you, stand up and try to figure out why. Are the decoys not facing into the wind? Is there some moisture on the decoys that is making them shine unnaturally? Is one of the laying-out gunners showing a shadow or moving? Always pick up your empty shell casings and keep everything as natural as possible.

A choice of shotgun for waterfowling is a matter of personal choice. There are a few factors, though, that I think a goose hunter should keep in mind while picking a weapon. Personally, I love pretty guns. They complement a day in the field after upland birds. Sadly, for waterfowl, and especially geese, they are a pain in the rear and if a serious goose hunter uses one for any length of time, they won't stay pretty. A goose gun, which is going to spend most of the hunting day laying in the dirt and mud, should have a synthetic stock and forearm and be parkerized or camouflaged. It should be equipped with a sling so that the weapon can be slung over a hunter's shoulder on the trip out to the blind, leaving hands free for decoy bags. At the end of the hunt, on the trip back from the blind, those same hands are also going to need extra room to carry a few dead geese. Lastly, the gun should be the most powerful gauge and shoot the most powerful loads a shooter can handle accurately. A 12-gauge will suffice, a 10-gauge is better. Take your shots no further than you are capable of killing cleanly.

Like shotguns, the type of retriever a waterfowler uses depends on several factors, with personal preference being the most influential. For the dog to hold up when a hunter concentrates on goose hunting, he is going to have to be stout. Springers and setters can pick up the occasional small goose, but it takes a waterfowl dog to do it day in and day out at 5 degrees Fahrenheit, with a wet coat. The big three—Labs, Chessies, and Goldens—should be on the short list. Just for shear cussedness, I personally would pick the Chessie, although a Lab or a field-bred Golden will also be up to the job.

A word about killing geese on water: The one place that a goose figures he's safe is in the middle of an unbroken piece of water. This is why geese roost at night on large reservoirs and loaf there during midday. The old time waterfowlers knew how to kill birds, their livelihood depended on it. To kill open water birds, you must go back to the knowledge they had, which we have sadly mostly lost in these modern times (see the section on recommended reading for a list of relevant early water-fowling books).

A portrait of Larry Anderson's extraordinary Labrador, Jessie.

The same methods that apply for open water diving ducks will work just as well on geese. Even more so, in some instances, because they just don't expect it. The two tools of choice are layout boats and scull boats (see the section on hunting diving ducks).

The exciting development in Kansas' goose hunting is the liberalization of snow goose hunting regulations. The continental snow goose population has been estimated at 6 million birds, which is double the number their nesting areas can sustain. The central flyway snow goose numbers are censused at 3 million. The current central flyway population objective is 1.5 million, which is half of where the numbers stand now. The central flyway produces an estimated average annual harvest of 220,000 snows and blues; 5,000 of those birds are taken in Kansas. Canadian and U.S. gunners produce a continent-wide annual kill of 500,000, but the experts feel that the bird take would have to double or even triple in order to reduce the population substantially. Meanwhile, the fragile far northern nesting areas are being stripped and destroyed at an alarming rate, and the damage is beginning to impact other nesting bird species.

Larry Anderson and Jay McDorman of Wichita show off a pair of big birds.

To aid in reducing total snow goose numbers, snow goose bag limits were increased a few years ago to allow a take of 10 birds a day and 40 birds in possession. In addition, along with the liberalization of hunting methods, the season was extended to run from late January to early March and allows hunters to take birds on their return trip north. None of this has reduced the overall numbers, and a whole host of additional liberalizations are being proposed. The list of possibilities the Central Flyway Council recommended to the U. S. Fish and Wildlife Service for consideration under the provisions of the special conservation hunt includes:

- No bag and possession limit.
- Legalized electronic callers.
- Legalized partial baiting (along the lines of what is currently legal for mourning dove; by way of explanation, this means that you can do whatever you want with the crop as long as the crop never leaves the field)
- Legalize live decoys.
- Eliminate tagging requirements.
- Extend shooting hours until one half-hour after sunset.

In addition, there has been a proposal to issue a flyway-wide license to hunt snows and blues, and another to eliminate magazine plug requirements. Any of this got you goose hunters out there daydreaming? It could sure be fun to turn the calendar back a hundred years. The difficulty is that snows travel in such large flocks that they are just plain hard to kill. Their movements are random and hard to pattern. Certainly, mitigating factors occasionally kick in, and birds lose their advantage and end up hitting the ground. Weather plays an important part in giving hunters the occasional edge. In a recently completed study where electronic call success was being monitored, the hunter success ratio was 6 to 1: 6 birds killed with electronics as opposed to 1 killed with conventional calling. Successful hunters claim it takes 700 or 800 decoys to pull the big flocks. I wonder what effect live decoys would have in fooling these wary birds?

Table Preparations

Over the years, we have eaten a fair amount of goose meat from Canadas, snows, Ross', black brant, and specs and have always enjoyed it. Geese have dark meat and a large, flat breast. There is actually less meat on a goose than their large size would tend to indicate. These big birds can be reduced down to a pretty small package if freezer space is a concern, and if a person does much goose hunting during the season, the freezer is going to fill up. If a person is fortunate enough to harvest multiple geese in a year, it is more practical to skin the birds and save the breast fillets and the leg meat. The breast can be filleted into two boneless steaks that can be butterflied and barbecued on a hot grill with butter and pepper. Whatever is left can be served cold, thin-sliced for sandwiches or salads. Fillets can be frozen individually and later partially thawed and thin-sliced for stir-fry meals.

Skinned geese are very flavorful when smoked. Once smoked and cooled, the bird can be transferred to the refrigerator and devoured at a person's leisure.

For those who take only a few geese per season, birds can be handled in the time-honored manner of plucking and cooking with the skin on. If the feathers are pulled while the bird is still warm, the job goes much easier. Once the skin is clean of feathers and the majority of fluffy down, a hand-held propane torch does a good job of flashing off any remaining down. Just a very quick pass of the flame, and the bird is ready to prepare or freeze. It is a lot of work to pluck a goose and roast it, but the reward is a beautiful presentation and a fine meal.

There are commercially made, electric, rubber-fingered plucking drums that work well if adequately powered. If a bird cleaning service is available in your hunting area, and a person wants to keep a couple of plucked birds for the table, a hunter might consider having the birds done commercially. Other birds can be skinned and prepared accordingly.

Gun and Shot Suggestions

- **Gauge:** 10, 12
- **Choke:** Modified and improved modified for doubles, modified for single barrels.
- **Shot:** For small geese shot sizes in BB and BBB will suffice. For large geese or extended range step up to BBB and T shot.

Hunter approaches a pointed single bobwhite.

The Prairie Wingshooter

The Kansas Gun Dog

Kansas is a big gun dog state. Driving through its cities and towns, it seemed that every tenth house had one or two dog kennels out back, or a Lab or Britt guarding the front yard. Kansas has a lot of birds, a lot of water, and a lot of big country to cut a dog loose in.

There are three classes of gun dogs: retrievers, pointers, and flush dogs. All of them chase birds in Kansas. Each type of dog does a very different job, and, according to their respective owners, each type is the one and only world's best. I am not going to enter into that debate. To paraphrase Will Rogers, I have never met a dog I didn't like. How many dogs are too many dogs? I tell my training clients, when they talk about getting an additional dog, "It is a slippery slope." A hunter could always get a few of each breed.

The bobwhite hunters I met who look upon pheasants with disdain, like the classic bird dogs, pointers and setters. Bobwhite hunters who also like to hunt pheasants, however, run versatile breeds such as German shorthairs, wire hairs, and such. Those who spend their time primarily chasing pheasants will probably be best served by a flushing dog such as a springer. A waterfowler living in Kansas and chasing mostly geese will do well to own a Chessie (one from a breeding pair that didn't like to bite). Finally, for those who want only one gun dog to hunt everything, one can't go too far wrong with a Lab.

Equipment Needs for the Prairie Gun Dog

Electronic dog gear is used regularly by many hunters in Kansas. Beeper collars, in particular, are very commonly heard out in the bird fields. Let me confess up front that I dislike this annoying electronic invasion into quiet hunting time. Although I myself seldom use a beeper, I'm certain that not using one in typical Kansas quail cover will cost a hunter birds. For those unfamiliar with beeper collars, they are an electronic collar unit containing a mercury switch. The collar monitors when the dog is, or is not, moving. Collars can be programmed to beep in different sequences and with different sounds or tones. For example, the collar can be set to beep at 8 second intervals while the dog is running, and then switch to 4 second intervals when the dog stops moving and establishes a point. This allows the following hunter to keep track of the dog's location at all times. In addition, the collar can be programmed to beep only when movement has stopped, forgoing the full-time running noise. This allows a hunter quiet time until birds are found. Then, the hunter can zero in on the sound of the point signal and get to the birds immediately. In heavy cover, the other option is to wander around for ten minutes, hunting the dog, and ultimately lose the opportunity for the shot.

One of the new Innotek systems allows a hunter to run with a silent beeper until he can't locate the dog. Then, a program button is available which will activate a loud

Off and running: the search for birds begins.

single chirp. By having the option of pushing this button, a hunter can locate a missing dog when necessary, yet have blessed silence for the rest of the time. Tri-Tronics has also developed a collar system with remote beeper capability.

Also available are collars with a tone button which allows a hunter to silently recall the dog without needing to use any other cues—no whistling or yelling. This feature works well on spooky birds that tend to run at a hunter's approach. The quieter a hunter and dog can work, the closer they can get before that old long-tailed rooster decides to start making tracks.

Dog First Aid Kit List

A hunter is well advised to carry a few first aid items with him in the field. However, after water and shells, there isn't much space left in a game vest. Fortunately, just a few essential things will cover most contingencies. My list includes a leather sheath containing a pair of needlenosed pliers and suture forceps for dealing with cactus and cholla (this is covered in more detail in the section on cactus and cholla). I also wear a Swiss army knife that includes tweezers and a pair of scissors. Additionally, I include a bit of cord for use as a tourniquet. In the back of my game bag, I carry a roll of "Vetrap" (an elastic self-sticking tape used by horse fanciers and available in most feed stores) in a ziplock bag for use on tears in the skin, and as a pressure wrap to control bleeding on the extremities.

Back at the truck, I keep a large first aid kit housed in a watertight, steel, army surplus ammo can. It is fairly complete (see list) and includes a copy of *A Field Guide: Dog First Aid,* by Randy Acker, D. V. M., and Jim Fergus.

Dog First Aid Kit List
- Vetrap bandaging tape in assorted widths
- Gauze
- Johnson and Johnson waterproof tape
- 12 fl. oz. aerosol can of saline (for contact lens) to clean debris from wounds
- Panolog ointment
- Benadryl (for insect and snake bite)
- Aspirin
- Nolvasan Otic cleansing solution (for cleaning ears)
- Opticlear (eyewash)
- Wound-kote spray wound dressing
- Cut-Heal medication
- Hydrocortisone cream
- Wound powder
- Styptic pencils
- Ear, nose, throat med-check light
- Thermometer
- 3-inch and 6-inch tweezers
- Canine nail cutter
- Disposable razors
- Assorted scissors
- Rubber tubing (for tourniquet)
- Several cotton socks
- Tarp or sheet plastic (for transporting a bleeding dog in a vehicle)
- Wood dowel (for holding a dog's mouth open while pulling cactus or quills)
- Wire muzzle
- Book: *A Field Guide: Dog First Aid*, by Randy Acker, D.V.M., and Jim Fergus
- Booklet: "A Field Guide to Dog Care" by Arizona Game and Fish Department
- Note pad and pencil

When a dog is in serious trouble, what you have in the way of first aid supplies may bridge the gap, but what he needs is a vet. If the dog can walk, I snap a lead on his collar and walk him out. When a dog goes down, he has to be carried. This is really a team effort, with one person carrying gear and the other the dog. Unfortunately, disaster has struck a time or two when I have been alone. In those situations, I dumped most of my water to shed weight, broke down my shotgun into two pieces and laid the pieces cross-ways in the back of my game bag, picked up the dog and walked the straightest line out.

Caring for the Prairie Gun Dog Afield

There seems to be an endless array of gear that a dog owner cannot live with-out. Some things are more necessary than others. One of the items typically billed as critical gear is dog boots. They come in different styles and different materials. The most well-made boots I have used were from the Lewis dog boots company in

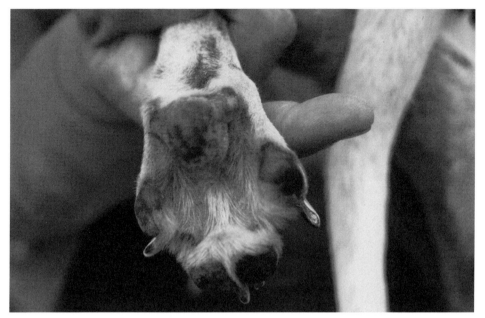

A dog's foot that's been on the ground too long; he won't be running tomorrow.

Enid, Oklahoma. They are made of a rubber welt similar to tire tread construction, and the tops will tear before the bottoms wear out. I have several sets of four set aside and bagged. I know that the first dog boots I ever bought from Lewis, twenty-odd years ago, are still in one of the bags and still serviceable.

The boots are held on with white medical tape or duct tape. They will come off when the dogs are running if they are not, as I was once told, "put on right." When I used to run boots a lot, years ago, I put them on as "right" as I could and would still lose a boot now and then.

One problem area is the side of a dog's front foot (where the dew claws are, if the dew claws still remain on the dog). After a few days of running, this area can be rubbed raw and thus becomes very painful for a dog. The trick is to use the tape to wrap the dog's lower legs in stockings, like you would wrap a horse's feet. Slide the boots on over that foundation layer of wrapping and then tape over it again. When removing the upper layer of tape to take the boots off, leave the stocking layer intact for the following day.

Dog boots made of leather with lace-up fronts and nylon boots held on with velcro don't hold up well nor do they stay on well. My experience with them was in rocky country where the bottoms wore through after a couple of weeks hunting. In the grass country of Kansas, however, they may last much longer. I don't have personal experience with them in grass.

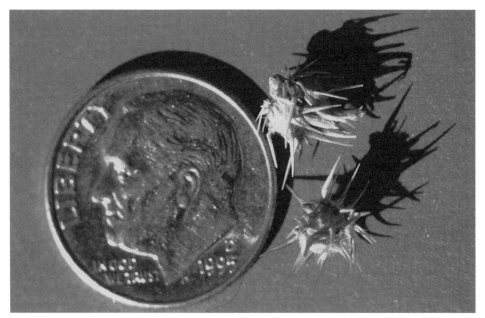

Sand burrs.

In my opinion, boots are really a pain to use, and most of the time dogs do fine without them. However, if a dog has bad pads or a foot injury, they can be used to buy some time. Boots are typically recommended to fend off cactus and cholla spines. Over time, however, dogs eventually learn to avoid these stickers and can hunt cactus/cholla areas more effectively without boots on. This is not to deny that the learning curve can get a little grim, but the problem area is not with the dog's feet but rather their mouths. A stickered dog will invariably bite the offending cactus/cholla segment to pull it off and end up with a mouthful. They generally learn not to do this after the first 2 or 3 times.

Sand burrs are the other plague of dogdom that reputably mandates the use of dog boots. If sand burrs lay as a blanket cover, then that would be the case (and they may in some places—I don't know). My experience in Kansas was that the burrs were only present in broken ground areas like road shoulders and parking areas. I brought dog boots with me, but did not use them. Once out onto a hunting area with an intact grass cover, burrs were not an issue.

Bear in mind, my prairie experience is limited, although I did find out how painful sand burrs can be when they were in my fingers. One of the spots where I parked to chain-out dogs had a sand burr carpet, and I got most of the dogs out on the ground before I realized no one was doing any moving. The dogs stood there like they had been whoaed. Every one of them had half a dozen burrs in each foot. I laid the dogs on top of the trailer, one by one, and cleaned their feet. In the process, I managed to load up my own fingers until I wised up and got out a pair of needle nose pliers. Those little burrs hurt like hell. If they covered the ground in a hunting area, the dogs would have to be booted.

Another thing I read about prior to my visit was saw grass and how hard it can be on dogs. After several weeks of running, much of it in heavy CRP grass, the dogs' cheek bones and eye ridges looked like they had been rough sanded, but were otherwise fine.

It is important at the end of a hunt to check a dog over. Things like barbed wire or other human related refuse can inflict injuries that are not readily apparent. Gun dogs will hunt with such determination and enthusiasm that often a dog won't acknowledge a wound until she has laid up for a time and stiffened up. Wounds that are tended to early, before they become contaminated or the edges dry out, heal more quickly. I once had a setter go through a barbed wire fence and, unbeknownst to me, lay her chest wide open. She then jumped into a marsh and stayed mostly submerged for the next hour while we walked the edge for ducks. By the time I noticed the wound, it was an opaque brown, waterlogged mess. I got her out of the water and back home. We laid her on the table and sewed her back up. Despite my best efforts at cleaning and disinfecting, by morning a roaring infection was at work. It required a vet to get her healthy. If I had caught it early, we could have saved some money and spared her some misery.

Let me tell you about another thing I started doing at the beginning of last season. My wife came home with a product called a "Power Bar." It is an athletic energy supplement that looks like a candy bar. It comes in different flavors, and really isn't too bad once a person gets used to it. Her intention was to find an easy snack for me when my energy started crashing. Now during the hunting season, I always keep my game bag stocked with 3 or 4 of them. I will eat half of one, and then offer any shooting companion one in order to get us through whatever death march we have undertaken. What I found, subsequently, is that they also work great for the dogs. I have always carried snacks for my dogs, but these bars are a no muss, no fuss alternative. A little goes a long way. I take a bite and chew it up to soften the normally stiff consistency, and then give it to the dog. Two to three small bites is enough to give them a 45 minute boost. They seem to enjoy the taste, and once introduced eat it immediately.

The instructions on the "Power Bar" label suggest that water should be taken when consuming the product. Water is always a concern when running dogs. Many of the areas where I hunted in Kansas had ample water available, so I didn't have to supplement with water I carried. Some of the areas, particularly the more arid western portions of the state, were dry and without water. If I hadn't carried water, the dogs would have been in trouble. Just as a matter of course, I always carry some water with me. If I don't have to use it, so much the better.

Containers used for carrying water are a matter of personal preference. I often run 2 or 3 dogs at a time, so I need to carry a lot of water. What has worked well for me are the long, salami-shaped, clear plastic water bottles that bottled water is sold in. They come in several sizes. I generally use the largest-sized bottle that fits perfectly, lying

*If a dog can get wet,
he's good for another hour.*

flat, in the bottom of a Filson game bag. A bottle of water costs about a buck and is available in supermarkets, anywhere in the country. These bottles are very light and very tough. They generally will remain watertight for a couple of seasons, and when you forget them or they wear out, all you have to find is the supermarket.

In my game bag, I also carry a water cup for the dogs to drink from. I prefer that the dogs drink from a container, rather than my squirting water into the dog's mouth with a bota bag or sports bottle. In my opinion, it chokes the dog and wastes a lot of water. When I'm carrying it, I want it to go to good use.

Another indispensible part of a dog handler's uniform is a belt clip and a short dog lead for every dog running. These items are available through mail order supply outfits. It won't happen often, but every once in a while it will be imperative to get the dog under control and out of an area immediately. This will be in cases such as: a dog fight, the approach of a rabid animal, finding a rattlesnake in the field, or finding yourself in a steel trap area. In such occasions, it is important that the lead is right at hand, hanging from the belt.

Equipment Needs for the Prairie Wingshooter

Some people have made the observation that the best way to learn what equipment works best in a given area is not to waste time asking questions, but instead to watch what other hunters are using. To that end, I was curious about what gear I'd find in use in Kansas.

Most of the shotguns used are three-shot models, be it auto or pump. Most of those long guns are 12-gauge, with Winchester model 12's being well represented. The presence of larger quarry such as pheasants, chickens and waterfowl, as well as the chance for a third shot, no doubt account for the three shot, 12-bore's popularity.

For those shooters focusing on bobwhites over dogs, light double guns in smaller gauges are in order. Flushes over points are the norm, and a fast pointing 28 or 20 fills the bill.

Many of the shotguns I saw in use were equipped with a sling. While slings have never really developed a following in this country, they make a lot of sense when a hunter is traveling the number of miles it sometimes takes to find open-country birds. They are also useful when a hunter has his hands otherwise full with an exhausted dog, decoy bags, or the like. Some shotguns I saw looked like they had seen some hard times, and may have been on their second or third generation of family service.

Much of the clothing I saw being worn came straight from farm work and was serving double duty. Carhartt and Walls overalls are very popular in Kansas. When I returned home from my first trip, I dug out an old pair of Carhartt overalls and put them in my clothes bag. With polypropylene long underwear underneath, they both kept me warm and cut the wind which always seemed to be blowing. A T-shirt and a knit turtleneck with an optional polar fleece on top completed my basic uniform. I could then layer above that as the weather conditions dictated, although if I was walking and remaining active, I usually stayed warm with the turtleneck alone. A pair of the high dollar, Thinsulate insulated, GoreTex-lined bird hunting overalls would also work well if a person had them.

Most outfits were covered in some way with a fluorescent orange outer shell. Much of the bird hunting in Kansas is communal in nature, with large parties going afield after pheasant. During the opening week of the pheasant season, I saw some fields with literally a dozen guns walking abreast towards a line of blockers. We had other hunting parties approach to within a hundred yards of us, as we were working the same ground, before we were aware of their presence. The value of wearing orange clothing cannot be overemphasized. An orange vest, sweatshirt, or jacket outlines the body. Orange head gear shows well above heavy cover and is available in a wide range of styles. I wore an orange balaclava that rolled up into a watch cap when I got warm (which was not too often). Most of the time, I needed a Yazoo style hat stretched over the balaclava to keep my ears from going numb.

My hands were perpetually cold in Kansas, and I found that there is a balance point between gloves thin enough to shoot in and thick enough to keep fingers from freezing. At home in Arizona, I use unlined goatskin gloves when I'm hunting.

Tailgate sitting at the end of a long walk.

However, I found that in Kansas, except on the warmest days, they were just not warm enough. I just about wore out a pair of thinsulate-lined deerskin gloves. They weren't quite warm enough on the coldest days, but they were close and they allowed me the freedom of movement to find a trigger or work the snap on a chain gang. Also, deerskin stays soft after getting wet, and my gloves seemed to get wet quite a lot.

One of the new gizmos on the market is a product called HotHandS-2 (HandWarmer). These are little chemical packettes that, when kneaded together with your fingers, produce a chemical reaction which generates heat. The little warmers can then be slipped into gloves, the toes of boots, or jacket pockets and are a Godsend in extreme cold. The packettes are a one-time use, disposable product, and sold through most sporting goods stores. I found them in Kansas Wal-Mart stores, in the sporting goods department.

I took along a pair of neoprene gloves. They can keep a person's hands dry when handling decoys, but they don't have much application past that. I found that if the neoprene is heated toasty warm before the gloves are put on, then they will hold the heat. If a pair are put on cold, however, they stay cold.

I included in my clothes box a pair of fluorescent orange polarfleece gloves. Although they were reasonably warm and got some use, their one drawback was they collected burrs and seed heads that poked through, and it seemed I was always trying to fish something or other out of them.

One piece of clothing that was a Godsend in the extreme cold of December and January was a face mask. They are available in several different styles, including camouflage, orange, and white. They are advertised for use by ice fishermen and snowmobilers. Wearing a face mask does restrict visibility and can handicap a walking upland bird hunter. However, on those days when the temperature reads minus 15 and the wind is gusting at 30 miles per hour, a person who wants to keep the tips of his ears and nose doesn't have a choice but to wear one.

For waterfowl hunting, a mask is standard equipment as it camouflages the face. Also, decoy hunting is predominantly a sedentary endeavor, and because of the lack of movement, a person has a lot of trouble staying warm. When I was laying out in open fields for geese, the wind was brutal and a face mask was an absolute necessity.

I wore a Filson shoulder strap model vest when I wasn't carrying a camera, but I saw a wide range of styles being worn. I packed a Filson waxed-cloth hunting jacket and just about lived in it. A hunting jacket with a game bag and shell pockets was a good choice on those cold rainy days when I knew it wasn't going to get any better.

I am a believer in Filson products. They make good stuff. Once, Don and I were driving through the southwestern corner of the state in late November and drove straight into a tornado warning. The sky around us was ringed with black, inverted dome clouds and rain fell in squall lines. As we raced to beat the storm, evening fell and the landscape around us flashed into view with each lightning crack. Gusting wind rocked and swayed the truck as we flew down the highway trying to beat the storm.

The dogs, however, had not been out since midday and they really needed to be aired and fed and watered. Somewhere near the Oklahoma line, the sky cleared. We spotted a small strip of bare ground between a gas station and an agricultural field. Light poles ringed the asphalt of the gas pump area and provided enough light to illuminate the dirt strip. We pulled in and stretched a chain. We had been racing against the storm and figured we had bought ourselves 30 to 45 minutes to get everybody tended to. We got all the dogs out and half of the food bowls filled when a black wall hit us. There was about a minute's worth of light rain drops as a warning. Then, the wind slammed in and lightning went off directly overhead, as if we were standing in the middle of an artillery barrage. The rain came down sideways in thimble-sized drops. The food bowls immediately filled up with water. The dogs panicked and we scrambled to get everybody back on the bus. Visibility was at 60 yards, and I knew that if a dog got loose in the middle of this maelstrom, he would run through three counties before he thought about slowing down. Don and I relayed back and forth to get the 12 dogs back on the trailer. By the time everyone was loaded, there were two inches of water standing on the ground and the storm was hanging on top of us. I began reeling in the 30 feet of chain and had one of those moments of clarity where I thought about the implications of standing submerged to my ankles in water, in the middle of a lightning storm, holding onto 30 feet of steel chain. During all the confusion, there had only been time to react. I stored the last of the gear, closed up the door, and jumped into the camper shell.

Although I was soaked to the skin everywhere, the Filson wasn't. I wrung out my Yazoo hat. The rain had filled up my boots and gone through my gloves and Carhartt

Emma burns up some country.

pants. The collar of the polar fleece that stuck up above the collar of the Filson was sopping wet, saturated like a sponge. I took off my boots and poured the water out. I took off the Filson jacket and found everything underneath bone dry.

In more reasonable weather, I wore upland boots with crepe soles as the fields were often muddy and a lug-pattern soled boot could feel as heavy as a cement block in short order. In the cold stuff, felt-lined Sorrels are the ticket for boots.

Traveling with Dog and Gun

The old adage, "There's a long way between here and there," is especially true in Kansas. The state is 98% private land and much of those private holdings are of a size that provide only a few hours worth of ground to hunt. A hunter after bobwhites or pheasants might hit a half-dozen places in a day's travels.

For a hunter with only two or three dogs, a pickup truck and some travel kennels will get the job done. With more than four dogs, a person is probably looking at either

On the road with the dogs in the middle of nowhere.

truck-mounted kennel boxes or a dog trailer. There is not much in print about the in's and out's of taking a large number of dogs across country. I guess I should qualify "large": some pros travel with an 18-wheeler, 40 dogs, and a few horses thrown in for good measure. A person traveling with that kind of entourage is more than likely not hunting and is either a professional dog trainer, traveling the field trial circuit, or both. Contrary to what some might think, these rigs are no threat to the local bird population. The handlers are too busy tending to dogs to be chasing birds, although the surest way to turn a landowner ashen gray is to pull up to the front of a farm house with a 14-hole dog trailer and ask permission to hunt. One gentleman we hunted with, who had arranged for some private land access, tactfully procured a barn to stash the dog trailer in so we would be welcome on the adjoining properties.

On my first trip in November of '96, I took 12 dogs in a 14-place dog trailer. We kept two holes free for a water jug and bucket. I traveled with a friend, Don Prentice, and it was all the two of us could do to keep everybody watered, fed, scooped, doctored, inspected, etc., etc., etc. There were days when our road show had all the qualities of a traveling circus, and some of our stops drew similar crowds.

On my second trip that December, I brought a 6-place trailer with only 6 dogs on board. I traveled alone, and the dog chores kept me pretty busy. My third trip was principally for waterfowl and greater prairie chickens. The thought of again pulling a trailer through the type of weather I had in December caused me to leave the rig at home. I brought only my male tricolor setter, Concho. He rode shotgun or in a crate in the camper shell.

When I'm traveling with dogs, I run a chain gang to air out dogs and to feed and water. I feed once a day in the evenings. While visiting with fellow hunters, I was told

The circus comes to town: a McDonald's in downtown Topeka.

that dog theft was a concern. Therefore, while unattended, I always keep the trailer doors padlocked.

For watering dogs, I use the spigoted, five-gallon water jugs that are available through the camping supply sections in sporting goods stores. I find that with several dogs, they expedite the process of getting everybody watered. I offer dogs water whenever we stop. I use black rubber watering bowls and buckets commonly sold in feed stores, and most competitively priced in the equine department at Wal-Mart. These rubber containers come in several sizes and are virtually indestructible. They stack inside each other (helping to conserve space) and serve double-duty for both food and water.

Some states are all private land and it can therefore be a real problem to find a place off the road where you can cut dogs loose safely and let them run. I find, when traveling on the interstate, that many of the fast food restaurants have large, developed RV and diesel truck parking areas adjoining the main parking lots. With the exception of one McDonald's in Santa Rosa, New Mexico, I have always been able to stretch a chain gang and tend to dogs. I make it a point to have a trash bag-lined bucket and shovel at the ready to pick up after the dogs. Weather permitting, I take care of the dogs first and then leave them out while I grab something to eat for myself. The dogs typically need at least an hour on the chain per stop to water and give them a stretch. When I am traveling straight through and they are not going to be exercised, I stop three times per day.

Hazards

Kansas is much more settled than some of our more "western" states. While there are some genuinely dangerous situations in those wild western states, Kansas' tame rural landscape holds its own unique set of concerns.

The one thing that just scared the hell out of me was the sheer number of roads. Large tracts of the state are gridded off by section with dirt access roads. Many farm fields we hunted were defined on at least one side by a public thoroughfare. The one common trait I observed was that nearly everyone drove like they had somewhere to be. A dog stepping out off the shoulder of the road would not stand a chance.

Often, I saw the dust cloud of an approaching vehicle and would pull the dogs in. Many times, however, there was no indication until a vehicle was right on top of us. The scary times were when we were working thick cover for bobwhite. I would pop out, with no forewarning, onto a farm road only to see or hear a car fast approaching. I would have no idea where the dogs were, or, worse yet, I would spot the dogs standing on the far shoulder of the road, looking for me and waiting to cross back once they had located my position, unaware of the vehicle's approach.

Some of the people I hunted with outfitted their dogs with electric collars for the main purpose of whoa control in these situations. I live, hunt, and train in an area with very few roads, and I make a point of not allowing my dogs on pavement or near a dirt road. Unfortunately, in Kansas, that lack of familiarity could get a dog killed.

Since 1992, when we lost a dog to the highway while hunting, I have been road breaking our dogs. We snake break all of our dogs during their initial training because of the numbers of rattlers found where we live. With that method, we use an electric shock collar and a defanged diamondback to convince the dog he doesn't ever want to approach another snake as long as he lives. There is a comprehensive explanation of snake breaking in the *Wingshooter's Guide to Arizona*, a companion book in this series published by Wilderness Adventures Press.

What I've done is modified the methods used for snake breaking to teach a dog to not step in front of a moving vehicle. While my results with car breaking have not been as uniformly permanent as with snake breaking, it does get the message across, for at least a while.

I start by locating off the side of a reasonably traveled, two lane, paved, curving rural road. The direction the car will be approaching from needs to be obscured from sight until the vehicle is within 100 to 150 yards. The dog needs to hear the vehicle approaching before she can physically see the vehicle.

Secondly, I make sure that the presence of myself or a dog is not going to constitute a dangerous situation for an approaching motorist. The ideal situation, of course, is when the driver of the approaching training vehicle is part of the training team. The dog is controlled by an attached check cord that does not allow her access to the roadway.

In snake breaking we work off of three cues: the sound (rattling), sight, and smell of the snake. Once the dog is perceiving all three stimuli, we shock the dog with the collar's highest level of intensity. In car breaking, we use two stimuli: first a horn tap and the "swoosh" sound of the approaching car, and secondly the sight of the vehicle approaching.

A dog isn't sure what caused the shock, but she knows that the road and the car have something to do with it and will approach both with much more caution in the future. It's not a hundred percent, but with some dogs it has a lasting effect.

There are poisonous snakes in Kansas, but according to locals they don't constitute a serious problem. Snakes are seen mostly during the summer before the onset of most of the bird seasons. Early dove and prairie chicken season, at the beginning of September, could still find snakes out and about. The snake most often encountered is a Massasaugas, found statewide with the exception of the northwestern corner. These are a small species of rattlesnake that pack some potent venom. The severity of a bite is mitigated by the small size of the snake and corresponding low venom yield of a strike. There are also a few Western (Prairie) rattlers ranging statewide. On the extreme eastern border, copperheads and seldom-seen timber rattlers are found. Apparently, cottonmouths are thought to be a very rare inhabitant of the extreme southeastern corner of Kansas. With all this in mind, it sure won't hurt to snake break as a precautionary measure. However, by all reports, poisonous snakes are rarely seen in Kansas, and antivenin is not normally stocked by veterinarians there.

Weather is a big factor in Kansas hunting—both in the amount of birds brought to bag and in the comfort level of those hunter/dog teams doing the bagging. I have never before been so cold for such an extended period of time. I was curious about the effects of cold on a working dog. The good news is that dogs can take a great deal of cold without any serious effects. If a dog is kept dry and out of the wind, he can withstand extreme cold.

Under severe conditions, canines are subject to the same maladies that afflict humans. Frostbite of the feet, toes, ears, tips of the tail, nose, and any areas of exposed skin are seen in dogs. When a dog is wet and in extreme cold, frostbite becomes a very real possibility. A dog's caloric requirements are higher during cold because calories are being used to maintain body heat. Without adequate food intake, hypothermia and exhaustion are a possibility. With sound conditioning and good health, a dog can be hunted at zero degrees, a little bit lower on the wind chill side.

On cold, wet days when the thermometer is hovering around zero, dog boots can be used to protect against frostbite. When ice forms in the hair of the dog's feet and lays against the skin for extended periods of time, the dog is in danger of frostbite. Dog boots will keep a dog's feet dry and protect against his pads cracking and tearing from cold.

Be sure, when bringing dogs to Kansas, that they are adequately protected from heartworm, as it is found statewide. In some areas of the country, heartworm is not a problem and therefore dogs are not given the proper medication to prevent infestation when they travel to other states. Currently two medications are available: Heartguard and Interceptor. Both require a veterinarian's assistance and prescription.

Landowner Ralph Clark sits ahorse and visits with bird hunters on his property.

Lyme disease is not an issue in Kansas at this time. A few cases have shown up in the large cities and in the future it may be prudent to vaccinate dogs against the ailment. As of now, it is not considered necessary.

Rabies, on the other hand, is not uncommon in Kansas, with skunks being the most common carrier. It is a good idea, for several reasons, not to let a dog approach any skunk seen in the field. Be sure your dog's vaccination status is current.

Region 1

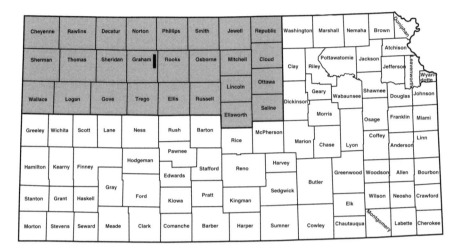

Historically, Region 1 has contained the best ring-necked pheasant hunting in the state of Kansas. The western half of the region falls in the High Plains country of Kansas; the land is flat and used for wheat production. Many of the agricultural fields are plowed from road edge to road edge. As a result, the birds have relied on winter wheat fields to survive the winters and raise their young in the spring. As a result of current agricultural practices, including the expanded use of herbicides and a shortening of stubble height for weed eradication, the area pheasant populations have experienced dramatic population declines. However, all things are relative, and good hunting can still be found locally.

The eastern half of the region still contains Kansas' pheasant stronghold, and hunters annually travel from the east coast population centers of Kansas and make the trek westward to hunt the long-tailed birds.

Bobwhite quail hunting can be very good in Region 1. However, the area is more prone to severe winter weather patterns, and this can affect bobwhite quail population numbers. This problem is more severe in the western High Plains, where the flat topography offers little escape for birds trapped in the throes of a winter storm. The Flint Hills country in the eastern portion of Region 1 is hillier and provides better survival rates.

Mourning dove hunting can be good region wide. Water and feed fields are the key to locating doves. Hunting can be short-lived, however, as the birds are generally gone on their way south before the early season gunning ends.

Greater prairie chickens are found in the eastern two-thirds of Region 1, and currently their range is reported to be expanding westward.

There are several Army Corps of Engineers lake projects scattered throughout the eastern half of the region, and all of them can offer good hunting opportunities for both ducks and geese.

Turkeys are found in suitable habitat regionwide.

Area Hunting Guides

Hideout Hunting Lodge
Richard R. Anderson
PO Box 415
Allen, KS 66833
Business 316-528-3354
Home 785-528-4440

C Diamond Ranch
Lee G. Couture
2680 3 Road
Palco, KS 67657
Business & Home 785-737-5651

Hancock Farms
Douglas L. Hancock
RR 1, Box 76
Ebson, KS 66941
Business & Home 785-725-3901

Golden Prairie Outfitters
Keith A. Horney
2803 County Road 2
Brewster, KS 677332
Business & Home 913-694-2808

Ken Kammer
1851 CR-2
Brewster, KS 67732
Business & Home 785-694-2725

Beaks, Beards, & Bucks
Terry L. Kiser
Rt. 2, Box S-9
Beloit, KS 67420
Business & Home 785-439-6468

Double 'K' Pheasant Hunt
Kevin L. Kline
PO Box 117
Delphos, KS 67436
Business & Home 913-523-4653

Golden Prairie Outfitters
Wayne F. Luckert
647 County Road 1
Brewster, KS 67732
Business & Home 785-694-2755

Crow's Roost Outfitters
Chris O'Hare
Rt. 1, Box 15
Norcatur, KS 67653
Business & Home 913-693-4229

High Plains Guide Service
Neal A. Shane
724 Melbert
Gypsum, KS 67448
Business & Home 785-536-4848

Curtis L. Smith
4585 West Schilling Road
Salina, KS 67401
Business & Home 785-825-8113

United States Outfitters
David B. Weinland
325 Santistaran Lane, Box 4204
Taos, NM 87571
Business & Home 505-758-9774

LaSada Hunting Service
Scott A. Young
3720 183 Street
Russell, KS 67665
Business & Home 785-483-3758

Area Hunting Preserves

Beaver Creek Outfitter
Brad Leitner
103 North 3rd
Atwood, KS 67730
1-800-250-5999

Ringneck Ranch, Inc.
Keith & Laura Rothgeb
Rt. 1, Box 229C
Independence, KS 67301
913-373-4835

Solomon Valley Game Ranch
1161 W. 30th Drive
Osborne, KS 67473
913-346-2707

Spillman Creek Lodge
Merrill Nielsen
785-277-3424

Region 1
Bobwhite Quail Distribution

Cheyenne	Rawlins	Decatur	Norton	Phillips	Smith	Jewell	Republic
Sherman	Thomas	Sheridan	Graham	Rooks	Osborne	Mitchell	Cloud
Wallace	Logan	Gove	Trego	Ellis	Russell	Lincoln	Ottawa
						Ellsworth	Saline

Good to Excellent Distribution

Fair to Good Distribution

Locally Good Distribution

Region 1
Greater Prairie Chicken Distribution

Cheyenne	Rawlins	Decatur	Norton	Phillips	Smith	Jewell	Republic
Sherman	Thomas	Sheridan	Graham	Rooks	Osborne	Mitchell	Cloud
						Lincoln	Ottawa
Wallace	Logan	Gove	Trego	Ellis	Russell	Ellsworth	Saline

Secondary Distribution

Region 1
Mourning Dove Distribution

Cheyenne	Rawlins	Decatur	Norton	Phillips	Smith	Jewell	Republic
Sherman	Thomas	Sheridan	Graham	Rooks	Osborne	Mitchell	Cloud
Wallace	Logan	Gove	Trego	Ellis	Russell	Lincoln	Ottawa
						Ellsworth	Saline

Mourning Dove Distribution

Region 1
Pheasant Distribution

Cheyenne	Rawlins	Decatur	Norton	Phillips	Smith	Jewell	Republic
Sherman	Thomas	Sheridan	Graham	Rooks	Osborne	Mitchell	Cloud
Wallace	Logan	Gove	Trego	Ellis	Russell	Lincoln	Ottawa
						Ellsworth	Saline

■ **Good to Excellent Distribution**

□ **Fair to Good Distribution**

□ **Locally Good Distribution**

Region 1
Sandhill Crane Hunting Area

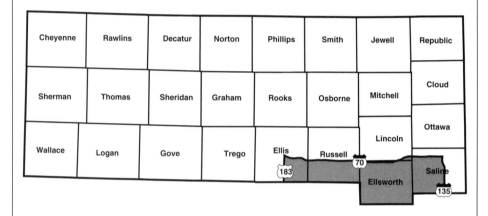

■ **Legal Sandhill Crane Hunting Area**

Region 1
Turkey Distribution

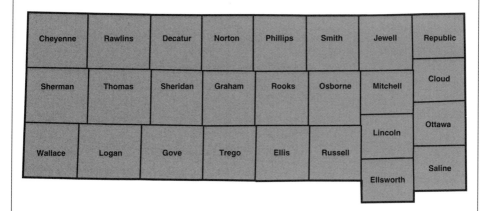

Turkey Distribution

Colby and Thomas County

Population–5,510	Elevation–3,138
County Population–8,258	October Temperature–53.1
County Area–1,075 sq. mi.	Acres in WIHA–3,600
	Acres in CRP–15,986

Found on the High Plains region of northwestern Kansas, Colby is a trade and service center that supports the area's wheat producers. The town is accessed via Interstate 70.

Northwestern Kansas was formerly one of the state's best ring-necked pheasant areas. Although pheasant populations have declined, birds can still be found in good numbers. No managed public hunting wildlife areas are found in the county. The 1997 Walk-In Hunting Area Atlas lists 6 enrolled properties totaling 3,600 acres.

UPLAND BIRDS
Pheasant, Bobwhite Quail,
Greater Prairie Chicken, Mourning Dove

WATERFOWL
Ducks & Geese

ACCOMMODATIONS
Best Western Crown Motel, I-70 & K-25 Highway, Colby, 67701 / 913-462-3943 / Dogs allowed / $$

Budget Host Inn, 1745 West 4th Street, Colby, 67701 / 913-462-3338 / Dogs allowed / $$

Days Inn, 1925 South Range Avenue, Colby, 67701 / 913-462-8691 / Dogs allowed / $$

Econo Lodge, 1985 South Range Avenue, Colby, 67701 / 913-462-8201 / Dogs allowed / $$

CAMPGROUNDS AND RV PARKS
Bourquins Farm Market & Trade Co, I-70 Frontage Road, Colby, 67701 / 913-462-3300

RESTAURANTS
Big Wong Restaurant, 1745 West 4th Street, Colby, 67701 / 913-462-7722
Mr C's Steak House, 1195 South Range Avenue, Colby, 67701 / 913-462-6776
Village Inn Restaurant, 2215 South Range Avenue, Colby, 67701 / 913-462-6683
White's Landing, 2290 Harry Lazarous Road, Colby, 67701 / 913-462-2481

VETERINARIANS
Colby Animal Clinic, 810 East 4th Street, Colby, 67701 / 913-462-8621

SPORTING GOODS STORES
Sports Shoppe, 400 North Franklin Avenue, Colby, 67701 / 913-462-8342
Wal-Mart Discount Cities, 1915 South Range Avenue, Colby, 67701 / 913-462-8651

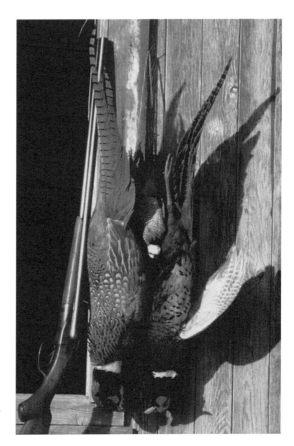

*A pair of pheasants
in the bag.*

AUTO REPAIR
C & C Auto Repair, 335 North Lake Avenue, Colby, 67701 / 913-462-6201

AIR SERVICE
Municipal Airport, RR 1, Colby, 67701 / 913-462-4438
Roesch Aviation Inc, RR 1, Box 295, Colby, 67701 / 913-462-2657

MEDICAL
Citizens Medical Center, 100 East College Drive, Colby, 67701 / 913-462-7511

FOR MORE INFORMATION
Colby Chamber of Commerce Inc
265 East 5th Street
Colby, KS 67701
913-462-3401

Concordia and Cloud County

Population–6,152	Elevation–1,363
County Population–11,023	October Temperature–55.5
County Area–716 sq. mi.	Acres in WIHA–2,370
	Acres in CRP–16,464

Concordia in Cloud County is a popular base of operations for area ring-necked pheasant and bobwhite quail hunters. The town is hunter friendly and provides any needed amenities. Agricultural crops include cash grain and livestock.

Jamestown Wildlife Area is found in the northwestern corner of Cloud County.

The 1997 Walk-In Hunting Area Atlas lists 11 enrolled properties totaling 2,370 acres.

UPLAND BIRDS
Pheasant, Bobwhite Quail, Greater Prairie Chicken, Mourning Dove

WATERFOWL
Ducks & Geese

ACCOMMODATIONS
Best Western Thunderbird Motel, North81 Highway, Concordia, 66901 / 913-243-4545 / Dogs allowed / $$
Super 8 Motel, 1320 Lincoln Street, Concordia, 66901 / 913-243-4200 / $$

CAMPGROUNDS AND RV PARKS
Nearest are in Mankato

RESTAURANTS
Brown's Kountry Kitchen, 217 West 6th Street, Concordia, 66901 / 913-243-1633
Chicken Georges, 135 East 13th Street, Concordia, 66901 / 913-243-1000
Cookhouse Cafe, 512 State Street, Concordia, 66901 / 913-243-1158
Jammer's Steak Haus, 1431 East 6th Street, Concordia, 66901 / 913-243-3100

VETERINARIANS
Don Hutchinson, 716 West 8th Street, Concordia, 66901 / 913-243-7967

SPORTING GOODS STORES
Coppoc Sports & Awards, 126 West 6th Street, Concordia, 66901 / 913-243-4284
Wal-Mart, 1502 Lincoln Street, Concordia, 66901 / 913-243-2602

AUTO REPAIR
Rick's Apco Service, 1302 Lincoln Street, Concordia, 66901 / 913-243-2728

A stylish setter on a covey of bobwhites.

AIR SERVICE
Blosser Municipal Airport, Concordia

MEDICAL
St. Joseph's Hospital, Concordia

FOR MORE INFORMATION
Chamber of Commerce
606 Washington Street
Concordia, KS 66901
913-243-4290

Hays and Ellis County

Population–17,814	Elevation–1,997
County Population–26,004	October Temperature–55.9
County Area–900 sq. mi.	Acres in WIHA–6,953
	Acres in CRP–33,547

Hays was known as Fort Hays in the 1860s when the settlement guarded the edge of U.S. expansion. Hays is a college town with an abundance of services for visiting hunters. The Region 1 office of the Kansas Department of Wildlife and Parks is found to the west of the Fort Hays State University campus; any necessary licenses and permits are available there.

Northwestern Kansas was formerly one of the state's best ring-necked pheasant areas. Although pheasant populations have declined, birds can still be found in good numbers. No managed public hunting wildlife areas are found in the county. The 1997 Walk-In Hunting Area Atlas lists 25 enrolled properties totaling 6,953 acres.

UPLAND BIRDS
Pheasant, Bobwhite Quail, Greater Prairie Chicken, Mourning Dove

WATERFOWL
Ducks & Geese

ACCOMMODATIONS
Best Western Vagabond Motel, 2524 Vine Street, Hays, 67601 / 913-625-2511 / Dogs allowed / $$$
Comfort Inn, 2810 Vine Street, Hays, 67601 / 913-628-8008 / Dogs allowed / $$$
Days Inn, 3205 Vine Street, Hays, 67601 / 913-628-8261 / Dogs allowed / $$
Hampton Inn, Highway 183 North, Hays, 67601 / 913-625-8103 / Dogs allowed / $$
Holiday Inn, 3603 Vine Street, Hays, 67601 / 913-625-7371 / Dogs allowed / $$$

CAMPGROUNDS AND RV PARKS
Circle S Overnight Trailer Park, Hays, 913-625-6119 / 45 sites

RESTAURANTS
Bamboo Garden, 117 Anita Drive, Haysville, 67060, 316-524-0840
Cafe Royal, 124 Stewart Avenue, Haysville, 67060, 316-554-1887
Pheasant Run, 3201 Vine Street, Hays, 67601 / 913-628-1044
Ted's Steak House & Club, 2505 Vine Street, Hays, 67601 / 913-628-6418
Vagabond Family Restaurant, 2522 Vine Street, Hays, 67601 / 913-625-5914
Village Inn Pancake House, 3402 Vine Street, Hays, 67601 / 913-628-1938

VETERINARIANS
Hays Veterinary Hospital, 1016 East 8th Street, Hays, 67601 / 913-625-2719
Pet Health Clinic, 1014 Cody Avenue, Hays, 67601 / 913-628-8603

SPORTING GOODS STORES
Goodwin Sporting Goods, 109 West 11th Street, Hays, 67601 / 913-625-2419
Sportsman's Supply, 2520 Vine Street Suite 1, Hays, 67601 / 913-628-2618
Wal-Mart Discount Cities, 3300 Vine Street, Hays, 67601 / 913-625-0001

AUTO REPAIR
Jerry's Service & Repair, 2814 Vine Street, Hays, 67601 / 913-628-6188
R & R Auto Repair, 500 Vine Street, Hays, 67601 / 913-628-8632

AIR SERVICE
Hays Municipal Airport, Hays / Served by USAirways

MEDICAL
Hays Medical Center, Hays, 67601 / 913-623-5000

FOR MORE INFORMATION
Chamber of Commerce
1301 Pine Street
Hays, KS 67601
913-628-8201

Mankato and Jewell County

Population–1,037	Elevation–1,740
County Population–4,251	October Temperature–54.1
County Area–909 sq. mi.	Acres in WIHA–3,320
	Acres in CRP–26,320

Mankato is situated off the beaten track, in an agricultural area that produces livestock and cash grain crops. The town is located in the northcentral pheasant belt, where Kansas' largest pheasant populations are located. Accommodations are at a minimum. The Lovewell Reservoir with its accompanying Lovewell Wildlife Area, and the Jewell State Fishing Lake and Wildlife Area are located in Jewell County. Both sites provide managed public hunting for visiting bird hunters. The 1997 Walk-In Hunting Area Atlas lists 5 enrolled properties totaling 3,320 acres.

UPLAND BIRDS
Pheasant, Bobwhite Quail, Greater Prairie Chicken, Mourning Dove

WATERFOWL
Ducks & Geese

ACCOMMODATIONS
Crest-Vue Motel, RR 1, Mankato, 66956 / 913-378-3515 / Dogs allowed / $
Dreamliner Motel, RR 2 Box 8, Mankato, 66956 / 913-378-3107 / Dogs allowed / $$

CAMPGROUNDS AND RV PARKS
Lovewell State Park, Mankato, 66956 / 913-753-4971 / 163 sites

RESTAURANTS
Buffalo Roam Steak House, Highway 36, Mankato, 66956 / 913-378-3971
The Red Rooster, West Highway 36, Mankato, 66956 / 913-378-3735

VETERINARIANS
Jewell County Veterinary Clinic, 510 East North Street, Mankato, 66956 /
913-378-3091

SPORTING GOODS STORES
Nearest are in Concordia and Osborne

AUTO REPAIR
Matt's Automotive, 414 East South Street, Mankato, 66956 / 913-378-3911

AIR SERVICE
Mankato Airport, Mankato

MEDICAL
Jewell County Hospital & Long Term Care, 100 Crestvue Avenue, Mankato, 66956 /
913-378-3137

Norton and Norton County

Population–3,017	Elevation–2,284
County Population–5,947	October Temperature–54.8
County Area–878 sq. mi.	Acres in WIHA–17,588
	Acres in CRP–42,589

Norton is located in the northcentral pheasant belt, where Kansas' largest pheasant populations are found. The county contains extensive areas of wheat farming. Norton County is a popular destination for Kansas hunters living in the populous eastern edge of the state, and therefore pressure can be heavy. An adequate range of amenities will provide choices to those visiting the area. Keith Sebelius Reservoir and the Norton Wildlife Area are located within the county, southeast of Norton. The 1997 Walk-In Hunting Area Atlas lists 50 enrolled properties totaling 17,588 acres.

UPLAND BIRDS
Pheasant, Bobwhite Quail, Greater Prairie Chicken, Mourning Dove

WATERFOWL
Ducks & Geese

ACCOMMODATIONS
Best Western Brooks Motel, Highway 36 & 283, Norton, 67654 / 913-877-3381 / Dogs allowed / $$
Budget Host Hillcrest Motel, West Highway 36, Norton, 67654 / 913-877-3343 / Dogs allowed / $$

CAMPGROUNDS AND RV PARKS
Prairie Dog State Park, Norton, 913-877-2953 / 192 sites / Open 4/15–10/15

RESTAURANTS
Adventures in Eating, 903 West Armory Drive, Norton, 67654 / 913-877-3491
The Beacon Cafe, 209 East Holme Street, Norton, 67654 / 913-877-2665
Prairie Dog Restaurant & Lounge, RR 3, Norton, 67654 / 913-877-3643
State Street Steakhouse, 402 South State Street, Norton, 67654 / 913-877-5222

VETERINARIANS
Norton Veterinary Clinic, West Holme, Norton, 67654 / 913-877-2411

SPORTING GOODS STORES
Ward's Sporting Goods, West Highway 36, Norton, 67654 / 913-877-2611

Hunters form a skirmish line to drive pheasants in heavy cover.

AUTO REPAIR

Hawk Repair & Service Inc, 210 South Norton Avenue, Norton, 67654 / 913-877-3561

Heller Auto Service, 209 West Lincoln Street, Norton, 67654 / 913-877-3391

AIR SERVICE

Miller Aviation Inc, RR 1, Norton, 67654 / 913-877-2201

MEDICAL

Norton County Hospital, 102 East Holme Street, Norton, 67654 / 913-877-3351

FOR MORE INFORMATION

Chamber of Commerce
3 Washington Square
Norton, KS 67654
913-877-2501

Oakley and Logan County

Population–2,045	Elevation–3,049
County Population–3,081	October Temperature–53
County Area–1,073 sq. mi.	Acres in WIHA–2,560
	Acres in CRP–32,396

The town of Oakley is located at the junction of Interstate 70, Highway 83, and Highway 40. The town's economy is tied to the region's heavy dependence upon wheat production. The area is sparsely populated, but amenities are available. Extreme western Kansas is west of the main bulk of the state's pheasant habitat, but birds are still available locally. No managed public hunting wildlife areas are found in the county. The 1997 Walk-In Hunting Area Atlas lists 6 enrolled properties totaling 2,560 acres.

UPLAND BIRDS
Pheasant, Bobwhite Quail, Mourning Dove

WATERFOWL
Ducks & Geese

ACCOMMODATIONS
1st Travel Inn, 708 Center Avenue, Oakley, 67748 / 913-672-3226 / Dogs allowed / $

Annie Oakley Motel, 428 Center Avenue, Oakley, 67748 / 913-672-3223 / Dogs allowed / $

Best Western Golden Plains Motel, Highway 40, Oakley, 67748 / 913-672-3254 / Dogs allowed / $$

First Interstate Inn, I-70 & Highway 40, Oakley, 67748 / 913-672-3203 / Dogs allowed / $$

CAMPGROUNDS AND RV PARKS
Camp Inn Trailer Park, 170 & 83rd, Oakley, 67748 / 913-672-3538

RESTAURANTS
Colonial Steak House, I-70 & Highway 83, Oakley, 67748 / 913-672-4720

Don's Drive-in Cafe, Highway 40 & 83, Oakley, 67748 / 913-672-3965

Shelli's Family Dining, 413 South Freeman Avenue, Oakley, 67748 / 913-672-3939

VETERINARIANS
Oakley Veterinary Service, Highway 83 South, Oakley, 67748 / 913-672-3411

SPORTING GOODS STORES
Nearest are in Colby

AUTO REPAIR
Bryan's Service Center, 203 Center Avenue, Oakley, 67748 / 913-672-4550
Ron's Automotive, 503 US Highway 83, Oakley, 67748 / 913-672-3008

AIR SERVICE
Municipal Airport, East Highway 40, Oakley, 67748 / 913-672-4621

MEDICAL
Nearest is in Colby

FOR MORE INFORMATION
Oakley Area Chamber of Commerce
313 Center Avenue
Oakley, KS 67748
913-672-4862

Osborne and Osborne County

Population–1,778	Elevation–1,700
County Population–4,867	October Temperature–56
County Area–893 sq. mi.	Acres in WIHA–6,408
	Acres in CRP–22,145

Osborne is located in north central Kansas. The region is sparsely settled and the principal occupations are in agriculture. Accommodations and services are at a minimum. The large Glen Elder Reservoir and Wildlife Area is found to the east on the Mitchell County line. The 1997 Walk-In Hunting Area Atlas lists 25 enrolled properties totaling 6,408 acres.

UPLAND BIRDS
Pheasant, Bobwhite Quail, Greater Prairie Chicken, Mourning Dove

WATERFOWL
Ducks & Geese

ACCOMMODATIONS
Camelot Inn, Highway 24 & 281, Osborne, 67473 / 913-346-5413 / Dogs allowed / $$

CAMPGROUNDS AND RV PARKS
Nearest are in Mankato

RESTAURANTS
Bossynova Steak House, 1106 West US Highway 24, Osborne, 67473 / 913-346-5622
C & J Diner, 118 East New Hampshire Street, Osborne, 67473 / 913-346-2711
The Huddle, 119 South 1st Street, Osborne, 67473 / 913-346-5880

VETERINARIANS
Osborne Veterinary Clinic, 989 South US Highway 281, Osborne, 67473 / 913-346-5545

SPORTING GOODS STORES
Roadhouse Sporting Goods, 216 South Oak Street, Osborne, 67473 / 913-346-5842

AUTO REPAIR
Robert Brummer Repair, North Locust, Osborne, 67473 / 913-346-5848
Roenne Motors, 214 W Connecticut Avenue, Osborne, 67473 / 913-346-2679

AIR SERVICE
Municipal Airport, 1027 C 388th Drive, Osborne, 67473 / 913-346-9632

John Leonard of Topeka walking up the line.

MEDICAL

Osborne County Memorial Hospital, 424 West New Hampshire Street, Osborne, 67473 / 913-346-2121

FOR MORE INFORMATION

Decatur County Area Chamber of Commerce
132 South Penn
Oberlin, KS 67749
785-475-3441

St. Francis and Cheyenne County

Population–1,495	Elevation–3,360
County Population–3,243	October Temperature–52.9
County Area–1,020 sq. mi.	Acres in WIHA–13,970
	Acres in CRP–45,090

St. Francis is located in the extreme northwestern corner of Kansas. This sparsely populated, high plains area is what one Kansas resident jokingly referred to as the "wheat ranching" part of the state. As the quote infers, large wheat fields cover the area. Accommodations and services are at a minimum.

The St. Francis Wildlife Area is found t o the southwest along the south fork of the Republican River. The South Fork Wildlife Area is located northeast of St. Francis, also on the south fork of the Republican River. The 1997 Walk-In Hunting Area Atlas lists 13 enrolled properties totaling 13,970 acres.

UPLAND BIRDS
Pheasant, Bobwhite Quail, Mourning Dove

WATERFOWL
Ducks & Geese

ACCOMMODATIONS
Empire Motel, Highway 36, St. Francis, 67756 / 913-332-2231
Homesteader Motel & Trailer Park, West Highway 36, St. Francis, 67756 /
913-332-2168

CAMPGROUNDS AND RV PARKS
Mid-America Camp Inn, South Highway 27, Goodland, 67735 / 913-899-5431 /
129 sites, 91 full hook-ups

RESTAURANTS
Captain Hooks, Highway 36, St. Francis, 67756 / 913-332-3275
Country Pantry, RR 1, St. Francis, 67756 / 913-332-3467
Park Hill Restaurant & Fiesta Room, Highway 36, St. Francis, 67756 /
913-332-2255
Peg's Family Dining, Highway 36, St. Francis, 67756 / 913-332-2212

VETERINARIANS
Republican Valley Veterinary Clinic, Highway 36, St. Francis, 67756 /
913-332-2262

SPORTING GOODS STORES
Nearest are in Colby

AUTO REPAIR
Austin P & D Repair, Highway 36, St. Francis, 67756 / 913-332-2384
Morrow's Garage, Highway 36, St. Francis, 67756 / 913-332-3941

AIR SERVICE
Cheyenne County Municipal Airport, St. Francis

MEDICAL
Cheyenne County Hospital, 210 West 1st, St. Francis, 67756 / 913-332-2104

FOR MORE INFORMATION
St. Francis Chamber of Commerce
212 Washington Street
St. Francis, KS 67756
913-332-2961

Salina and Saline County

Population–42,299	Elevation–1,222
County Population–49,301	October Temperature–57
County Area–720 sq. mi.	Acres in WIHA–320
	Acres in CRP–21,868

Salina is a large city that supports a multitude of businesses and services. Both Kansas Wesleyan University and a branch of Kansas State University make their home here. Centrally located at the junction of Interstates 70 and 135, the city provides ready freeway access to other parts of the state. Saline County is Flint Hills country and provides habitat for greater prairie chickens.

Pheasant, bobwhites, and dove are also area staples. No managed public hunting wildlife areas are found in the county. The 1997 Walk-In Hunting Area Atlas lists 2 enrolled properties totaling 320 acres.

UPLAND BIRDS
Pheasant, Bobwhite Quail, Greater Prairie Chicken, Mourning Dove

WATERFOWL
Ducks & Geese

ACCOMMODATIONS
Best Western Heart of America Inn, 632 Westport Boulevard, Salina, 67401 /
   913-827-9315 / Dogs allowed / $$
Best Western Mid-America Inn Inc, 1846 North 9th Street, Salina, 67401 /
   913-827-0356 / Dogs allowed / $$
Comfort Inn, 1820 West Crawford Street, Salina, 67401 / 913-826-1711 / Dogs
   allowed / $$-$$$
Howard Johnson Motel, 2403 South 9th Street, Salina, 67401 / 913-827-5511 /
   Dogs allowed / $$
Red Coach Inn and Restaurant, 2110 West Crawford Street, Salina, 67401 /
   913-825-2111 / Dogs allowed / $$
Super 8 Motel of Salina, 1640 West Crawford Street, Salina, 67401 / 913-823-9215 /
   Dogs allowed / $$

CAMPGROUNDS AND RV PARKS
KOA of Salina, 1109 West Diamond Drive, Salina, 67401 / 913-827-3182 / 82 sites
Sundowner West Park, 2745 North Hedville Road, Salina, 67401 / 913-823-8335 /
   100 sites

RESTAURANTS

Bayard's Cafe, 2301 North 9th Street, Salina, 67401 / 913-825-4351
Grandma Max's Restaurant, 1944 North 9th Street, Salina, 67401 / 913-825-5023
Gutierrez Mexican Restaurant, 1935 South Ohio Street, Salina, 67401 / 913-825-1649
Hickory Hut, 1707 West Crawford Street, Salina, 67401 / 913-825-1588
Ranger's Steak & Seafood, 716 North 12th Street, Salina, 67401 / 913-823-3491
Shang-hai Chinese Restaurant, 453 South Broadway Boulevard, Salina, 67401 /
    913-825-2288
Shooter's Bar & Grill, 107 North Santa Fe Avenue, Salina, 67401 / 913-827-0992
The Phoenix, 100 North 5th Street, Salina, 67401 / 913-825-8877

VETERINARIANS

Atherton Veterinary Clinic, 645 South Ohio Street, Salina, 67401 / 913-823-3322
Town and Country Animal Hospital, 1001 Schippel Drive, Salina, 67401 /
    913-823-2217

SPORTING GOODS STORES

Rusty's Outdoor Sports, 2259 South 9th Street Unit 117, Salina, 67401 /
    913-827-7924
K-Mart, 2900 South 9th Street, Salina, 67401 / 913-825-6800

AUTO REPAIR

Austin Auto Repair, 755 North 12th Street, Salina, 67401 / 913-825-8399
D & P Auto Repair, 400 North 5th Street, Salina, 67401 / 913-827-5901
Precision Automotive, 540 North 7th Street, Salina, 67401 / 913-827-6621
S & K Automotive, 2846 Centennial Road, Salina, 67401 / 913-823-1899

AIR SERVICE

Salina Airport Authority, 3237 Arnold Avenue, Salina, 67401 / 913-827-3914 /
    Served by USAirways

MEDICAL

Salina Regional Health Center, 400 South Santa Fe, Salina, 67401 / 785-452-7000

FOR MORE INFORMATION

Chamber of Commerce
120 West Ash Street
Salina, KS 67401
913-827-930

Region 2

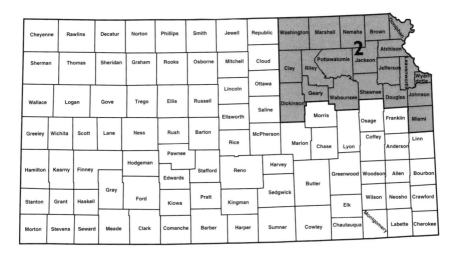

Region 2 is Kansas' most heavily populated region, and contains the capital city of Topeka, Kansas. The western third of the region is Flint Hills country and is characterized by rolling, short grass hills. This is the home of the greater prairie chicken. The Flint Hills land is used primarily for the ranging of livestock. Hardwood-lined watersheds vein the region, and the bottomlands give way to agricultural fields. Bobwhite quail hunting is very good to excellent in the Flint Hills, depending on the year. Pheasants are found in the agricultural fields and along the water courses.

Moving east, the region gives way to traditional small farms. The country is flatter and more heavily wooded. Pheasants and bobwhite quail are the principal upland birds hunted.

Mourning dove are found region-wide, as are waterfowl. There are several large water impoundments, and these areas are used by migrating ducks and geese. With the build-up of snow goose populations, whose traditional migratory pattern has been to follow the eastern edge of the state, birds now can be found on any of the large reservoirs in Region 2.

Turkeys are found region-wide, in suitable habitat.

Area Hunting Guides

Bell Wildlife Specialities
Daniel D. Bell
155 Oak Street, Box 147
Harveyville, KS 66431
Business & Home 785-589-2321

North Central Kansas Guide Service
Brian D. Blackwood
1624 Meadow Lane
Clay Center, KS 67432
Business 913-632-2085
Home 913-632-5302

Extreme Upland Adventures
Guy D. Caster
308 West Allen Street
Springhill, KS 66083
Business & Home 913-592-4102

Dague's Hunting
Murray L. Dague
1267 Quivira Road
Washington, KS 66968
Business & Home 785-325-2858

Stan Fisher Outfitting
Stan Fisher
PO Box 1493
Trout Creek, MT 59874
Business & Home 406-827-4812

RMF Guide Service
Ronald M. Ford
PO Box 1924
Manhattan, KS 66502
Business 785-537-4682
Home 913-537-4682

Carry Creek Outfitters
Bart L. Hettenbach
2095 1600 Avenue
Woodbine, KS 67492
Business & Home 785-257-3583

Morris Guns, Dogs, & Guided Hunts
Jeff R. Morris
2104 Browning Avenue
Manhattan, KS 66502
Business & Home 785-539-1622

Philip A. Niblock
16943 West 68th Street
Shawnee, KS 66217
Business & Home 9113-268-8733

Nickels' Quarters
Michael L. Nickels
17100 Fairview Road
McLouth, KS 66054
Business & Home 785-863-2037

Wolfriver Outfitters
Larry A. Olmstead
Rt. 5, Box 10
Hiawatha, KS 66434
Business 785-742-3277
Home 785-742-7935

Fetch Dog and Guide
Mark A. Pirozzoli
7405 SW 27th Street
Topeka, KS 66614
Business & Home 785-478-9685

Joe Rush Guide & Outfitter
Joe Rush
RR 1, PO Box 354
Eskridge, KS 66423
Business & Home 913-449-2409

Kitten Creek English Springer Spaniels
Steven E. Salzman
1208 East 2100 Road
Eudora, KS 66025
Business & Home 785-542-3823

Prairie Winds Guide Service
Thomas D. Slick
1611 K-157 Highway
Junction City, KS 66441

Uhlik Hunting Grounds
Mark G. Uhlik
1548 17th Road
Washington, KS 66968
Business & Home 785-325-2747

KCV Outdoors
K. Craig Vaughn
4857 Fairlawn Circle
Boulder, CO 80301
Business & Home 303-530-4479

Area Hunting Preserves

Blue Line Club
Bernie Janssen
Rt. 1, Box 139A
Solomon, KS 67480
785-488-3785

Cokeley Farms Hunting Preserve
RR 1
Delia, KS 66418
913-771-3817

Ravenwood Hunting & Clay
Ken Corbet
10147 SW 61
Topeka, KS 66610
913-256-6444

Region 2
Bobwhite Quail Distribution

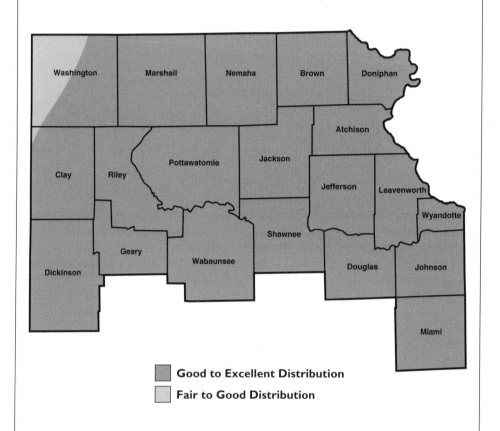

■ Good to Excellent Distribution
□ Fair to Good Distribution

Region 2
Greater Prairie Chicken Distribution

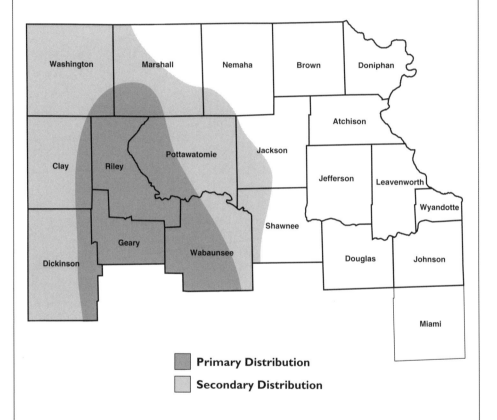

Primary Distribution

Secondary Distribution

Region 2
Mourning Dove Distribution

Mourning Dove Distribution

Region 2
Pheasant Distribution

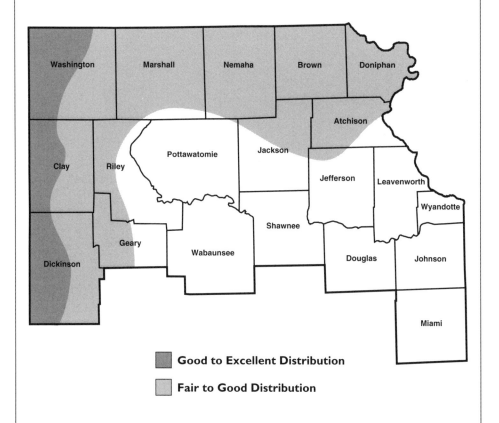

Good to Excellent Distribution

Fair to Good Distribution

Region 2
Turkey Distribution

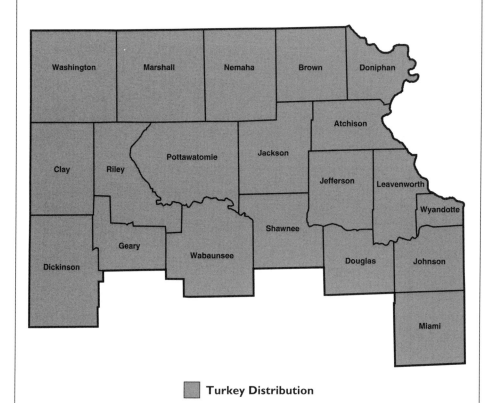

Turkey Distribution

Abilene and Dickenson County

Population–6,242	Elevation–1,155
County Population–18,958	October Temperature–57
County Area–848 sq. mi.	Acres in WIHA–4,207
	Acres in CRP–24,694

Abilene, that famous cow town of old, is now a respectable farming community. The town supports a host of accommodations and services. Close proximity to Interstate 70 allows quick access to other areas in central Kansas. The city is located in the Flint Hills region of Kansas. Milford Lake Project containing Milford Wildlife Area is found on the northeastern corner of Dickenson County. The 1997 Walk-In Hunting Area Atlas lists 19 enrolled properties totaling 4,207 acres.

UPLAND BIRDS
Pheasant, Bobwhite Quail, Greater Prairie Chicken, Mourning Dove

WATERFOWL
Ducks & Geese

ACCOMMODATIONS
Best Western Abilene's Pride, 1709 North Buckeye Avenue, Abilene, 67410 / 913-263-2800 / Dogs allowed / $$
Best Western Inn, 2210 North Buckeye Avenue, Abilene, 67410 / 913-263-2050 / Dogs allowed / $$
Diamond Motel, 1407 NW 3rd Street, Abilene, 67410 / 913-263-2360 / Dogs allowed / $
Super 8 Motel, 2207 North Buckeye Avenue, Abilene, 67410 / 913-263-4545 / Dogs allowed / $$

CAMPGROUNDS AND RV PARKS
Covered Wagon RV Park and CampGround, 803 South Buckeye Avenue, Abilene, 67410 / 913-263-2343 / 45 sites
Four Seasons RV Acres, 2502 Mink Road, Abilene, 67410 / 913-598-2221 / 100 sites

RESTAURANTS
Cornucopia, 115 West 1st Street, Abilene, 67410 / 913-263-8335
Green Acres Restaurant & Lounge, I-70 & K-15, Abilene, 67410 / 913-263-1001
Kirby House Restaurant, 205 NE 3rd Street, Abilene, 67410 / 913-263-7336
Midway Cafe, RR 5, Abilene, 67410 / 913-263-8955
Mr. K's Buckboard, 849 East 1st Street, Abilene, 67410 / 913-263-7995
Texan Cafe, 123 North Spruce Street, Abilene, 67410 / 913-263-2373

VETERINARIANS
Abilene Animal Hospital, 320 NE 14th Street, Abilene, 67410 / 913-263-2301
Alan Myers, 1126 Eden Road, Abilene, 67410 / 913-479-2256

SPORTING GOODS STORES
Sweats Sporting Goods, 317 North Broadway Street, Abilene, 67410 / 913-263-2910

AUTO REPAIR
H & H Repair, 1000 South Buckeye Avenue, Abilene, 67410 / 913-263-4222
Rodda's Auto Clinic, 315 West 1st Street, Abilene, 67410 / 913-263-3383

AIR SERVICE
Abilene Municipal Airport, Abilene

MEDICAL
Abilene Memorial Hospital, 511 NE 10th Street, Abilene, 67410 / 785-263-2100

FOR MORE INFORMATION
Chamber of Commerce
201 NW 2nd Street
Abilene, KS 67410
913-263-1770

Hiawatha and Brown County

Population–3,603	Elevation–1,085
County Population–11,128	October Temperature–55
County Area–571 sq. mi.	Acres in WIHA–2080
	Acres in CRP–9,337

Hiawatha services the agricultural and livestock producing business of Brown County. The town is off the beaten path and services are at a minimum. Brown State Fishing Lake and Wildlife Area is to the east of town on Highway 36; the large flocks of snow geese that travel the flyway are known to occasionally frequent the lake. Squaw Creek National Wildlife Refuge, one of the important snow goose stops on the central flyway, is to the northwest in Missouri. The Iowa Indian Reservation sits to the north on the Nebraska Border and allows hunting with a tribal hunting permit (see the section on Indian Reservations). The 1997 Walk-In Hunting Area Atlas lists 13 enrolled properties totaling 2,080 acres.

UPLAND BIRDS
Pheasant, Bobwhite Quail, Mourning Dove

WATERFOWL
Ducks & Geese

ACCOMMODATIONS
Hiawatha Heartland Restaurant and Inn, Jct Highway 36 & 73, Hiawatha, 66434 / 913-742-7401 / Dogs allowed / $$

CAMPGROUNDS AND RV PARKS
Country Squire Motel and RV Park, Rt. 4, Box 10, Hiawatha, 66434 / 913-742-2877 / 16 sites

RESTAURANTS
Danny's Restaurant, 606 Oregon Street, Hiawatha, 66434 / 913-742-2900
Heartland Restaurant, Jct Highway 36 & 73, Hiawatha, 66434 / 913-742-7760
Maple Leaf Restaurant, 208 North 1st Street, Hiawatha, 66434 / 913-742-3166

VETERINARIANS
Nearest are in St. Joseph, MO

SPORTING GOODS STORES
Wal-Mart Discount Cities, US Highway 36 West, Hiawatha, 66434 / 913-742-7445

AUTO REPAIR
Bill's Auto Repair, 200 South 12th Street, Hiawatha, 66434 / 913-742-3667
Vonderschmidt Repair, 708 North 1st Street, Hiawatha, 66434 / 913-742-3016

Pheasant hunting.

AIR SERVICE
Hiawatha Airport Ted Gore Municipal, RR 1, Hiawatha, 66434 / 913-742-9081

MEDICAL
Hiawatha Community Hospital, 300 Utah Street, Hiawatha, 66434 / 913-742-2131

FOR MORE INFORMATION
Hiawatha Chamber of Commerce
413 Oregon Street
Hiawatha, KS 66434
785-742-7136

Junction City and Geary County

Population–20,642	Elevation–1,080
County Population–30,453	October Temperature–57
County Area–384 sq. mi.	Acres in WIHA–160
	Acres in CRP–2,933

Junction City is the gateway to Fort Riley Military Reservation. Both services and accommodations are extensive. There are many public hunting opportunities available in the general vicinity, including Tuttle Creek Wildlife Area, Milford Wildlife Area, Geary State Fishing Lake and Wildlife Area, and of course, Fort Riley. The 1997 Walk-In Hunting Area Atlas lists 1 enrolled property totaling 160 acres.

UPLAND BIRDS
Pheasant, Bobwhite Quail, Greater Prairie Chicken, Mourning Dove

WATERFOWL
Ducks & Geese

ACCOMMODATIONS
Best Western Jayhawk Inn Motel, 110 East Flint Hills Boulevard, Junction City, 66441 / 913-238-5188 / Dogs allowed / $$
Days Inn, 1024 South Washington Street, Junction City, 66441 / 913-762-2727 / Dogs allowed / $$
Econo Lodge, 211 West Flint Hills Boulevard, Junction City, 66441 / 913-238-8181 / Dogs allowed / $-$$
Golden Wheat Budget Inn, 820 South Washington Street, Junction City, 66441 / 913-238-5106 / Dogs allowed / $-$$
Harvest Inn, 1001 East 6th/4th Street, Junction City, 66441 / 913-238-8101 / Dogs allowed / $$-$$$

CAMPGROUNDS AND R.V. PARKS
Curtis Creek Campground, Junction City, 913-238-5714 / 80 sites
Thunderbird Marina Campground, Junction City, 913-238-5864/ 80 sites
West Rolling Hills/Milford Lake, Junction City, 913-238-5714 / 98 sites

RESTAURANTS
Chubby's Bar-B-Q, 203 South Washington Street, Junction City, 66441 / 913-762-2773
Denny's Restaurant, 1032 South Washington Street, Junction City, 66441 / 913-238-8166
Gasthaus Erika, 610 North Washington Street, Junction City, 66441 / 913-762-6414
Kimchee House, 1000 Grant Avenue, Junction City, 66441 / 913-762-3335

Palm Tree Restaurant, 306 South Jefferson Street, Junction City, 66441 /
913-238-5872

Peking Restaurant, 836 South Washington Street, Junction City, 66441 /
913-238-2336

Riverside Bar & Grill, 122 Grant Avenue, Junction City, 66441 / 913-238-6051

Soup House, 1118½ North Washington Street, Junction City, 66441 / 913-762-7789

Top's Burgers Brats & Beer, 1111 Grant Avenue, Junction City, 66441 / 913-223-0550

Town House Cafe, 127 West 7th Street, Junction City, 66441 / 913-238-6638

VETERINARIANS

Nedrick L Price, 106 North Eisenhower Drive, Junction City, 66441 / 913-762-5631

Casey L Thomas, 2206 Prospect Circle, Junction City, 66441 / 913-762-3310

SPORTING GOODS STORES

JD's Sports Center, 18th & Jackson Street, Junction City, 66441 / 913-238-1425

Wal-mart Discount Cities, 521 East Chestnut Street, Junction City, 66441 /
913-238-8229

AUTO REPAIR

Affordable Mechanics, 1004 Price Street, Junction City, 66441 / 913-762-6617

Ed's Auto Repair, 1038 Grant Avenue, Junction City, 66441 / 913-238-2517

M & N Motors, 121 East 5th Street, Junction City, 66441 / 913-762-5111

Reich's Foreign Car Service, 305 North Washington Street, Junction City, 66441 /
913-238-1181

AIR SERVICE

Municipal Airport, 540 West 18th Street, Junction City, 66441 / 913-238-2020

MEDICAL

Geary Community Hospital, 1102 Saint Mary's Road, Junction City, 66441 /
913-238-4131

FOR MORE INFORMATION

Chamber of Commerce
814 North Washington Street
Junction City, KS 66441
913-762-2632

Greater Kansas City Area, Wyandotte and Johnson Counties

Population–859,946	Elevation–763
Wyandotte County Population–162,026	October Temperature–58
Johnson County Population–355,054	October Temperature–58
Wyandotte County Area–151 sq. miles	Acres in WIHA–0
	Acres in CRP–170
Johnson County Area–477 sq. mi.	Acres in WIHA–0
	Acres in CRP–1,869

The Greater Kansas City Area is a veritable metropolis, with many small towns and suburbs radiating out from the twin giants of Kansas City, Missouri, and Kansas City, Kansas. The two cities are divided by the Missouri River, which flows north to south. For the sake of organization, I have listed all the area cities under the Greater Kansas City listing. A full range of goods and services are available throughout the area. The Kansas City Office of the Kansas Department of Wildlife and Parks is located in Lenexa, Kansas.

Hillsdale Lake Project and Wildlife Area is found on the southern Johnson County border.

UPLAND BIRDS
Pheasant, Bobwhite Quail, Mourning Dove

WATERFOWL
Ducks & Geese

Kansas City, Kansas

ACCOMMODATIONS
Civic Centre Hotel, 424 Minnesota Avenue, Kansas City, KS 66101 / 913-342-6919 / Dogs allowed / $$-$$$

Best Western Flamingo Motel, 4725 State Avenue, Kansas City, KS 66102 / 913-287-5511 / $$

Best Western Inn, 501 Southwest Boulevard, Kansas City, KS 66103 / 913-677-3060 / Dogs allowed / $$$

Home & Hearth Inn, 3930 Rainbow Boulevard, Kansas City, KS 66103 / 913-236-6880 / Dogs allowed / $$

RESTAURANTS
Fee Fee's Fish & International Cuisine, 500 Parallel Parkway, Kansas City, KS 66101 / 913-342-7211

International House of Pancakes, 7901 State Avenue, Kansas City, KS 66112 / 913-788-3195

La Hacienda Restaurant, 320 Kansas Avenue, Kansas City, KS 66105 / 913-371-1324

Nefertiti Restaurant & Banquet Hall, 1314 Quindaro Boulevard, Kansas City, KS 66104 / 913-321-6677

Perkins Restaurants, 7262 State Avenue, Kansas City, KS 66112 / 913-788-7101

Ponderosa Steak House, 5001 State Avenue, Kansas City, KS 66102 / 913-287-3757

Rosedale Barbeque, 600 Southwest Boulevard, Kansas City, KS 66103 / 913-262-0343

Sesame Chinese Restaurant, 1017 North 7th Street, Kansas City, KS 66101 / 913-371-5523

Trackside Restaurant & Lounge, 8919 Leavenworth Road, Kansas City, KS 66109 / 913-788-3838

Wyandotte Cafe, 7731 State Avenue, Kansas City, KS 66112 / 913-788-7851

VETERINARIANS

Bethel Animal Hospital & Kennel, 7100 Leavenworth Road, Kansas City, KS 66109 / 913-334-2792

Gates Mobile Vet, 335 North 38th Street, Kansas City, KS 66102 / 913-621-1836

Mellissa A Irwin, 6014 Mission Road, Kansas City, KS 66103 / 913-432-7611

Gary R Stallings, 7100 Leavenworth Road, Kansas City, KS 66109 / 913-334-2792

James Swanson, 1930 North 77th Streeet, Kansas City, KS 66112 / 913-334-6770

SPORTING GOODS STORES

K-Mart Stores, 7836 State Avenue, Kansas City, KS 66112 / 913-299-1434

Wal-Mart Discount Cities, 612 South 130th Street, Bonner Springs, KS 66012 / 913-441-6751

Wal-Mart Discount Cities, 6565 State Avenue, Kansas City, KS 66102 / 913-788-3331

AUTO REPAIR

Car Doctor, 905 Troup Avenue, Kansas City, KS 66104 / 913-321-0801

Johnson Motors & Tow Service, 5500 Leavenworth Road, Kansas City, KS 66104 / 913-287-9897

Luna Auto Repairing, 301 North 7th Street, Kansas City, KS 66101 / 913-321-3633

Maple Hill Garage & Service, 4200 Metropolitan Avenue, Kansas City, KS 66106 / 913-262-6818

Walker Brothers Automotive, 969 Kansas Avenue, Kansas City, KS 66105 / 913-281-4002

AIR SERVICE

See Kansas City, MO

MEDICAL

Bethany Medical Center, 51 North 12th Street, Kansas City, KS 66102 / 913-281-8400

Providence Medical Center, 8929 Parallel Parkway, Kansas City, KS 66112 / 913-596-4000

University of Kansas Medical Center, 3901 Rainbow Boulevard, Kansas City, KS 66160 / 913-588-5000

FOR MORE INFORMATION
Chamber of Commerce Kansas City
727 Minnesota Avenue
Kansas City, KS 66101
913-371-3070

Bonner Springs

RESTAURANTS
Binkle's, 13100 Kansas Avenue, Bonner Springs, 66012 / 913-422-4700
Evergreen Chinese Restaurant, 13034 Kansas Avenue, Bonner Springs, 66012 /
    913-441-6484
Fortune Red Chinese Restaurant, 121 Oak Street, Bonner Springs, 66012 /
    913-441-1988
Granny Grump's, 220 Cedar Street, Bonner Springs, 66012 / 913-422-3121
Papa Mingos Mexican Restaurant, 228 Oak Street, Bonner Springs, 66012 /
    913-422-7665

AUTO REPAIR
Hoffine's Automotive, 112 Cornell Avenue, Bonner Springs, 66012 / 913-422-5791
Kenny's Automotive, 13900 State Avenue, Bonner Springs, 66012 / 913-721-2200

FOR MORE INFORMATION
Bonner Springs, Edwardsville Chamber of Commerce
205 East 2nd Street
Bonner Springs, KS 66012
913-422-5044

Kansas City, Missouri

ACCOMMODATIONS
American Inn, I-35 & Armour Road, Kansas City, MO 64116 / 816-471-3451 / Dogs
    allowed / $$
Best Western Airport Inn, I-29 Exit 19, Kansas City, MO 64163 / 816-464-2300 /
    Dogs allowed / $$
Days Inn North, 2232 Taney Street, Kansas City, MO 64116 / 816-421-6000 / Dogs
    allowed / $$
Drury Inn, I-70 & Blue Ridge Cutoff, Kansas City, MO 64133 / 816-923-3000 / Dogs
    allowed / $$$
Econo Lodge, 5100 East Linwood Boulevard, Kansas City, MO 64128 / 816-923-7777 /
    Dogs allowed / $-$$
Motel 6, 8230 NW Prairie View Road, Kansas City, MO 64151 / 816-741-6400 /
    Dogs allowed / $-$$

Park Place Hotel, I-435 & Front, Kansas City, MO 64120 / 816-483-9900 / Dogs allowed / $$$

Sleep Inn, 7611 NW 97th Terrace, Kansas City, MO 64153 / 816-891-0111 / Dogs allowed / $$-$$$

CAMPGROUNDS AND RV PARKS

KOA Kansas City East, PO Box 191, Oakgrove, MO 64075 / 816-625-7515

Interstate RV Campground, RR 2, Box 227, Higginsville, MO 64037 / 800-690-CAMP

Best Western Airport Inn RV Park, PO Box 319, Platte City, MO 64079 / 819-858-4588

RESTAURANTS

Apple Tree Inn Restaurant, 5755 North Northwood Road, Kansas City, MO 64151 / 816-587-9300

Ararat Temple Restaurant, 5100 Ararat Drive, Kansas City, MO 64129 / 816-923-1995

Bo Ling's Chinese Restaurant, 4800 Main Street, Ste G26, Kansas City, MO 64112 / 816-753-1718

Cafe Allegro, 1815 West 39th Street, Kansas City, MO 64111 / 816-561-3663

Cafe Nile, 8433 Wornall Road, Kansas City, MO 64114 / 816-361-9097

Callahan's Bar & Grill, 323 West 8th Street, Ste 100, Kansas City, MO 64105 / 816-474-7070

Denny's Restaurant, 1400 Burlington Street / 1600 Broadway Street / 3832 Blue Ridge Cutoff / 6220 East 87th Street / 8810 East 350th Highway / Kansas City, MO

Don Fajita's Mexican Restaurant, 2532 NW Vivion Road, Kansas City, MO 64150 / 816-741-0555

El Cerro Grande Mexican Restaurant, 1144 West 103rd St, Kansas City, MO 64114 / 816-941-2855

Georgia's Greek Restaurant, 10236 Wornall Road, Kansas City, MO 64114 / 816-942-8135

VETERINARIANS

Bannister Veterinary Clinic, 8201 East 87th Street, Kansas City, MO 64138 / 816-765-7979

James Cupp and Thomas R Noyes, 4825 NW Gateway Avenue, Kansas City, MO 64151 / 816-741-2345

G Mark Daniels and David R. McGhee, 8343 Wornall Road, Kansas City, MO 64114 / 816-363-4922

Corey Entriken, Larry M Richards, Jeffrey Schlager, and Cheryl Talken, 7027 North Oak, Kansas City, MO 64118 / 816-436-1100

Gregory Raytown Animal Health Center and Mobile Vet, 7037 Raytown Road, Kansas City, MO 64133 / 816-353-6681

Michael L Hodgson and Todd G. McCracken, 5200 NE Vivion Road, Kansas City, MO 64119 / 816-453-7272

Northland Mobile Veterinary Clinic, 4207 North Colorado Avenue, Kansas City, MO 64117 / 816-223-1772

F J Schroeder and Waybern D Yates, 10401 East 63rd Street, Kansas City, MO 64133 / 816-353-3666

SPORTING GOODS STORES
Backwoods, 3936 Broadway Street, Kansas City, MO 64111 / 816-531-0200
CR Gun Specialty Inc, 1701 Baltimore Avenue, Kansas City, MO 64108 / 816-221-3550
K-Mart Discount Store, I-435 & Eastwood Tfwy, Kansas City, MO 64138 /
  816-921-5911
K-Mart Stores, 2821 NE Vivion Road, Kansas City, MO 64119 / 816-454-4929
K-Mart Stores, 5615 East Bannister Rd, Kansas City, MO 64137 / 816-763-8700
K-Mart Stores, 600 NE Barry Road, Kansas City, MO 64155 / 816-468-6000
K-Mart Stores, 7100 NW Prairie View Road, Kansas City, MO 64151 / 816-587-8050
Mc Sporting Goods, 400 NW Barry Road, Kansas City, MO 64155 / 816-468-7477
Mc Sporting Goods, 4200 Blue Ridge Boulevard, Kansas City, MO 64133 /
  816-737-5533
Mc Sporting Goods, 8600 Ward Pky, Kansas City, MO 64114 / 816-444-1554
Outdoor Tradition, 5338 NW 64th Street, Kansas City, MO 64151 / 816-741-0208
Shelby's Sports Shop, 3111 Prospect Avenue, Kansas City, MO 64128 / 816-921-4910
Wal-Mart Hypermart USA, 9051 Hillcrest Road, Kansas City, MO 64138 / 816-767-1200

AUTO REPAIR
Blue Ridge Auto Repair, 8623 Blue Ridge Blvd, Kansas City, MO 64138 /
  816-356-6690
Clay Platte Auto Repair & Tow Service, 4001 Prather Road, Kansas City, MO 64116 /
  816-454-1800
Leibrand's Riverside Automotive, Jct A Highway & Vivion Road, Kansas City, MO
  64150 / 816-741-9892
National Car Care, 1905 East Truman Road, Kansas City, MO 64127 / 816-474-4144
One Stop Auto Service, 9717 NE 35th Street, Kansas City, MO 64161 / 816-737-8803

AIR SERVICE
Heart Airport, 7000 East 40th Highway, Kansas City, MO 64129 / 816-923-4112
Kansas City International Airport, Kansas City, MO 64163 / 816-243-5237 / Served
  by Air Canada, AirTran, American Airlines, America West, Comair, Continental,
  Delta, Midwest Express, Northwest, Redwing, Southwest, TransWorld Airlines,
  United, USAirways, Vanguard, and Western Pacific
Kansas City Missouri City Aviation Dept, 1 International Square, Kansas City, MO
  64153 / 816-243-5205
Midwest ATC Service Inc, Richards Gebaur Airport, Kansas City, MO 64147 /
  816-322-2472
Noah's Ark Airport, 7620 NW River Road, Kansas City, MO 64152 / 816-891-7010

MEDICAL
Baptist Medical Center, 6601 Rockhill Road, Kansas City, MO 64131 / 816-276-7000
Cameron Community Hospital, 1015 East 4th Street, Kansas City, MO 64106 /
  816-472-7313
Crittenton, 10918 Elm Avenue, Kansas City, MO 64134 / 816-767-1112

Menorah Medical Center, 4949 Rockhill Road, Kansas City, MO 64110 / 816-276-8000

North Hills Hospital of Kansas City, 4800 NW 88th Street, Kansas City, MO 64154 / 816-436-3900

Park Lane Medical Center, 5151 Raytown Road, Kansas City, MO 64133 / 816-358-8000

Saint Joseph Health Center, 1000 Carondelet Drive, Kansas City, MO 64114 / 816-942-4400

Saint Luke's Hospital of Kansas City, 4401 Wornall Road, Kansas City, MO 64111 / 816-932-2000

Trinity Lutheran Hospital, 3030 Baltimore Avenue, Kansas City, MO 64108 / 816-753-4600

Truman Medical Center, 2301 Holmes Street, Kansas City, MO 64108 / 816-556-3000

Vencor Hospital-Kansas City, 8701 Troost Avenue, Kansas City, MO 64131 / 816-995-2000

FOR MORE INFORMATION
The Convention and Visitors Bureau of Greater Kansas City at City Center Square
1100 Main, Suite 2550
Kansas City, MO 64105
816-221-5242 or 1-800-767-7700

Lenexa

ACCOMMODATIONS
Day's Inn, 9630 Rose Hill Road, Lenexa, 66215, 800-325-2525 / Dogs allowed / $$-$$$

La Quinta Inn, 9461 Lenexa Drive, Lenexa, 66215 / 913-492-5500 / Dogs allowed / $$-$$$

Motel 6, 9725 Lenexa Drive, Lenexa, 66215 / 913-541-8558 / Dogs allowed / $-$$

RESTAURANTS
Hawley's Restaurant & Bar, 9126 Hall Street, Lenexa, 66219 / 913-492-4894

Longbranch Saloon, 87th & I-35, Lenexa, 66215 / 913-894-5334

Montana Steak Company, 9391 Lenexa Drive, Lenexa, 66215 / 913-492-5310

Zarda Bar-B-Q & Catering Co, 87th & Quivira, Lenexa, 66215 / 913-492-2330

AUTO REPAIR
Apa, 9441 Noland Road, Lenexa, 66215 / 913-492-7232

Lenexa Automotive, 13311 Walnut Street, Lenexa, 66215 / 913-492-8250

FOR MORE INFORMATION
Lenexa Convention & Visitors Bureau
11900 West 87th Street Parkway, Suite 115 / P.O. Box 15626
Lenexa, KS 66215
913-888-1414, 1-800-950-7867

Merriam

ACCOMMODATIONS

Comfort Inn, 6401 Frontage Road, Merriam, 66202 / 913-262-2622 / Dogs allowed / $$-$$$

Drury Inn, I-35 & Shawnee Mission Parkway, Merriam, 66202 / 913-236-9200 / Dogs allowed / $$-$$$

CAMPGROUNDS AND RV PARKS

Walnut Grove Mobile Home RV Park, 10218 Johnson Dr., Merriam, 66203 / 913-262-3023 / 56 sites

RESTAURANTS

International House of Pancakes, 8701 West 63rd, Merriam, 66202 / 913-362-8663
Shoney's Restaurants, 9001 West 63rd, Merriam, 66202 / 913-362-2204

AUTO REPAIR

Apa, 5541 Merriam Drive, Merriam, 66203 / 913-262-1594

FOR MORE INFORMATION

Merriam Chamber of Commerce
6505 Frontage Road
Shawnee Mission, KS 66200-3246
912-236-6471

Mission

RESTAURANTS

Captain D's Seafood Restaurants, 6751 Johnson Drive, Mission, 66202 / 913-262-6733

Town Topic Inc Sandwich Shops, 6018 Johnson Drive, Mission, 66202 / 913-362-8830

VETERINARIANS

Mission Medvet, 5501 Johnson Drive, Mission, 66202 / 913-722-5566

FOR MORE INFORMATION

Greater Kansas City Chamber of Commerce
1601 East 18th Street
Kansas City, MO 64108-1609
816-221-2424

Olathe

ACCOMMODATIONS

Best Western Hallmark Inn, I-35 & 150 Highway, Olathe, 66061 / 913-782-4343 / Dogs allowed / $$

Econo Lodge Olathe, 209 East Flaming Road, Olathe, 66061 / 913-829-1312 / Dogs allowed / $$

Royal Manor Motel, 1641 South Main, Olathe, 66067 / 913-242-4842 / Dogs allowed / $-$$

Village Inn Motel, 2520 South Main, Olathe, 66067 / 913-242-5512 / Dogs allowed / $

RESTAURANTS

Chinese Lantern Restaurant, 409 East Santa Fe Street, Olathe, 66061 / 913-764-2200

Denny's Restaurant, 205 North Rawhide Road, Olathe, 66061 / 913-764-0920

El Pollo Rico, 12755 South Mur Len Road, Olathe, 66062 / 913-764-6700

Gourmet Pizza Kitchen, 16657 West 151st Street, Olathe, 66062 / 913-768-4400

Jumpin' Catfish, 151 & Ridgeview Road, Olathe, 66061 / 913-829-3474

Perkins Restaurants, 1828 East Santa Fe Street, Olathe, 66062 / 913-764-7288

Pickering's Restaurant & Pub, 11922 South Strang Line Road, Olathe, 66062 / 913-782-6464

Ponderosa Steak House, 1109 East Santa Fe Street, Olathe, 66061 / 913-782-8497

VETERINARIANS

Affordable Pet Hospital, 413 East Santa Fe Street, Olathe, 66061 / 913-829-9009

David C Gray and R J Schieffer, 231 East Dennis Avenue, Olathe, 66061 / 816-781-0173

Winchester Place Pet Care Center, 15070 West 116th Street, Olathe, 66062 / 913-451-2827

SPORTING GOODS STORES

K-Mart Stores, 2000 East Santa Fe Street, Olathe, 66062 / 913-782-8080

Wal-Mart, 16630 West 135th Street, Olathe, 66062 / 913-829-2913

AUTO REPAIR

Hankle's Automotive, 820 East Dennis Avenue, Olathe, 66061 / 913-782-2922

Heartland Automotive Group, 2018 East Spruce Circle, Olathe, 66062 / 913-780-6967

Moore Mobile Service, 823 East Highway 56, Olathe, 66061 / 913-782-3940

Ross Automotive Inc, 1139 West Dennis Avenue, Olathe, 66061 / 913-782-7677

AIR SERVICE

Johnson County Airports, 15335 South Pflumm Road, Olathe, 66062 / 913-782-1245

FOR MORE INFORMATION

Olathe Area Chamber of Commerce
128 South Chestnut / P.O. Box 98
Olathe, KS 66051
913-764-1050

Overland Park

ACCOMMODATIONS

Best Western Hallmark Inn, I-435 & Metcalf, Overland Park, 66212 / 913-383-2550 / Dogs allowed / $$$

Comfort Inn, 6401 East Frontage Road, Merriam, 66202, 800-221-2222 / Dogs allowed / $$-$$$

Marriott-Overland Park, 10800 Metcalf Avenue, Overland Park, 66212 / 913-339-9900 / Dogs allowed / $$$

Red Roof Inns, I-435 & Metcalf Road, Overland Park, 66211 / 913-341-0100 / Dogs allowed

Residence Inn By Marriott, 6300 West 110th Street, Overland Park, 66211 / 913-491-3333 / Dogs allowed / $$$

White Haven Motor Lodge, 8039 Metcalf Avenue, Overland Park, 66204 / 913-649-8200 / Dogs allowed / $$

RESTAURANTS

Bennigan's, 9520 Metcalf Avenue, Overland Park, 66212 / 913-341-0103

Chili's Grill & Bar, 7001 West 119th Street, Overland Park, 66209 / 913-341-6567

Dragon Inn, 7500 West 80th Street, Overland Park, 66204 / 913-381-7299

Hoagie's Hero Sandwich Shoppe, 10450 Metcalf Avenue, Overland Park, 66212 / 913-341-8308

Longbranch Saloon, 9095 Metcalf Avenue, Overland Park, 66212 / 913-642-2042

May Vietnamese Restaurant, 8841 West 75th Street, Overland Park, 66204 / 913-648-1688

Nag's Head Bar & Grill, 13460 West 105th Terrace, Overland Park, 66215 / 913-491-4664

Steak N Shake Restaurants, 7510 Shawnee Mission Pky, Overland Park, 66202 / 913-262-1800

SPORTING GOODS STORES

K-Mart Stores, 9401 Metcalf Avenue, Overland Park, 66212 / 913-381-7300

Mc Sporting Goods, 11461 West 95th Street, Overland Park, 66214 / 913-599-5400

Wal-Mart Discount Cities, 11701 Metcalf Avenue, Overland Park, 66210 / 913-338-2202

Wal-Mart Discount Cities, 7701 Frontage Rd, Overland Park, 66204 / 913-648-5885

AUTO REPAIR

Apa, 4860 Merriam Dr, Overland Park, 66203 / 913-384-0900

Roe Amoco Service, 10701 Roe Avenue, Overland Park, 66211 / 913-381-9772

MEDICAL

The Kansas Institute, 5808 West 110th Street, Overland Park, 66211 / 913-451-1700

FOR MORE INFORMATION

Overland Park Chamber of Commerce
P.O. Box 12125
Overland Park, KS 66282-21225
913-491-3600

Shawnee Mission

ACCOMMODATIONS

Red Roof Inn, 6800 West 108th Street, Shawnee Mission, 66211, 800-843-7663 /
Dogs allowed

Super 8 Motel, 9601 Westgate Street, Shawnee Mission, 66215 / 913-888-8899

CAMPGROUNDS AND RV PARKS

Walnut Grove RV Park, 10218 Johnson Drive, Shawnee Mission, 66203 /
913-262-9737

RESTAURANTS

Denny's Restaurant, 10480 Metcalf Avenue and 9471 Lenexa Drive, Shawnee
Mission, KS

Governor's Mansion Restaurant, 10910 West 60th Street, Shawnee Mission, 66203 /
913-962-9999

La Cocina Del Puerco, 9097 Metcalf Avenue, Shawnee Mission, 66212 /
913-341-2800

Mother India Restaurant Inc, 9036 Metcalf Avenue, Shawnee Mission, 66212 /
913-341-0415

Outback Steak House, 9501 Quivira Road, Shawnee Mission, 66215 / 913-894-5115

Perkins Restaurants, 10200 West 63rd and 7401 Frontage Road, Shawnee Mission

Ricco's Italian Restaurant, 11801 College Boulevard, Shawnee Mission, 66210 /
913-469-8405

Scallop's Bar & Grill, 6508 Martway Street, Shawnee Mission, 66202 / 913-236-4300

VETERINARIANS

Dearborn Animal Clinic, 6100 Johnson Drive, Shawnee Mission, 66202 /
913-722-2800

F M Gaddie, Kenneth G Huggins, and Dean E. Small, 9550 Quivira Road, Shawnee
Mission, 66215 / 913-888-3939

Highland Animal Hospital, 10160 West 119th, Shawnee Mission, 66213 /
913-451-9555

Parkway Animal Hospital, 8734 Lackman Road, Shawnee Mission, 66219 /
913-492-5300

SPORTING GOODS STORES

Center Sporting Goods, 119th & Quivira, Shawnee Mission, 66210 / 913-345-2882

K-Mart Stores, 8540 Maurer Road, Shawnee, 66219 / 913-894-1294

K-Mart Stores, 8703 Shawnee Mission Parkway, Shawnee Mission, 66202 /
913-236-6205

AUTO REPAIR

Adkins Auto Service, 24005 West 95th Street, Shawnee Mission, 66227 /
913-782-3084

Certified Automotive, 6400 Carter Street, Shawnee Mission, 66203 / 913-236-9910

D & L Auto Service, 9115 Elmhurst Drive, Shawnee Mission, 66212 / 913-649-0102
L & L Automotives, 6315 Larsen Lane, Shawnee Mission, 66203 / 913-268-6142

MEDICAL
CPC College Meadows Hospital, 14425 College Boulevard, Shawnee Mission, 66215 /
913-469-1100
Crittenton, 4601 West 109th Street, Shawnee Mission, 66211 / 913-345-1551
Shawnee Mission Medical Center, I-35 & 75th Street, Shawnee Mission, 66201 /
913-676-2000

FOR MORE INFORMATION
Shawnee Area Chamber of Commerce
10913 Johnson Drive / P.O. Box 3449
Shawnee, KS 66203
913-631-6545

Lawrence and Douglas County

Population–65,608	Elevation–822
County Population–81,798	October Temperature–57.2
County Area–457 sq. mi.	Acres in WIHA–0
Acres in CRP–5,492	

Lawrence is an upscale college town on the Kansas River in northeastern Kansas. The city is serviced by two of the great travel arteries of the Sunflower State: the Kansas River and Interstate 70. One moves vehicles and the other guides trading flocks of waterfowl. Lawrence has all the services and accommodations that a large city could offer.

The large Clinton Lake Project with its public hunting site, the Clinton Wildlife Area, is a few short miles southwest of Lawrence.

UPLAND BIRDS
Pheasant, Bobwhite Quail, Greater Prairie Chicken, Mourning Dove

WATERFOWL
Ducks & Geese

ACCOMMODATIONS
Best Western Hallmark Inn, 730 Iowa Street, Lawrence, 66044 / 913-841-6500 / Dogs allowed / $$$

Day's Inn, 2309 Iowa Street, Lawrence, 66046 / 913-843-9100 / Dogs allowed / $$$

Holiday Inn Holidome, 200 West Turnpike Access Road, Lawrence, 66044 / 913-841-7077 / Dogs allowed / $$$

Ramada Inn of Lawrence, 2222 West 6th Street, Lawrence, 66049 / 913-842-7030 / Dogs allowed / $$$

Super 8 Motel of Lawrence, 515 McDonald Drive, Lawrence, 66049 / 913-842-5721 / Dogs allowed

Travelodge, 801 Iowa Street, Lawrence, 66044 / 913-842-5100 / Dogs allowed / $$

Westminster Inn, 2525 West 6th Street, Lawrence, 66049 / 913-841-8410 / Dogs allowed / $$

CAMPGROUNDS AND RV PARKS
KOA Campgrounds of Lawrence, 1473 Highway 40, Lawrence, 66044 / 913-842-3877 / 75 sites

RESTAURANTS
Border Bandido, 1528 West 23rd Street, Lawrence, 66046 / 913-842-8861

The Jade Garden, 15th & Kasold Drive, Lawrence, 66047 / 913-843-8650

Kaspar's Bar & Grill, 3115 West 6th Street, Lawrence, 66049 / 913-843-9621

Mad Greek Restaurant, 907 Massachusetts Street, Lawrence, 66044 / 913-843-2441
Perkins Restaurant, 1711 West 23rd Street, Lawrence, 66046 / 913-842-9040
The Rivercity Smokehouse, 406 East 9th Street, Lawrence, 66044 / 913-865-3858
Scott's Brass Apple Grill & Bar, 3300 West 15th Street, Lawrence, 66049 /
    913-841-0033
Valentino's Ristorante, 544 West 23rd Street, Lawrence, 66046 / 913-749-4244
Village Inn Pancake House Restaurant, 821 Iowa Street, Lawrence, 66044 /
    913-842-3251

VETERINARIANS
Jarrett Small Animal Clinic, 2201 West 25th Street, Ste J, Lawrence, 66047 /
    913-749-2993
W W Wempe Hospital, 219 East 9th Street, Lawrence, 66044 / 913-843-4066

SPORTING GOODS STORES
Ballard's Sporting Good Outlet, 1 Riverfront Plaza, Lawrence, 66044 / 913-749-0111
Ernst & Son, 826 Massachusetts Street, Lawrence, 66044 / 913-843-2373
Francis Sporting Goods, 731 Massachusetts Street, Lawrence, 66044 / 913-843-4191
K-Mart Stores, 3106 Iowa Street, Lawrence, 66046 / 913-841-6557
K-Mart Stores, Lawrence, 66046 / 913-841-4774
Lunker Bait, Tackle & Hunting, 941 East 23rd Street, Lawrence, 66046 /
    913-842-6338
Wal-Mart, 3300 Iowa Street, Lawrence, 66046 / 913-832-8600

AUTO REPAIR
Freeman Automotive, 2858 Four Wheel Drive, Lawrence, 66047 / 913-842-8665
Gateway Auto Service, 534 Gateway Drive, Lawrence, 66049 / 913-841-5700
James Gang Automotive, 304 Locust Street, Lawrence, 66044 / 913-842-7051
Precision Automotive, 1209 East 23rd Street, Lawrence, 66046 / 913-841-0888

AIR SERVICE
Lawrence Municipal Airport, Lawrence

MEDICAL
Lawrence Memorial Hospital, 325 Maine Street, Lawrence, 66044 / 913-749-6100

FOR MORE INFORMATION
Lawrence Convention and Visitors Bureau
Visitor Information Center / PO Box 586
Lawrence, KS 66044
785-865-4499, 1-888-529-5267

Manhattan and Riley County

Population–37,737	Elevation–1,019
County Population–67,139	October Temperature–57.8
County Area–610 sq. mi.	Acres in WIHA–760
	Acres in CRP–4,539

Manhattan sits in the heart of Kansas' Flint Hills country. The area is a series of rolling, grass-covered hills and hardwood-lined creek bottoms. Manhattan sits in one of the areas of Kansas blessed with a great deal of publicly accessible hunting ground. The city is poised on the Kansas River, just south of the Tuttle Creek Lake Project and its public hunting area, Tuttle Creek Wildlife Area. The large, sprawling Ft. Riley Military Reservation (which provides public access) and Milford Lake Project with the accompanying Milford Wildlife Area, are found to the west of Manhattan. The 1997 Walk-In Hunting Area Atlas lists 2 enrolled properties totaling 760 acres.

Manhattan offers all the services and amenities of a medium-sized city. Interstate 70 is located to the south of Manhattan and is accessible by a short route on easily traveled state highway.

UPLAND BIRDS
Pheasant, Bobwhite Quail, Greater Prairie Chicken, Mourning Dove

WATERFOWL
Ducks & Geese

ACCOMMODATIONS
Best Western Continental Inn, 100 Bluemont Avenue, Manhattan, 66502 / 913-776-4771 / Dogs allowed / $$-$$$

Day's Inn, 1501 Tuttle Creek Boulevard, Manhattan, 66502 / 913-539-5391 / Dogs allowed / $$

Manhattan Holiday Inn & Holidome, 530 Richards Drive, Manhattan, 66502 / 913-539-5311 / Dogs allowed / $$$

Motel 6, 510 Tuttle Creek Boulevard, Manhattan, 66502 / 913-537-1022 / Dogs allowed / $-$$

Ramada Inn, 17 & Anderson, Manhattan, 66506 / 913-539-7531 / Dogs allowed / $$$

Super 8 Motel, 200 Tuttle Creek Boulevard, Manhattan, 66502 / 913-537-8468 / $$

CAMPGROUNDS AND RV PARKS
Tuttle Creek State Park, 913-539-7941 / 604 sites

RESTAURANTS
Bowinkle's Sports Bar & Grill, 3043 Anderson Avenue, Manhattan, 66503 / 913-776-1022

Chicago Bar & Grill, 3003 Anderson Avenue, Manhattan, 66503 / 913-537-1515
Diamond B Restaurant, 230 Riley Avenue, Manhattan, 66502 / 913-776-2002
Giorgio's Italian Restaurant, 100 Bluemont Avenue, Manhattan, 66502 /
    913-537-0444
Hibachi Hut, 608 North 12th Street, Manhattan, 66502 / 913-539-9393
La Palme French Cuisine, 3003 Anderson Avenue, Manhattan, 66503 / 913-539-9300
Panda Paradise Chinese Restaurant, 1135 Westport Drive, Manhattan, 66502 /
    913-539-2551
Raoul's Escondido, 215 Seth Childs Road, Manhattan, 66502 / 913-539-3410
Village Inn Restaurant, 204 Tuttle Creek Boulevard, Manhattan, 66502 / 913-537-3776

VETERINARIANS
Eastside Veterinary Clinic, 210 Tuttle Creek Boulevard, Manhattan, 66502 /
    913-537-3719
Little Apple Veterinary Clinic, 525 Richards Drive, Manhattan, 66502 /
    913-539-0191
Penner Veterinary Service, 2621 Marion Avenue, Manhattan, 66502 /
    913-539-8765

SPORTING GOODS STORES
Don Morton Sports, 2040 Tuttle Creek Boulevard, Manhattan, 66502 / 913-776-5551
K-Mart Stores, 401 East Poyntz Avenue, Manhattan, 66502 / 913-776-4026
Ole Mikes Shooters Supplies & Tackle, 1111 North 3rd Street, Manhattan, 66502 /
    913-537-9815
Wal-Mart, 628 Tuttle Creek Boulevard, Manhattan, 66502 / 913-776-4897

AUTO REPAIR
Abernathy Foreign & Domestic Auto Repair, 1461 Zeandale Road, Manhattan,
    66502 / 913-539-3740
C W Pierce Auto Service, 1422 Colorado Street, Manhattan, 66502 / 913-537-7438
Flint Hills Automotive, 1621 Pillsbury Drive, Manhattan, 66502 / 913-587-1807

AIR SERVICE
Manhattan Municipal Airport, 1725 South Airport Road, Manhattan, 66503 /
    913-537-0058 / Served by USAirways

MEDICAL
Saint Mary Hospital, 1823 College Avenue, Manhattan, 66502 / 913-776-3322
Memorial Hospital, 1105 Sunset Avenue, Manhattan, 66502 / 913-776-3300

FOR MORE INFORMATION
Manhattan Convention and Visitors Bureau
501 Poyntz Avenue
Manhattan, KS 66502
785-776-8829, 1-800-7590134

Marysville and Marshall County

Population–3,359	Elevation–1,154
County Population–11,705	October Temperature–55.2
County Area–903 sq. mi.	Acres in WIHA–5,352
	Acres in CRP–22,336

Marysville is located on the Kansas/Nebraska line, in the northeastern quarter of Kansas. While it is far removed from the easy access of the freeway interstate system, it does offer a wealth of services and accommodations for the traveling hunter. In addition, it does have a Wal-Mart—which means that if you need it, you can find it in Marysville.

Marysville is in Kansas' Flint Hills country, and surrounding private lands offer the promise of greater prairie chickens. Tuttle Creek Wildlife Area provides public hunting ground to the south of Marysville, in southern Marshall County. The 1997 Walk-In Hunting Area Atlas lists 18 enrolled properties totaling 5,352 acres.

UPLAND BIRDS
Pheasant, Bobwhite Quail, Greater Prairie Chicken, Mourning Dove

WATERFOWL
Ducks & Geese

ACCOMMODATIONS
Best Western Surf Motel, 2005 Center Street, Marysville, 66508 / 913-562-2354 / Dogs allowed / $$
Super 8 Motel, 1155 Pony Express Highway, Marysville, 66508 / 913-562-5588 / Dogs allowed / $$
Thunderbird Motel, US 36 West, Marysville, 66508 / 913-562-2373 / Dogs allowed / $-$$

CAMPGROUNDS AND RV PARKS
Nearest are in Manhattan

RESTAURANTS
Carolyn's Kitchen, 1806 Center Street, Marysville, 66508 / 913-562-2830
Fiesta Lagrande, 308 Center Street, Marysville, 66508 / 913-562-5395
June's Bar & Grill, 612 Broadway, Marysville, 66508 / 913-562-9817
Nine-twelve Broadway Inc, 912 Broadway, Marysville, 66508 / 913-562-3232

VETERINARIANS
Nearest are in Manhattan

Two Flint Hills hunters prospecting for chickens.

SPORTING GOODS STORES
Wal-Mart, 1115 Pony Express Highway, Marysville, 66508 / 913-562-2390

AUTO REPAIR
R and K Service, 200 North 12th Street, Marysville, 66508 / 913-562-3336

AIR SERVICE
Marysville Municipal Airport, Marysville

MEDICAL
Marysville Community Memorial Hospital, 708 North 18th, Marysville, 665008 / 758-562-2311

FOR MORE INFORMATION
Marysville Chamber of Commerce
101 North 10th Street / PO Box 16
Marysville, KS 66508
785-562-3101

St. Joseph, Missouri

Population–71,852	Elevation–813
County Population–83,083	County Area–410 sq. miles

While not within the state of Kansas, St. Joseph, Missouri, is listed because of its importance as a service center in this border area of the state. Hunters may readily avail themselves of what St. Joseph has to offer in terms of accommodations and amenities and then head west, across the Missouri River, to chase the game birds of Kansas. St. Joseph is strategically located under one of the great waterfowling flyways, and seasonally large flocks of migrating birds funnel up and down the Missouri. The Squaw Creek National Wildlife Refuge is an important snow and blue goose hunting area and is located across the border in Missouri, northwest of St. Joseph.

ACCOMMODATIONS

Day's Inn, 4312 Frederick Avenue, St. Joseph, 64506 / 800-325-2525 / Dogs allowed / $$

Drury Inns, I-29 Frederick 6, St. Joseph, MO 64506 / 816-364-4700 / Dogs allowed / $$-$$$

Holiday Inn St. Joseph-Downtown, 102 South 3rd Street, St. Joseph, MO 64501 / 816-279-8000 / Dogs allowed / $$$

Ramada Inn, 4016 Frederick Avenue, St. Joseph, MO 64506 / 816-233-6192 / Dogs allowed / $$

Super 8 Motel of St. Joseph, 4024 Frederick Avenue, St. Joseph, MO 64506 / 816-364-3031 / Dogs allowed / $$

CAMPGROUNDS AND RV PARKS

A-Ok Campground, RR 3, St. Joseph, MO 64505 / 816-324-4263

Beacon RV, 822 South Belt Highway, St. Joseph, MO 64507 / 816-279-5417

RESTAURANTS

China House Restaurant, 2604 North Belt Highway, St. Joseph, MO 64506 / 816-233-9116

Dantes Pizza Pasta & Cappuccino, 809 Francis Street, St. Joseph, MO 64501 / 816-233-5000

Denny's Restaurant, 4015 Frederick Avenue, St. Joseph, MO 64506 / 816-232-1369

Frederick Inn Steakhouse, 1627 Frederick Avenue, St. Joseph, MO 64501 / 816-364-5151

Palma's Authentic Mexican Restaurant, 2715 North Belt Highway, St. Joseph, MO 64506 / 816-279-9445

Perkins Restaurant, 3901 Frederick Avenue, St. Joseph, MO 64506 / 816-364-6188

Sunset Grill, 4012 River Road, St. Joseph, MO 64505 / 816-364-6500

Valentino's, 2204 North Belt Highway, St. Joseph, MO 64506 / 816-233-7725

VETERINARIANS

Countryside Veterinary Clinic, 5025 Frederick Avenue, St. Joseph, MO 64506 /
816-233-2005

Twin Pines Veterinary Clinic Inc, 6108 North 71 Highway, St. Joseph, MO 64506 /
816-364-1089

SPORTING GOODS STORES

Ed's Sporting Goods, 2327-a North Belt Highway, St. Joseph, MO 64506 /
816-232-0587

K-Mart Stores, 2901 North Belt Highway, St. Joseph, MO 64506 / 816-233-5101

K-Mart Stores, US 169 & Pear Street, St. Joseph, MO 64503 / 816-364-3499

Wal-Mart Supercenter, 4201 North Belt Highway, St. Joseph, MO 64506 /
816-390-8855

AUTO REPAIR

Advanced Auto Service, 3306 Chippewa Lane, St. Joseph, MO 64503 / 816-364-3601

Benitz Service Center, 902 Faraon Street, St. Joseph, MO 64501 / 816-233-8781

Hines Auto & Wrecking Service, 1211 Wilton Drive, St. Joseph, MO 64504 /
816-238-5641

Keith Auto Service, 528 West Market Street, St. Joseph, MO 64505 / 816-279-7550

South Park Auto Body, 2827 South 21st Street, St. Joseph, MO 64503 / 816-233-
7593

AIR SERVICE

St. Joseph-Rosecran Memorial Airport, St. Joseph, MO

MEDICAL

Heartland Health System, 5325 Faraon Street, St. Joseph, MO 64506 / 816-271-6563

North Hills of St. Joseph, 1202 Village Drive, St. Joseph, MO 64506 / 816-233-9159

FOR MORE INFORMATION

St. Joseph Convention and Visitors Bureau
109 South Fourth Street / PO Box 445
St. Joseph, MO 64502
816-233-6688, 1-800-785-0360

Topeka and Shawnee County

Population–119,883	Elevation–940
County Population–160,976	October Temperature–56.2
County Area–550 sq. mi.	Acres in WIHA–0
	Acres in CRP–6,495

Topeka is the capital of the state of Kansas, and befitting its station it hosts traveling bird hunters to a multitude of choices in accommodations and services. The Region 2 offices of the Kansas Department of Wildlife and Parks are located in Topeka; any necessary licenses and permits are available there.

The Kansas River flows north of the city, and several public hunting areas are available in close proximity. In Shawnee County is located Shawnee State Fishing Lake; outside of the county but still close at hand are Perry Lake Project with the Perry Wildlife Area and Clinton Lake Project with the Clinton Wildlife Area. In addition, Pomona Lake Project and Osage State Fishing Lake and Wildlife Area offer public hunting opportunities to the south in Osage County.

UPLAND BIRDS
Pheasant, Bobwhite Quail,
Greater Prairie Chicken, Mourning Dove

WATERFOWL
Ducks & Geese

ACCOMMODATIONS

Best Western Meadow Acres Motel, 2950 SW Topeka Boulevard, Topeka, 66611 / 913-267-1681 / Dogs allowed / $$

Day's Inn of Topeka, 1510 SW Wanamaker Road, Topeka, 66604 / 913-272-8538 / Dogs allowed / $$

Fairfield Inn By Marriott, 1530 SW Westport Drive, Topeka, 66604 / 913-273-6800 / Dogs allowed / $$-$$$

Holiday Inn West Holidome, 605 SW Fairlawn Road, Topeka, 66606 / 913-272-8040 / Dogs allowed / $$$

Liberty Inn, 3839 SW Topeka Boulevard, Topeka, 66609 / 913-266-4700 / Dogs allowed / $$

Motel 6, 709 SW Fairlawn Road, Topeka, 66606 / 913-272-8283 / Dogs allowed / $

Plaza Inn, 3802 SW Topeka Boulevard, Topeka, 66609 / 913-266-8880 / Dogs allowed / $$

Super 8 Motel, 5968 SW 10th, Topeka, 66604 / 913-273-5100 / Dogs allowed / $$

*The bird season begins:
a hunter holds up
a mourning dove.*

CAMPGROUNDS AND RV PARKS

Lake Shawnee Camping Area, 3435 SE East Edge Road, Topeka, 66609 / 913-267-1859 / 154 sites

KOA of Topeka, RR1, Grantville, 66429 / 913-246-3419, 1-800-KOA-8717 / 72 sites

RESTAURANTS

Aboud's at Western Hills, 8533 SW 21st Street, Topeka, 66615 / 913-478-9290

Blind Tiger Brewery & Restaurant, 417 SW 37th Street, Topeka, 66611 / 913-267-2739

Denny's of Topeka, 1500 SW Wanamaker Road and 3210 SW Topeka Blvd, Topeka

Empress of China, 2920 South Kansas Avenue, Topeka, 66611 / 913-266-5222

Giorgio's Italian Restaurant, 425 SW 30th Street, Topeka, 66611 / 913-266-2772

Heidelberger Cafe, 1409 NW Topeka Boulevard, Topeka, 66608 / 913-233-9065

Perkins Restaurant, 1720 SW Wanamaker Road, Topeka, 66604 / 913-273-0300

Rosa's Mexican Restaurant, 2025 SE California Avenue, Topeka, 66607 /
913-233-9842
Steak Escape, 1801 SW Wanamaker Road, Topeka, 66604 / 913-271-5733
The Downtowner, 119 SE 6th Avenue, Topeka, 66603 / 913-232-5775

VETERINARIANS

Carbondale Pet Clinic, 416 SW Topeka Boulevard, Topeka, 66603 / 913-836-7212
Michael T Cavanaugh and Robert P Trupp, 2147 SW Westport Drive, Topeka, 66614 /
913-272-3333
Topeka Veterinary Hospital, 5800 SW 21st Street, Topeka, 66604 / 913-272-3555
Westport Animal Clinic, 2800 SW Wanamaker Road, Ste 120, Topeka, 66614 /
913-272-2520

SPORTING GOODS STORES

Asay's Sportsman's Store, 834 SE Quincy Street, Topeka, 66612 / 913-354-7766
K-Mart Stores, 2240 NW Tyler Street, Topeka, 66608 / 913-233-1110
Reffner's Sporting Goods, West Ridge Mall, Topeka, 66604 / 913-271-1550
Rusty's Outdoor Sports, 2139 SW Fairlawn Plaza Drive, Topeka, 66614 /
913-273-9520
Topeka Shooter's Supply, 1301 South Kansas Avenue, Topeka, 66612 /
913-357-7319
Wal-Mart, 1301 SW 37th Street, Topeka, 66611 / 913-266-5757
Wal-Mart Discount Cities, US Highway 75, Holton, 66436 / 913-364-4619

AUTO REPAIR

A Auto Company, 1821 NE Grantville Road, Topeka, 66608 / 913-354-4565
Gros Auto Repair, 1001 NW Harrison Street, Topeka, 66608 / 913-232-4766
Keller Auto Service, 331 NW Reo Street, Topeka, 66617 / 913-232-3737
Whitey''s Auto Repair, 400 SE 45th Street, Topeka, 66609 / 913-862-0802

AIR SERVICE

Metro Topeka Airport Authority, 6700 SW Topeka Boulevard, Topeka, 66619 /
913-862-9250 / Served by USAirways

MEDICAL

Saint Francis Hospital & Medical Center, 1700 SW 7th Street, Topeka, 66606 /
913-295-8000
Stormont Vail Regional Medical Center, 1500 SW 10th Avenue, Topeka, 66604 /
913-354-6000
Topeka State Hospital, Topeka, 66604 / 913-296-4436

FOR MORE INFORMATION

Topeka Convention and Visitors Bureau
1275 SW Topeka Boulevard
Topeka, KS 66612
785-234-1030, 1-800-235-1030

Region 3

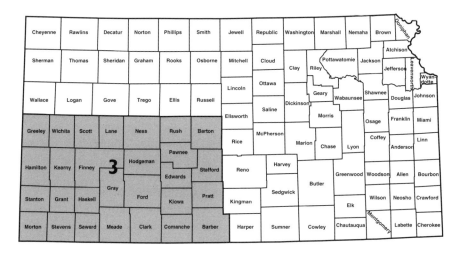

Region 3 contains the range of the lesser prairie chicken. The birds are found on two public huntings areas: the 108,000-acre Cimarron National Grasslands in the extreme southwestern corner of the region, and the 4,457-acre Pratt Sandhills Wildlife Area near the town of Pratt. Additionally, in this characteristically warmer and drier area of Kansas, scaled quail are present. These birds add an unusual dimension to a quail hunt, and when mixed with bobwhite make for a unique mixed bag.

The ring-necked pheasant is also found in Region 3, although its range is limited and its population density sporadic. The traditional stronghold of pheasants is found beginning in the eastern part of Region 3 and extending toward north central Kansas.

Since the beginning of sandhill crane hunting in Kansas, the sport has taken off. Only a portion of the state is open to the hunting of these birds, and that area falls within the boundaries of Region 3. As well as being important for waterfowl, the Cheyenne Bottoms Wildlife Area and the Quivira National Wildlife Refuge provides the roosting sites that hold sandhill crane populations within the area.

Mourning dove and waterfowl are a mainstay here. Depending upon the availability of feed and water, birds can be found throughout the region. Turkeys are found in suitable habitat throughout the region.

Area Hunting Guides

James's Guide Service
James E. Burnett
303 Point Rock, PO Box 1159
Elkhart, KS 67950
Business & Home 405-696-4735

Longneck Sportsman Club
Kenny Smith
319 NE 20th Avenue
Great Bend, KS 67530
Business & Home 316-792-1852

Wild Horse Creek Guide Service
Tommy B. Haynes
324 West Broadway, PO Box 403
Macksville, KS 67557
Business & Home 316-348-3902

Area Hunting Preserves

Pheasant Creek
Raymond Dienst, Jr.
PO Box 209
Lakin, KS 67860
316-355-7118

Pheasants Unlimited, Inc.
7589 South Road B
Ulysses, KS 67880
316-356-3737

Mid America Pheasant
11565 East Plymell Road
Pierceville, KS 67868
316-335-5522

Sullivan Sand & Sage
3019 North Road G
Ulysses, KS 67880
316-356-3924

Pheasants Galore Hunting Service
HC 1, Box 5
Sublette, KS 67877
316-675-8418

Region 3
Bobwhite Quail Distribution

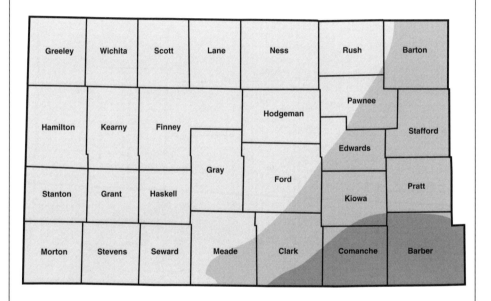

Good to Excellent Distribution

Fair to Good Distribution

Locally Good Distribution

Region 3
Lesser Prairie Chicken Distribution

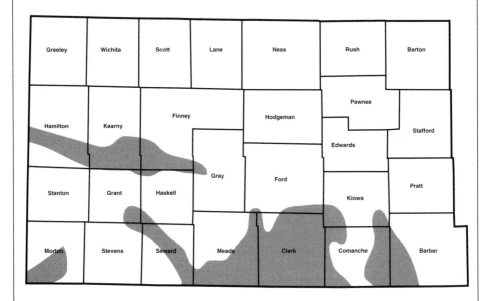

■ **Lesser Prairie Chicken Distribution**

Region 3
Mourning Dove Distribution

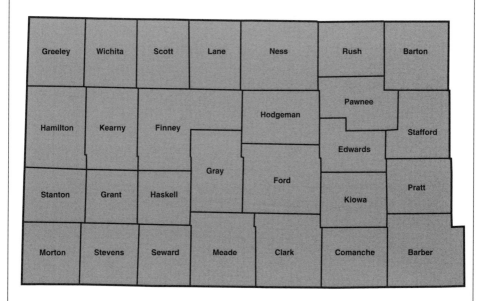

Mourning Dove Distribution

Region 3
Pheasant Distribution

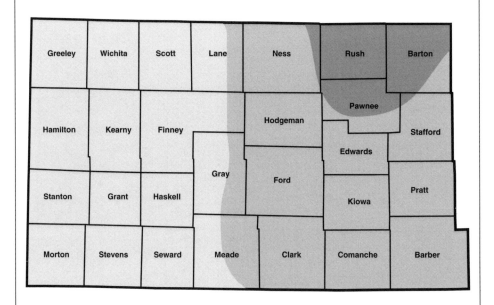

■	**Good to Excellent Distribution**
■	**Fair to Good Distribution**
□	**Locally Good Distribution**

Region 3
Scaled Quail Distribution

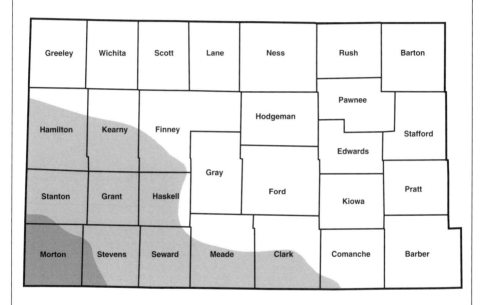

Primary Distribution   Secondary Distribution

Region 3
Sandhill Crane Hunting Area

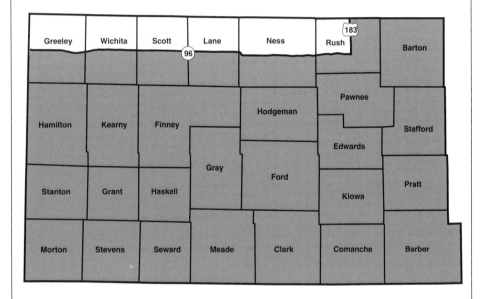

Legal Sandhill Crane Hunting Area

Region 3
Turkey Distribution

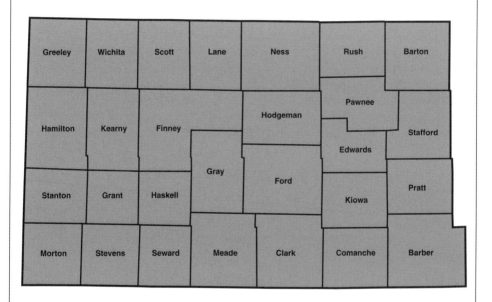

Turkey Distribution

Dodge City and Ford County

Population–21,129	Elevation–2,496
County Population–27,463	October Temperature–56.1
County Area–1,099 sq. mi.	Acres in WIHA–3,072
	Acres in CRP–49,329

The name Dodge City evokes images of cowboys and lawmen in a time gone by. The wild cowtown of the past has evolved into a modern city with a wealth of services and accommodations for a traveling bird shooter. The Region 3 Office of the Kansas Department of Wildlife and Parks is located in the southeastern section of town. There, a hunter can arrange for any necessary licenses and permits.

The Hain Wildlife Area is found to the northeast of Dodge City. Ford County lies within the open area for sandhill crane hunting. Shooting opportunities exist where cranes can be observed feeding in agricultural fields, and where permission to hunt can be obtained. The 1997 Walk-In Hunting Area Atlas lists 9 enrolled properties totaling 3,072 acres.

UPLAND BIRDS
Pheasant, Bobwhite Quail, Lesser Prairie Chicken, Mourning Dove, Sandhill Crane

WATERFOWL
Ducks & Geese

ACCOMMODATIONS
Astro Motel, 2200 West Wyatt Earp Boulevard, Dodge City, 67801 / 316-227-8146 / Dogs allowed / $-$$

Best Western Silver Spur Lodge, 1510 West Wyatt Earp Boulevard, Dodge City, 67801 / 316-227-2125 / Dogs allowed / $$

Dodge House Inn, 2408 West Wyatt Earp Boulevard, Dodge City, 67801 / 316-225-9900 / Dogs allowed / $-$$$

Econo Lodge Of Dodge City, 1610 West Wyatt Earp Boulevard, Dodge City, 67801 / 316-225-0231 / Dogs allowed / $$

Super 8 Motel, 1708 West Wyatt Earp Boulevard, Dodge City, 67801 / 316-225-3924 / Dogs allowed / $$

CAMPGROUNDS AND RV PARKS
Gunsmoke Campground, West Highway 50, Dodge City, 67801 / 316-227-8247 / 110 sites

RESTAURANTS
Casa Alvarez, 1701 West Wyatt Earp Boulevard, Dodge City, 67801 / 316-225-7164
Denny's Restaurant, 1005 West Wyatt Earp Boulevard, Dodge City, 67801 /
316-225-3226
Golden Corral Family Steak House, 700 West Wyatt Earp Boulevard, Dodge City,
67801 / 316-227-7455
Golden Pancake House, 2110 East Wyatt Earp Boulevard, Dodge City, 67801 /
316-227-6196
Hong Kong Restaurant, 2100 West Wyatt Earp Boulevard, Dodge City, 67801 /
316-227-7474
Los Laguneros, 810 East Wyatt Earp Boulevard, Dodge City, 67801 / 316-227-7517
Saigon Market, 1202 East Wyatt Earp Boulevard, Dodge City, 67801 / 316-225-9099
Taqueria Mexico, 1010 East Wyatt Earp Boulevard, Dodge City, 67801 /
316-227-2688

VETERINARIANS
JH Brands, Ft. Dodge Road, Dodge City, 67801 / 316-225-0443
Veterinary Hospital, 1007 East Trail Street, Dodge City, 67801 / 316-227-2751

SPORTING GOODS STORES
Wal-Mart, 2101 North 14th Avenue, Dodge City, 67801 / 316-225-3917

AUTO REPAIR
Cosmic Auto Repair, 1112 East Trail Street, Dodge City, 67801 / 316-227-2402
Heiland Auto Service, 112 Forrest Avenue, Dodge City, 67801 / 316-225-4716
Knight's Auto Repair, 2702 Colleen Avenue, Dodge City, 67801 / 316-225-2483
Sammons Auto Repair, 813 South 2nd Avenue, Dodge City, 67801 / 316-225-6528

AIR SERVICE
Dodge City Regional Airport, Dodge City / Served by USAirways
Wilroads Gardens Airport, Dodge City

MEDICAL
Western Plains Regional Hospital, 3001 Avenue A, Dodge City, 67801 / 316-225-8400

FOR MORE INFORMATION
Dodge City Convention and Visitors Bureau
400 West Wyatt Earp Boulevard / PO Box 1474
Dodge City, KS 67801
316-225-8186/ 1-800-653-9378

Elkhart and Morton County

Population–2,318	Elevation–3,600
County Population–3,480	October Temperature–55.7
County Area–730 sq. mi.	Acres in WIHA–12,720
	Acres in CRP–85,964

Elkhart is the gateway to the Cimarron National Grasslands, the largest public hunting area within the state of Kansas. Elkhart exhibits a small town charm, but still offers an acceptable range of accommodations and services. The Cimarron Grasslands Headquarters office is found heading out of town on Highway 56. A visit to the headquarters will help a visiting hunter acquaint himself with the Grasslands. Maps, printed literature, and books are available to help interested parties acquaint themselves with the history, flora, and fauna of this interesting piece of public ground.

The Cimarron Grasslands is one of two public areas in the state where lesser prairie chickens are available, Pratt Sandhills Wildlife Area being the other. Scaled quail are also found on the Grasslands, high up on the rolling grass flats south of the Cimarron River. Bobwhite quail are much more numerous and found along the river bottoms. While pheasants would be an oddity on the Grasslands themselves, they are found on surrounding private lands that are farmed and provide suitable habitat for them. Early season mourning doves frequent the many water sources dotting the Grasslands.

The 1997 Walk-In Hunting Area Atlas lists 29 enrolled properties totaling 12,720 acres.

UPLAND BIRDS
Pheasant, Bobwhite Quail, Scaled Quail, Lesser Prairie Chicken, Mourning Dove, Sandhill Crane

WATERFOWL
Ducks & Geese

ACCOMMODATIONS
El Rancho Motel, Highway 56 East, Elkhart, 67950 / 316-697-2117
Elkhart Motel, 329 Morton-downtown, Elkhart, 67950 / 316-697-2168

CAMPGROUNDS AND RV PARKS
Nearest is in Liberal

RESTAURANTS
Downtown Restaurant, 329 Morton, Elkhart, 67950 / 316-697-9895
The Lunch Box, 350 Morton Street, Elkhart, 67950 / 316-697-4644
Spangles Restaurant, 634 Highway 56, Elkhart, 67950 / 316-697-9886
The Trolley Car, 420 Morton, Elkhart, 67950 / 316-697-4755

*Ed Anderson checks out one of the 110 guzzlers
on the Cimarron National Grasslands.*

VETERINARIANS
Gene Berghaus, 752 Border Avenue, Elkhart, 67950 / 316-697-2089
Ellinwood Veterinary Clinic, 312 West 7th Street, Ellinwood, 67526 / 316-564-2730

SPORTING GOODS STORES
Nearest are in Liberal

AUTO REPAIR
Nearest is in Liberal

AIR SERVICE
Elkhart Airport, east of Elkhart, Elkhart, 67950 / 316-697-9803

MEDICAL
Morton County Hospital, 445 Hilltop, Elkhart, 67950 / 316-697-2141

FOR MORE INFORMATION
Elkhart Chamber of Commerce
316-697-4600

Garden City and Finney County

Population–24,097	Elevation–2,830
County Population–33,070	October Temperature–55
County Area–1,300 sq. mi.	Acres in WIHA–1,740
	Acres in CRP–57,232

In a land of wide open spaces and broad vistas, Garden City appears like the Emerald City on the horizon. Garden City sits on the Arkansas River and provides an important agricultural and livestock service center; the city is large and provides a wealth of accommodations and services. Finney County contains three areas managed for public hunting by the Department of Wildlife and Parks: Concannon Wildlife Area is 18 miles east of Garden City; the Finney Game Refuge is south of Garden City; and Finney State Lake and Wildlife Area is in the northeastern corner of the county. The entire county is open to sandhill crane hunting in season. The 1997 Walk-In Hunting Area Atlas lists 4 enrolled properties totaling 1,740 acres.

UPLAND BIRDS
Pheasant, Bobwhite Quail, Scaled Quail, Lesser Prairie Chicken, Mourning Dove, Sandhill Crane

WATERFOWL
Ducks & Geese

ACCOMMODATIONS
Best Western Red Baron Motor Inn, East Highway 50, Garden City, 67846 / 316-275-4164 / Dogs allowed / $$

Budget Host Village Inn, 123 Honeybee Ct, Garden City, 67846 / 316-275-0677 / Dogs allowed / $$

Continental Inn, 1408 Buffalo Jones Avenue, Garden City, 67846 / 316-276-7691 / Dogs allowed / $-$$

Garden City Plaza Inn, 1911 East Kansas Avenue, Garden City, 67846 / 316-275-7471 / Dogs allowed / $$$

National 9 Inn, 1502 East Fulton, Garden City, 67846 / 316-276-2394 / Dogs allowed / $$

Winchester Inn, 1818 Commanche Drive, Garden City, 67846 / 316-275-5095 / Dogs allowed / $-$$

CAMPGROUNDS AND RV PARKS
KOA Kampgrounds, East Highway 50, Garden City, 67846 / 316-276-8741 / 86 sites

RESTAURANTS

Cafe Melody, 1917 Buffalo Jones Avenue, Garden City, 67846 / 316-276-3959
Denny's Restaurant, 1505 East Kansas Avenue, Garden City, 67846 / 316-275-7608
Grain Bin Supper Club, 1301 East Fulton Street, Garden City, 67846 / 316-275-5954
La Hacienda Restaurant, 1601 West Mary Street, Garden City, 67846 / 316-275-0635
Pho Hoa One Restaurant, 107 North Jenny Barker Road, Garden City, 67846 /
    316-276-3393
Ranch Steak House & Saloon, 5730 East Mansfield Road, Garden City, 67846 /
    316-276-6652
Workman Cafe, 812 East Fulton Street, Garden City, 67846 / 316-276-4141

VETERINARIANS

Nearest are in Dodge City, Scott City, Syracuse, and Ulysses

SPORTING GOODS STORES

The Good Sport, 220 North Main Street, Garden City, 67846 / 316-276-8600
R T Sporting Goods Inc, 306 North Main Street, Garden City, 67846 / 316-275-5507
Wal-Mart, 2310 East Kansas Avenue, Garden City, 67846 / 316-275-0775

AUTO REPAIR

A & B Auto Service, 2708 North 11th Street, Garden City, 67846 / 316-276-7972
Daniel's Repair Shop, 203 East Hillside Avenue, Garden City, 67846 / 316-275-6713
Luis's Auto Repair, 107 South 13th Street, Garden City, 67846 / 316-276-6390
Ted Auto Repair, 3230 West Jones Avenue, Garden City, 67846 / 316-277-2248

AIR SERVICE

Garden City Regional Airport, Garden City / Served by USAirways
Seng Airport, Garden City

MEDICAL

St. Catherine's Medical Hospital, 410 East Walnut, Garden City, 67846 / 316-272-2222

FOR MORE INFORMATION

Garden City Area Chamber of Commerce
1511 East Fulton Terrace
Garden City, KS 67846-6165
316-276-3264

Great Bend and Barton County

Population–15,427	Elevation–1,843
County Population–29,382	October Temperature–53.3
County Area–894 sq. mi.	Acres in WIHA–2,640
	Acres in CRP–25,975

Great Bend is named for the sweeping bend in the channel of the Arkansas River. The world-famous Cheyenne Bottoms Wildlife Area is a few miles northeast of town. This site provides excellent hunting in season for ducks, geese, and sandhill cranes. In addition, pheasants are also available on the wildlife area for a hunter willing to do some walking. The 1997 Walk-In Hunting Area Atlas lists 8 enrolled properties totaling 2,640 acres. Visiting waterfowlers can find a full range of services in Great Bend. The area Wal-Mart can assist hunters needing licenses or other hunting equipment. Sandhill crane permits are available through the personnel at Cheyenne Bottoms.

UPLAND BIRDS
Pheasant, Bobwhite Quail, Greater Prairie Chicken, Mourning Dove, Sandhill Crane

WATERFOWL
Ducks & Geese

ACCOMMODATIONS
Best Western Angus Inn, 2920 10th Street, Great Bend, 67530 / 316-792-3541 / Dogs allowed / $$-$$$

Holiday Inn, 3017 West 10th Street, Great Bend, 67530, 800-528-1234 / Dogs allowed/ $$

Inn-4-Less, 4701 10th Street, Great Bend, 67530 / 316-792-8235 / Dogs allowed / $-$$

Super 8 Motel Of Great Bend, 3500 10th Street, Great Bend, 67530 / 316-793-8486 / Dogs allowed

Traveler's Budget Inn, 4200 10th Street, Great Bend, 67530 / 316-793-5448 / Dogs allowed / $

CAMPGROUNDS AND RV PARKS
Colossal Wash Systems, 835 East 10th, Great Bend, 67530 / 316-792-1483

RESTAURANTS
Granny's Kitchen, 925 10th Street, Great Bend, 67530 / 316-792-8344

The Pioneer Inn, 3322-a Railroad Avenue, Great Bend, 67530 / 316-793-5505

Sams Famous Mexican Restaurant, North Highway 281, Great Bend, 67530 / 316-793-5519
Twelfth Street Steak House, 12th & Main, Great Bend, 67530 / 316-793-6343
Victorian Garden, 4807 10th Street, Great Bend, 67530 / 316-792-6300
Wallace Ralph Buffet & Restaurant, 1203 Main Street, Great Bend, 67530 / 316-793-6162

VETERINARIANS
Animal Medical Center, 622 McKinley Street, Great Bend, 67530 / 316-792-1265
Ark Valley Veterinary Hospital, 1205 South Patton Road, Great Bend, 67530 / 316-793-5457
Countryside Veterinary Associates, 2900 Main Street, Great Bend, 67530 / 316-792-2551

SPORTING GOODS STORES
Action Sports Inc, 1915 Lakin Avenue, Great Bend, 67530 / 316-792-2538
Wal-Mart, 3503 10th Street, Great Bend, 67530 / 316-792-3632

AUTO REPAIR
DC's Auto Repair, 1410 Williams Street, Great Bend, 67530 / 316-793-9117
Hertel's Automotive Service & Repair Inc, 912 MacArthur Road, Great Bend, 67530 / 316-792-5105
Jenkins Automotive, 1720 Main Street, Great Bend, 67530 / 316-793-7681
Steve's Auto Repair, 151 South US Highway 281, Great Bend, 67530 / 316-792-3851

AIR SERVICE
Button Airport, Great Bend
Great Bend Municipal Airport, Great Bend / Served by USAirways

MEDICAL
Central Kansas Medical Center, 3515 Broadway Avenue, Great Bend, 67530 / 316-792-2511

FOR MORE INFORMATION
Great Bend Chamber of Commerce
1307 Williams / PO Box 400
Great Bend, KS 67530-0400
316-792-2401

Greensburg and Kiowa County

Population–1,792	Elevation–2,235
County Population–3,660	October Temperature–55.3
County Area–722 sq. mi.	Acres in WIHA–7,133
	Acres in CRP–54,835

Greensburg sits to the west of Pratt on Highway 54. The area is sparsely populated and the town offers a minimum of amenities. Two public hunting areas sit just over the county line, in Pratt County. The Pratt Sandhills Wildlife Area offers one of the few chances in the state for lesser prairie chickens and also provides an opportunity for other upland game birds. The Texas Lake Wildlife Area, in addition to hosting upland game birds, also has waterfowl hunting available. The 1997 Walk-In Hunting Area Atlas lists 19 enrolled properties totaling 7,133 acres.

UPLAND BIRDS
Pheasant, Bobwhite Quail, Lesser Prairie Chicken, Mourning Dove, Sandhill Crane

WATERFOWL
Ducks & Geese

ACCOMMODATIONS
Best Western J-Hawk Motel, 515 West Kansas Avenue, Greensburg, 67054 / 316-723-2121 / Dogs allowed / $$
Kansan Inn, 800 East Kansas Avenue, Greensburg, 67054 / 316-723-2141 / Dogs allowed / $-$$

CAMPGROUNDS AND RV PARKS
Pleasant View Motel and RV Park, 800 West Kansas Avenue, Greensburg, 67054 / 316-723-2105 / 15 sites

RESTAURANTS
Dave's Pizza Oven, 213 West Kansas Avenue, Greensburg, 67054 / 316-723-2801
Kansan Restaurant, 800 East Kansas Avenue, Greensburg, 67054 / 316-723-3092

VETERINARIANS
Robert G Skaggs, 513 North Maple Street, Greensburg, 67054 / 316-723-2462

SPORTING GOODS STORES
Nearest are in Dodge City and Pratt

A pair of shorthairs pin a single.

AUTO REPAIR
Kimble Auto Repair, 221 West Kansas Avenue, Greensburg, 67054 / 316-723-2742
LE Schmidt Service, 320 Scott Street, Greensburg, 67054 / 316-723-2892

AIR SERVICE
Greensburg Airport, 239 South Main Street, Greensburg, 67054 / 316-723-2751

MEDICAL
Kiowa County Memorial Hospital, 501 South Walnut, Greensburg

FOR MORE INFORMATION
Greensburg Chamber of Commerce
315 South Sycamore
Greensburg, KS 67054
316-723-2261

Larned and Pawnee County

Population–4,490	Elevation–2,002
County Population–7,555	October Temperature–57.1
County Area–754 sq. mi.	Acres in WIHA–14,295
	Acres in CRP–58,575

The town of Larned sits on the northern shore of the Arkansas River. The area consists of sparsely populated agricultural lands. Great Bend sits to the northeast. No managed public hunting areas exist within the County. However, the 1997 Walk-In Hunting Area Atlas, published by the Department of Wildlife and Parks, lists 51 different enrolled sites totaling 14,295.5 acres. Pawnee County is open to the hunting of sandhill cranes.

The town offers a minimum of services and accommodations. Great Bend, to the northeast, is a large city and contains a multitude of services.

UPLAND BIRDS
Pheasant, Bobwhite Quail, Mourning Dove, Sandhill Crane

WATERFOWL
Ducks & Geese

ACCOMMODATIONS
Best Western Townsman Inn, 123 East 14th Street, Larned, 67550 / 316-285-3114 / Dogs allowed / $$
Country Inn Motel, 135 East 14th Street, Larned, 67550 / 316-285-3216

CAMPGROUNDS AND RV PARKS
Larned Village Campground / 316-285-3261 / 24 sites

RESTAURANTS
The Chicken House, 415 West 14th Street, Larned, 67550 / 316-285-2644
Don-do Restaurant, 124 East 14th Street, Larned, 67550 / 316-285-6431
Doucette International Buffet, 628 West 7th Street, Larned, 67550 / 316-285-2268
Harvest Inn Restaurant & Grain Club, 718 Fry Street, Larned, 67550 / 316-285-3870
Paco's, 410 Main Street, Larned, 67550 / 316-285-3515

VETERINARIANS
Apley Veterinary Clinic, North Highway 156, Larned, 67550 / 316-285-3153

SPORTING GOODS STORES
Nearest are in Great Bend

Auto Repair
Nearest is in Great Bend

Air Service
Larned-Pawnee County Airport, Larned

Medical
Central Kansas Medical Center, 923 Carroll, Larned, 67550 / 316-285-3161

For More Information
Larned Area Chamber of Commerce
502 Broadway / PO Box 240
Larned, KS 67550
316-285-6916

Liberal and Seward County

Population–16,573	Elevation–2,839
County Population–18,743	October Temperature–56.9
County Area–640 sq. mi.	Acres in WIHA–880
	Acres in CRP–42,608

Liberal sits on the Oklahoma border in the extreme southwestern part of Kansas. As such, it is the access point where many hunters traveling from the south or southwest first access the Sunflower State. Liberal can provide a full range of services and accommodations for those wishing to hunt from Liberal as a base camp. There are no managed public wildlife areas within the county. The 1997 Kansas Walk-In Hunter Area Atlas lists 4 land holdings enrolled in the WIHA program, totaling 880 acres.

UPLAND BIRDS
Pheasant, Bobwhite Quail, Scaled Quail, Lesser Prairie Chicken, Mourning Dove, Sandhill Crane

WATERFOWL
Ducks & Geese

ACCOMMODATIONS
Best Western La Fonda Motel, 229 West Pancake Boulevard, Liberal, 67901 / 316-624-5601 / Dogs allowed / $$

Cimarron Inn, Highway 54 East, Liberal, 67901 / 316-624-6203 / Dogs allowed / $$

Liberal Inn, 603 East Pancake Boulevard, Liberal, 67901 / 316-624-7254 / Dogs allowed / $$

Liberal Super 8 Motel, 747 East Pancake Boulevard, Liberal, 67901 / 316-624-8880 / $$

Thunderbird Inn, 2100 North Highway 83, Liberal, 67901 / 316-624-7271 / Dogs allowed / $-$$

CAMPGROUNDS AND RV PARKS
B & B Overnite Park, Highway 54 West, Liberal, 67901 / 316-624-5581 / 38 sites

RESTAURANTS
Branding Iron Restaurant & Club, 603 East Pancake Boulevard, Liberal, 67901 / 316-624-7254

Casa Alvarez, 1010 South Kansas Avenue Ste B10, Liberal, 67901 / 316-624-5205

Denny's Restaurant, 741 East Pancake Boulevard, Liberal, 67901 / 316-624-3906

Golden Corral Family Steak House, 539 East Pancake Boulevard, Liberal, 67901 / 316-624-9589

Mandarin Restaurant, 300 East Pancake Boulevard, Liberal, 67901 / 316-624-1222
Mister Breakfast, 150 West Pancake Boulevard, Liberal, 67901 / 316-624-0458

VETERINARIANS
Liberal Animal Hospital, 730 South Kansas Avenue, Liberal, 67901 / 316-624-8461

SPORTING GOODS STORES
Wal-Mart, 1601 North Kansas Avenue, Liberal, 67901 / 316-624-0106

AUTO REPAIR
Amigo Auto Repair, 314 South Clay Avenue, Liberal, 67901 / 316-624-2002
Chrisenberry's Automotive Service, 16 East 5th Street, Liberal, 67901 /
   316-626-4613

AIR SERVICE
Liberal Municipal Airport, Liberal

MEDICAL
Southwest Medical Center, 15th and Persian, Liberal, 67905 / 316-624-1651

FOR MORE INFORMATION
Liberal Convention and Tourism Bureau
1 Yellow Brick Road / PO Box 2257
Liberal, KS 67905
316-626-0170 or 1-800-542-3725

Ness City and Ness County

Population–1,724	Elevation–2,200
County Population–4,033	October Temperature–57.2
County Area–1,075 sq. mi.	Acres in WIHA–7,933
	Acres in CRP–39,200

Ness City lies in the middle of Kansas' wheat producing heartland. Settlements are few and far between; Ness City offers a minimum amount of amenities. There are no managed public hunting wildlife areas found within the county. The 1997 Walk-In Hunting Area Atlas lists 25 enrolled properties totaling 7,933 acres. The southern portion of Ness County falls within the open area for sandhill crane hunting.

UPLAND BIRDS
Pheasant, Bobwhite Quail, Mourning Dove, Sandhill Crane

WATERFOWL
Ducks & Geese

ACCOMMODATIONS
Derrick Inn, East Highway 96, Ness City, 67560, 913-798-3617 / Dogs allowed / $$

CAMPGROUNDS AND RV PARKS
Nearest are in Great Bend, Dodge City, and Hays (see Region 1)

RESTAURANTS
Balloons West, 201 East Sycamore Street, Ness City, 67560 / 913-798-3701
Derrick Inn Motel & Restaurant, East Highway 96, Ness City, 67560 /
913-798-3617
Oriental Delight, 502 East Main Street, Ness City, 67560 / 913-798-2642

VETERINARIANS
Nearest are in Great Bend, Dodge City, and Hays (see Region 1)

SPORTING GOODS STORES
Werth Sport's Station, 202 East Sycamore Street, Ness City, 67560 / 913-798-3290

AUTO REPAIR
Earl's Service Center, K-96 & 5th, Ness City, 67560 / 913-798-2271
Joe's A-1 Service & Repair, 114 North Pennsylvania Avenue, Ness City, 67560 /
913-798-3173
Virg's Automotive Repair, 717 South Pennsylvania Avenue, Ness City, 67560 /
913-798-2660

AIR SERVICE
Ness City Municipal Airport, Ness City

MEDICAL
Ness City Medical Clinic, Ness City, 67560 / 785-798-2233

FOR MORE INFORMATION
Ness City Chamber of Commerce
Ness City, KS 67560
785-798-2413

Pratt and Pratt County

Population–6,687 County Population–9,702 County Area–735 sq. mi.	Elevation–1,896 October Temperature–58.6 Acres in WIHA–960 Acres in CRP–47,381

Pratt is the location of the Region 3 offices of the Kansas Department of Wildlife and Parks. This area is known as a wheat and livestock producing region. A good selection of services and accommodations are available in Pratt.

Two public hunting wildlife areas are managed by the state in Pratt County. Texas Lake Wildlife Area, west of Pratt, offers both waterfowl hunting and the hunting of ring-necked pheasant, bobwhite quail, and mourning dove. Pratt Sandhills Wildlife Area, also west of Pratt, houses populations of upland game birds. One of the most difficult birds to bag, the lesser prairie chicken, is located on the Pratt Sandhills Wildlife Area.

The 1997 Walk-In Hunting Area Atlas lists 6 enrolled properties totaling 960 acres.

UPLAND BIRDS
Pheasant, Bobwhite Quail, Lesser Prairie Chicken, Mourning Dove, Sandhill Crane

WATERFOWL
Ducks & Geese

ACCOMMODATIONS
Best Western Hillcrest Motel, 1336 East 1st Street, Pratt, 67124 / 316-672-6407 / Dogs allowed / $$

Budget Inn, 1631 East 1st Street, Pratt, 67124 / 316-672-6468 / Dogs allowed / $

Evergreen Motel, West Highway 54, Pratt, 67124 / 316-672-6431 / Dogs allowed / $-$$

Seville Inn Holiday Inn Express, 1401 West 54th Highway, Pratt, 67124 / 316-672-9433 / Dogs allowed / $$$

Super 8 Motel, 1906 East 1st Street, Pratt, 67124 / 316-672-5945 / Dogs allowed / $-$$

CAMPGROUNDS AND RV PARKS
Mound Street RV Park, 601 West Blaine Street, Pratt, 67124 / 316-672-3525

Evergreen Inn & RV Park, West Highway 54, Pratt, 67124 / 316-672-6431 / 12 sites

RESTAURANTS
Ay Chihuahua, 920 West 1st Street, Pratt, 67124 / 316-672-5599

Burke Restaurant, West Highway 54, Pratt, 67124 / 316-672-3681

Country Grill, 1600 East 1st Street, Pratt, 67124 / 316-672-9910

Uptown Cafe, 202 South Main Street, Pratt, 67124 / 316-672-6116

Because sandhill hunting is so new, not many styles of decoys are available. These are a pair from the author's spread.

VETERINARIANS
Nearest are in Greensburg and Kingman (see Region 4)

SPORTING GOODS STORES
Swishers Sporting Goods, East Highway 54, Pratt, 67124 / 316-672-3641
Wal-Mart, 1801 East 1st Street, Pratt, 67124 / 316-672-7548

AUTO REPAIR
Arnett Automotive, 308 Pedigo Drive Pratt, 67124 / 316-672-9241
Cline Automotive, 1002 North Jackson Street, Pratt, 67124 / 316-672-9314

AIR SERVICE
Pratt Airport, Pratt, 67124 / 316-672-3601

MEDICAL
Pratt Regional Medical Center, 200 Commodore Street, Pratt, 67124 /
  316-672-7451

FOR MORE INFORMATION
Pratt Area Chamber of Commerce
114 North Main Street / PO Box 469
Pratt, KS 67124
316-672-5501

Scott City and Scott County

Population–3,785	Elevation–249
County Population–5,289	October Temperature–55.4
County Area–718 sq. mi.	Acres in WIHA–1,788
	Acres in CRP–21,791

The land around Scott City is managed for wheat and range livestock. Services and accommodations are at a minimum. The Scott Wildlife Area is found on the northern boundary of Scott County. This site is managed for public hunting. The 1997 Walk-In Hunting Area Atlas lists 8 enrolled properties totaling 1,788 acres.

UPLAND BIRDS
Pheasant, Bobwhite Quail, Mourning Dove, Sandhill Crane

WATERFOWL
Ducks & Geese

ACCOMMODATIONS
Airliner Motel, 609 East 5th Street, Scott City, 67871 / 316-872-2125 / $$

CAMPGROUNDS AND RV PARKS
Lake Scott State Park / 316-872-2061 / 220 sites

RESTAURANTS
Broiler Steakhouse, 611 East 5th Street, Scott City, 67871 / 316-872-3495
Chaparral Inn Restaurant & Club, 102 Main Street, Scott City, 67871 / 316-872-5191
Homestead Restaurant, 324 North Main Street, Scott City, 67871 / 316-872-5620

VETERINARIANS
Spencer Randall Veterinary Clinic, West 96 Highway, Scott City, 67871 / 316-872-2185

SPORTING GOODS STORES
Cramers Sporting Goods, 406 Main Street, Scott City, 67871 / 316-872-7094

AUTO REPAIR
Matthies Service & Repair, 135 South Main, Scott City, 67871 / 316-872-5696

AIR SERVICE
Scott City Municipal Airport, Scott City

MEDICAL
Scott County Hospital, 310 E. 3rd., Scott City, 67871 / 316-872-5811

FOR MORE INFORMATION
Scott City Chamber of Commerce
221 West 5th Street
Scott City, KS 67871
316-872-3525

Syracuse and Hamilton County

Population–1,606	Elevation–3,240
County Population–2,388	October Temperature–55.4
County Area–997 sq. mi.	Acres in WIHA–8,282
	Acres in CRP–126,047

Syracuse is an agricultural community. This portion of the state has little in the way of population centers, and what small towns are available are few and far between. Services and accommodations are at a minimum. The town is located on the Arkansas River. The Hamilton Wildlife Area is north of Syracuse in Hamilton County. This area can be hunted for upland birds and waterfowl. Hunting is available on private lands throughout the county, provided that permission to trespass can be obtained. The 1997 Walk-In Hunting Area Atlas currently lists 14 enrolled properties totaling 8,282 acres.

UPLAND BIRDS
Pheasant, Bobwhite Quail, Scaled Quail, Lesser Prairie Chicken, Mourning Dove, Sandhill Crane

WATERFOWL
Ducks & Geese

ACCOMMODATIONS
Nearest are in Garden City

CAMPGROUNDS AND RV PARKS
Long's RV Camper Park, 700 East Highway 50, Syracuse, 67878 / 316-384-7414

RESTAURANTS
Dog House Restaurant, Highway 50 & Main, Syracuse, 67878 / 316-384-7709
Macaw's 66 Restaurant, 405 Highway 50 West, Syracuse, 67878 / 316-384-5666
Ramble-N-Restaurant, 606 Highway 50 West, Syracuse, 67878 / 316-384-7425
Uptown Cafe, 207 East Highway 50, Syracuse, 67878 / 316-384-7874

VETERINARIANS
Western Veterinary Services, Highway 50 East, Syracuse, 67878 / 316-384-5721

SPORTING GOODS STORES
Nearest are in Garden City

AUTO REPAIR
Jantz Repair Shop, 729 North Gardner, Syracuse, 67878 / 316-384-7359
Willis Auto, 310 West Avenue A, Syracuse, 67878 / 316-384-7371

Working a holding covey of scalies on the Cimarron National Grasslands.

AIR SERVICE
Syracuse Hamilton County Airport, 1301 North Main, Syracuse, 67878 /
316-384-5835

MEDICAL
Hamilton County Hospital, East G Street, Syracuse, 67878 / 316-384-7461

FOR MORE INFORMATION
Syracuse Chamber of Commerce
118 North Main
Syracuse, KS 67878
316-384-5459

Region 4

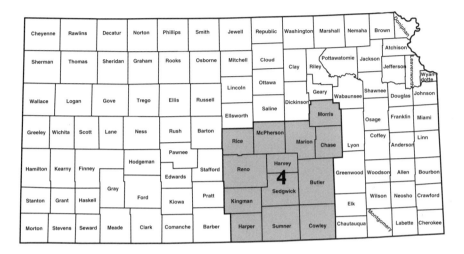

Region 4 contains Kansas' most populated city, Wichita. The region is divided by the Arkansas River. This, along with ample water, makes waterfowling a popular pursuit in Region 4. Populations of Canada geese winter through, along with opportunities for late season greenhead mallards.

Upland bird hunters find good populations of ring-necked pheasant and bobwhite quail. Much of the land is in agriculture, and the ample available feed can make for large game bird populations. The southern extension of the Flint Hills extends down through Region 4, providing opportunities for greater prairie chickens whose flocks also make use of the fallow grain left in late winter stubble fields.

Mourning doves are found early season on available food sources. Turkeys are found throughout the region, where suitable habitat is present.

Area Hunting Guides

Clark's Creek Outfitters, Inc.
Ronald L. Britt
812 S. 2700 Rd.
White City, KS 66872
Business & Home 913-349-2280

Ash Creek Upland Game Farm
Richard L. Case
1713 13th Ave.
McPherson, KS 67460
Business & Home 316-241-1849

Hett Hollow
John R. Hett
208 Hett Hollow
Marion, KS 66861
Business & Home 316-382-2903

Steven L. Hett
RR2
Marion, KS 66861
Business & Home 316-382-2080

Kansas Whitetail Outfitters
Roger M. King, JR.
4328 E. Lewis
Wichita, KS 67218
Business & Home 316-682-5911

Kansas Gun Dog & Supply
Michael B. Koehn
2707 S. Worthington
Burrton, KS 67020
Business & Home 316-463-2021

Blackdog Outfitter, Inc.
John M. Koslowsky
3448 N. Jeanette
Wichita, KS 67204
Business & Home 316-832-0589

R. L. Guide Service
Robert E. Landrum
2215 S. Sherry Ln.
Wichita, KS 67235
Business & Home 316-729-2520

Gerald Shivers Guide Service
Gerald M. Shivers, Jr.
482 V Ave.
Council Grove, KS 66846
Business & Home 316-767-5739

Goose Creek Guide Service
21307 S. Hodge Rd.
Arlington, KS 67514
Business & Home 316-538-3518

Diamond V Ranch
Thomas P. Sollner
Rt. 1, Box 15
Burdick, KS 66838
Business & Home 316-273-8535

Flint Hills Hunts
Danny J. Torrence
3209 Central
Winfield, KS 67156
Business 316-221-3767
Home 316-221-4741

Kansas Whitetail Outfitters
John P. Turner
4328 E. Lewis
Wichita, KS 67218
Business & Home 316-686-7007

Area Hunting Preserves

Quail Valley Farms Sports Clay
207 Chestnut
Moundridge, KS 67107
316-345-2947

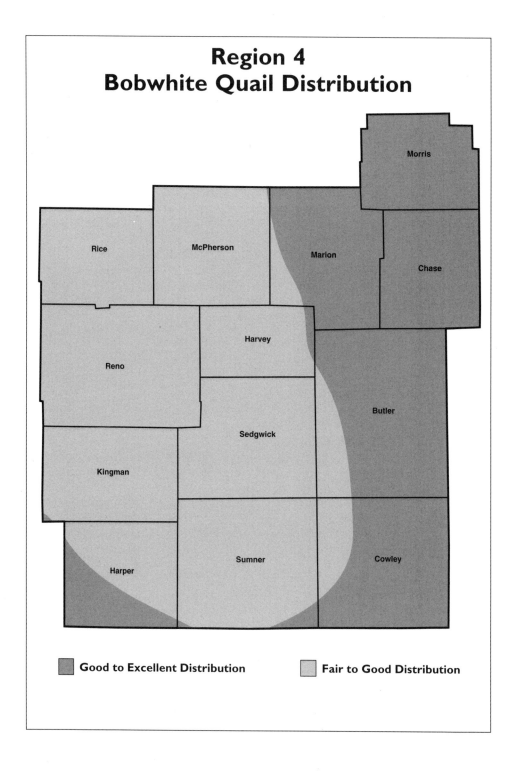

Region 4
Bobwhite Quail Distribution

Good to Excellent Distribution   Fair to Good Distribution

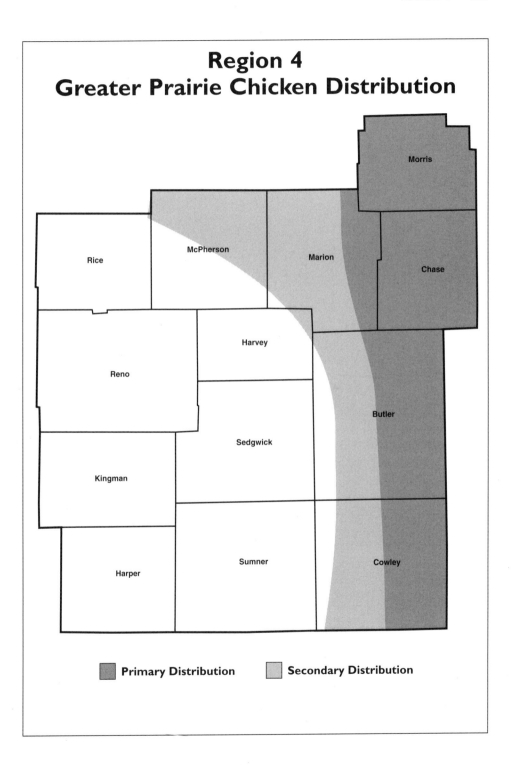

Region 4
Greater Prairie Chicken Distribution

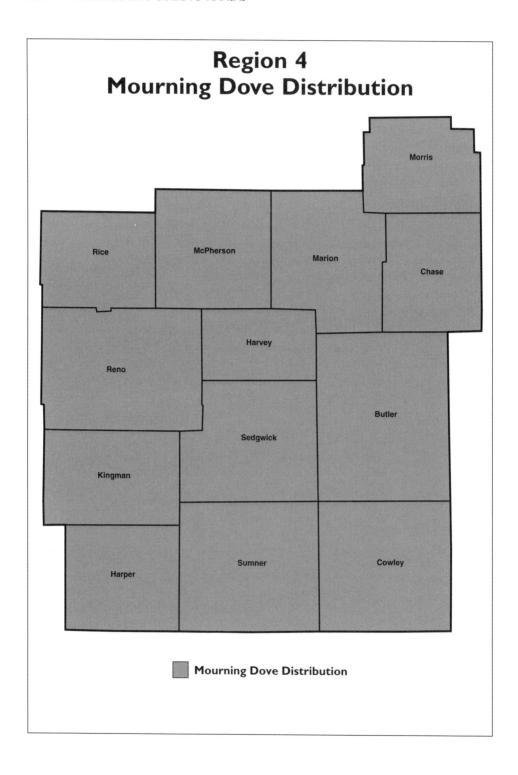

Region 4
Mourning Dove Distribution

Mourning Dove Distribution

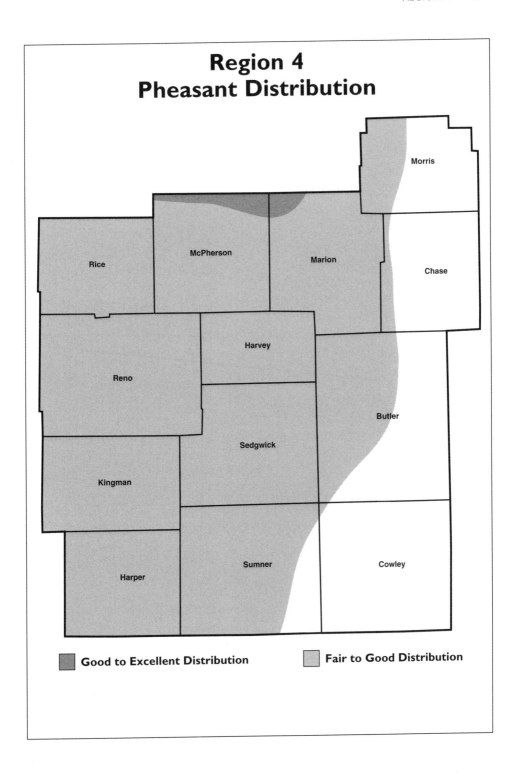

Region 4
Pheasant Distribution

Morris

Rice

McPherson

Marion

Chase

Harvey

Reno

Butler

Sedgwick

Kingman

Harper

Sumner

Cowley

Good to Excellent Distribution   Fair to Good Distribution

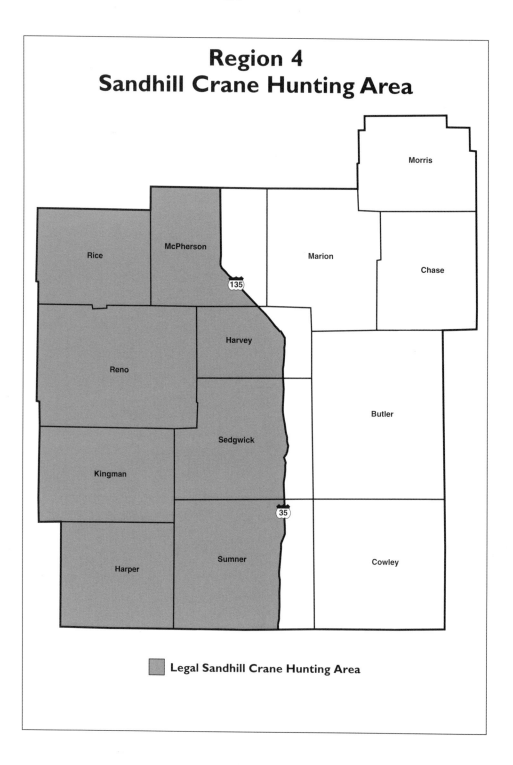

Region 4
Sandhill Crane Hunting Area

Legal Sandhill Crane Hunting Area

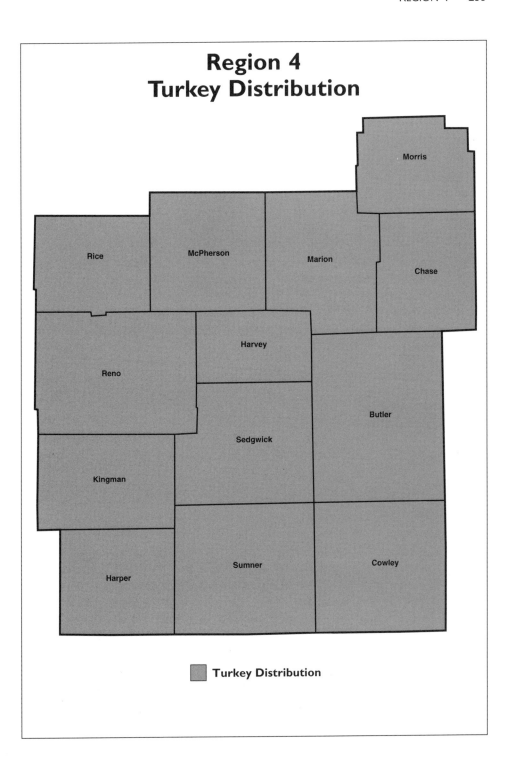

Region 4
Turkey Distribution

Turkey Distribution

Arkansas City and Cowley County

Population–12,762	Elevation–1,075
County Population–36,915	October Temperature–57.0
County Area–1,126 sq. mi.	Acres in WIHA–0
	Acres in CRP–7,387

    Arkansas City is found just above the Oklahoma line in south central Kansas. The city offers a full range of services and accommodations. Found on the Arkansas River, Arkansas City plays host to Caw Wildlife Refuge; Caw is an important snow goose area. A second public hunting area, the Cowley State Fishing Lake and Wildlife Area is found just to the east of Caw Wildlife Area. Both sites are in Cowley County. Hunting for waterfowl, bobwhite quail, dove, and turkey is available on the Caw Wildlife Area. Hunting for bobwhite quail, dove, and waterfowl is available on the Cowley Wildlife Area.

UPLAND BIRDS
Pheasant, Bobwhite Quail, Greater Prairie Chicken, Mourning Dove

WATERFOWL
Ducks & Geese

ACCOMMODATIONS
Best Western Hallmark Motor Inn, 1617 North Summit Street, Arkansas City, 67005 / 316-442-1400 / Dogs allowed / $$
Heritage Regency Court Inn, 3232 North Summit Street, Arkansas City, 67005 / 316-442-7700 / Dogs allowed / $$

CAMPGROUNDS AND RV PARKS
Nearest are in Wichita

RESTAURANTS
Best of the Orient, 1611 North Summit Street, Arkansas City, 67005 / 316-442-8802
Brick's Restaurant, 301 South Summit Street, Arkansas City, 67005 / 316-442-5390
The Firehouse Restaurant, 114 West 5th Avenue, Arkansas City, 67005 / 316-442-0911
Garden Restaurant & Lounge, 3232 North Summit Street, Arkansas City, 67005 / 316-442-7700
Greendoor Lafamilia, 714 West Madison Avenue, Arkansas City, 67005 / 316-442-1685
The Grinder Man, 101 South Summit Street, Arkansas City, 67005 / 316-442-6420

VETERINARIANS
Nearest are in Wichita

Setting up decoys for a goose hunt.

SPORTING GOODS STORES
JC & Earnie's Outdoor Sports, 1114 North C Street, Arkansas City, 67005 /
316-442-0848
Wal-Mart, 2715 North Summit Street, Arkansas City, 67005 / 316-442-2063

AUTO REPAIR
George Hain Auto Repair, 511 East Quincy Avenue, Arkansas City, 67005 /
316-442-3595
Pate's Auto Service, 918 South Summit Street, Arkansas City, 67005 / 316-442-6770

AIR SERVICE
Strother Field Airport & Industrial Park, Arkansas City, 67005 / 316-442-2061

MEDICAL
South Central Kansas Regional Medical Center, 216 West Birch Street, Arkansas
City, 67005 / 316-442-2500

FOR MORE INFORMATION
Arkansas City Chamber of Commerce
126 East Washington Avenue / PO Box 795
Arkansas City, KS 67005
316-442-0230

Council Grove and Morris County

Population–2,228	Elevation–1,234
County Population–6,198	October Temperature–55.8
County Area–697 sq. mi.	Acres in WIHA–2,205
	Acres in CRP–6,090

Council Grove is found north of Emporia in the Kansas Flint Hills country. A limited number of services and accommodations are available. Council Grove sits just below Council Grove Lake Project. Council Grove Wildlife Area, on the grounds of the Lake Project, offers public hunting.

The 1997 Walk-In Hunting Area Atlas lists 8 enrolled properties totaling 2,205 acres in Morris County.

UPLAND BIRDS
Pheasant, Bobwhite Quail, Greater Prairie Chicken, Mourning Dove

WATERFOWL
Ducks & Geese

ACCOMMODATIONS
Cottage House Hotel & Motel, 25 North Neosho Street, Council Grove, 66846 / 316-767-6828 / Dogs allowed / $$
Flint Hills Bed & Breakfast, 613 West Main Street, Council Grove, 66846 / 316-767-6655

CAMPGROUNDS AND RV PARKS
Canning Creek Cove, Council Grove Lake / 316-767-6745 / 54 sites
Richey Cove, Council Grove Lake / 316-767-5800 / 48 sites
Santa Fe Trail, Council Grove Lake / 316-767-7125 / 39 sites

RESTAURANTS
Hays House 1857 Restaurant, 112 West Main Street, Council Grove, 66846 / 316-767-5911
Saddlerock Cafe, 15 South 6th Street, Council Grove, 66846 / 316-767-6411
Trailside Diner, 209 West Main Street, Council Grove, 66846 / 316-767-6945

VETERINARIANS
The Veterinary Clinic, RR 3 Box 3, Council Grove, 66846 / 316-767-5914

SPORTING GOODS STORES
Nearest are in Emporia (see Region 5)

AUTO REPAIR
Nearest are in Emporia (see Region 5)

AIR SERVICE
Nearest are in Emporia (see Region 5)

MEDICAL
Morris County Hospital, 600 North Washington Street, Council Grove, 66846 / 316-767-6811

FOR MORE INFORMATION
Council Grove Convention and Visitors Bureau
200 West Main Street
Council Grove, KS 66846
316-767-5882

El Dorado and Butler County

Population–11,495	Elevation–1,285
County Population–50,580	October Temperature–59.4
County Area–1,428 sq. mi.	Acres in WIHA–1,396
	Acres in CRP–6,483

Set in the rolling Flint Hills country of south central Kansas, the city of El Dorado offers a host of services and accommodations for the traveling bird hunter. The large, sprawling El Dorado Lake with its State Park and Wildlife Area, sits directly above the city to the northeast. Public hunting opportunities within Butler County are available at both El Dorado Wildlife Area and the Butler State Fishing Lake and Wildlife Area.

The 1997 Walk-In Hunting Area Atlas lists 7 enrolled properties totaling 1,396 acres in Butler County.

UPLAND BIRDS
Pheasant, Bobwhite Quail, Greater Prairie Chicken, Mourning Dove

WATERFOWL
Ducks & Geese

ACCOMMODATIONS
Best Western Red Coach Inn, 2525 West Central Avenue, El Dorado, 67042 / 316-321-6900 / Dogs allowed / $$
Heritage Inn Motel, 2515 West Central Avenue, El Dorado, 67042 / 316-321-6800 / Dogs allowed / $-$$
Super 8 Motel of El Dorado, 2530 West Central Avenue, El Dorado, 67042 / 316-321-4888 / $$

CAMPGROUNDS AND RV PARKS
El Dorado State Park / 316-321-7180 / 1100 sites
Tarrant Overnight Camping / 316-321-6272 / 36 sites

RESTAURANTS
Dave's Soup & Sandwich Shoppe, 120 North Main Street, El Dorado, 67042 / 316-321-9062
El Sarape, 1111 West Central Avenue, El Dorado, 67042 / 316-321-1490
Gambino's Pizza, 1321 West Central Avenue, El Dorado, 67042 / 316-322-8827
House of Ghen Gis Khan, 626 North Main Street, El Dorado, 67042 / 316-321-0030
Rusty Bucket Cafe, 719 Main, El Dorado, 67042 / 316-536-2221
Silverado Restaurant, 151 North Main Street, El Dorado, 67042 / 316-321-9400

VETERINARIANS
Nearest are in Wichita

SPORTING GOODS STORES
Kohls' Sports, 103 North Main Street, El Dorado, 67042 / 316-321-6191
R J's Fishing & Hunting, 1220 North Main Street, El Dorado, 67042 / 316-321-3443
Wal-Mart, 2850 West Central Avenue, El Dorado, 67042 / 316-322-8100

AUTO REPAIR
Dolan Daniels Auto Repair, 326 South Main Street, El Dorado, 67042 /
    316-321-5752
Heartland Towing, 2235 West Towanda Avenue, El Dorado, 67042 / 316-321-2730

AIR SERVICE
Patty Field, El Dorado
Captain Jack Thomas, El Dorado Airport, El Dorado

MEDICAL
Susan B. Allen Hospital, 720 West Central Avenue., El Dorado, 67042 /
    316-321-3300

FOR MORE INFORMATION
El Dorado Chamber of Commerce
383 East Central
El Dorado, KS 67042
316-321-3150

Florence and Marion County

Population–636	Elevation–1,200
County Population–12,888	October Temperature–58.3
County Area–943 sq. mi.	Acres in WIHA–2,597
	Acres in CRP–18,105

Florence is a small town far off the beaten track. It is found north of Interstate 35 in the south central part of Kansas. It offers little in the way of amenities. While Marion County is a sparsely populated region, it does contain the Marion Reservoir Project. The Marion Wildlife Area is located on the Marion Reservoir Project and public hunting is available there. The 1997 Walk-In Hunting Area Atlas lists 14 enrolled properties totaling 2,597 acres in Marion County.

UPLAND BIRDS
Pheasant, Bobwhite Quail, Greater Prairie Chicken, Mourning Dove

WATERFOWL
Ducks & Geese

ACCOMMODATIONS
Holiday Motel, Highway 50 & 77, Florence, 66851 / 316-878-4246 / Dogs allowed / $

CAMPGROUNDS AND RV PARKS
Nearest are in El Dorado

RESTAURANTS
Town & Country Cafe, 410½ Highway 77, Florence, 66851 / 316-878-4452
Wagon Chuck, 503 Main Street, Florence, 66851 / 316-878-4382

VETERINARIANS
Florence Veterinary Clinic, 424 Main Street, Florence, 66851 / 316-878-4251

SPORTING GOODS STORES
Nearest are in El Dorado

AUTO REPAIR
Huntley Repair Shop, 306 West 4th Street, Florence, 66851 / 316-878-4527

AIR SERVICE
Nearest is in El Dorado

MEDICAL
Florence Health Care, 109 West 9th Street., Florence, 66851 / 316-878-4440

Hutchinson and Reno County

Population–39,308	Elevation–1,529
County Population–62,389	October Temperature–56.1
County Area–1,255 sq. mi.	Acres in WIHA–5,364
	Acres in CRP–94,055

Hutchinson is a large city that can provide a multitude of options for the traveling bird shooter. The town is found on the Arkansas River, to the northeast of Wichita. Both the Cheney Wildlife Area and State Park and the Sandhills State Park are found in Reno County and both are open to hunting. The 1997 Walk-In Hunting Area Atlas lists 25 enrolled properties totaling 5,364 acres.

UPLAND BIRDS
Pheasant, Bobwhite Quail,
Greater Prairie Chicken, Mourning Dove

WATERFOWL
Ducks & Geese

ACCOMMODATIONS
Astro Motel, 15 East 4th Avenue, Hutchinson, 67501 / 316-663-1151 / Dogs allowed / $

Comfort Inn, 1621 Super Plaza, Hutchinson, 67501, 800-221-2222 / Dogs allowed / $$

Holiday Inn, 1400 North Lorraine Street, Hutchinson, 67501, 800-465-4329 / Dogs allowed / $$$

Quality Inn City Center, 15 West 4th Street, Hutchinson, 67501, 800-424-6423 / Dogs allowed/ $$

Super 8 Motel, 1315 East 11th Avenue, Hutchinson, 67501 / 316-662-6394 / Dogs allowed

CAMPGROUNDS AND RV PARKS
Melody Acres Campground / 316-665-5048 / 47 sites

RESTAURANTS
Cafe Mexico, 1616 Nickerson Boulevard, Hutchinson, 67501 / 316-665-7409

Chelsea's Family Restaurant, 200 East 4th Avenue, Hutchinson, 67501 / 316-662-0037

The Main Street Diner, 422 South Main Street, Hutchinson, 67501 / 316-662-3773

Prime Thyme, 2803 North Main Street, Hutchinson, 67502 / 316-663-8037

Roy's Hickory Pit Bar-B-Q, 1018 East 5th Avenue, Hutchinson, 67501 / 316-663-7421

Taiwan Chinese Restaurant, 701 East 30th Avenue, Hutchinson, 67502 / 316-662-7878

Tommassi Italian Restaurant, 17 East 2nd Avenue, Hutchinson, 67501 / 316-663-9633

Village Inn Pancake House Restaurant, 2901 North Main Street, Hutchinson, 67502 / 316-662-3116

VETERINARIANS

Elden R Austin, 1201 East 30th Avenue, Hutchinson, 67502 / 316-665-8743

Country Junction Companion Animal Clinic, 2400 South State Road 61, Hutchinson, 67501 / 316-663-6150

Gerald D Schrater and Randall A Smith, 2909 Apple Ln, Hutchinson, 67502 / 316-662-0515

SPORTING GOODS STORES

Reffner's Sporting Goods, Hutchinson Mall, Hutchinson, 67501 / 316-662-0293

Rusty's Outdoor Sports, 1105 East 30th Avenue, Hutchinson, 67502 / 316-665-0380

Wal-Mart Discount Cities, 1905 East 17th Avenue, Hutchinson, 67501 / 316-669-0027

AUTO REPAIR

B & B Auto Repair, 308 Stevens Street, Hutchinson, 67501 / 316-662-6131

Franklin Automotive, 1800 East 4th Avenue, Hutchinson, 67501 / 316-669-8387

Rice's Auto Repair, 225 West 4th Avenue, Hutchinson, 67501 / 316-662-6939

Spitler's Service Center, 2601 North Main Street, Hutchinson, 67502 / 316-663-6302

AIR SERVICE

Hutchinson Municipal Airport, Hutchinson

Mills Field, Hutchinson

MEDICAL

Hutchinson Hospital, Hutchinson, 67501 / 316-663-7774

FOR MORE INFORMATION

Greater Hutchinson Chamber of Commerce
117 North Walnut / PO Box 519
Hutchinson, KS 67504-0519
316-662-3391

Kingman and Kingman County

Population–3,196	Elevation–1,560
County Population–8,292	October Temperature–57.5
County Area–864 sq. mi.	Acres in WIHA–1,850
	Acres in CRP–45,618

Kingman sits to the west of Wichita in south central Kansas. A limited number of services and accommodations are available. Within the confines of Kingman County, only one publicly managed wildlife area is available for area gunners, The Byron Walker Wildlife Area; both upland birds and waterfowl are available. To the north, sharing a common border with Reno County, lies the large Cheney Wildlife Area and State Park. This may give area gunners a chance to prospect new ground while still headquartering in Kingman. The 1997 Walk-In Hunting Area Atlas lists 12 enrolled properties totaling 1,850 acres in Kingman County.

UPLAND BIRDS
Pheasant, Bobwhite Quail, Greater Prairie Chicken, Mourning Dove,

WATERFOWL
Ducks & Geese

ACCOMMODATIONS
Budget Host Copa Motel, 1113 East US Highway 54, Kingman, 67068 / 316-532-3118 / Dogs allowed / $-$$
Econo Lodge, 504 North Main, Kingman, 67068 / 316-424-4777 / Dogs allowed / $$
Welcome Inn, 1101 East US Highway 54, Kingman, 67068 / 316-532-3144 / Dogs allowed / $

CAMPGROUNDS AND RV PARKS
Nearest are in Hutchinson, Wichita, and Pratt (see Region 3)

RESTAURANTS
Forbidden Fruit Cafe, 1640 North Broadway Avenue, Kingman, 67068 / 316-532-5654
Houdini's Pizza, 401 Avenue D East, Kingman, 67068 / 316-532-5117
Jeanett's, 1123 East US Highway 54, Kingman, 67068 / 316-532-5993
Ranch House Restaurant, 1122 East US Highway 54, Kingman, 67068 / 316-532-3733

VETERINARIANS
Kingman Veterinary Clinic, 633 North Marquette Street, Kingman, 67068 / 316-532-3472
Raida Veterinary Clinic, West Highway 54, Kingman, 67068 / 316-532-5271

*Setter keeping guard
over the day's bag.*

SPORTING GOODS STORES

Near's Country Store, 1020 Avenue D West, Kingman, 67068 / 316-532-2153

AUTO REPAIR

Harbert Automotive Service, 525 Avenue East, Kingman, 67068 / 316-532-3001

AIR SERVICE

Kingman Airport, Kingman, 67068 / 316-532-3864

MEDICAL

Kingman Community Hospital, 750 Avenue D West, Kingman, 67068 /
316-532-3147

FOR MORE INFORMATION

Kingman Chamber of Commerce
322 North Main
Kingman, KS 67068
316-532-1853

Lyons and Rice County

Population–3,688	Elevation–1,695
County Population–10,610	October Temperature–55.8
County Area–727 sq. mi.	Acres in WIHA–2,801
	Acres in CRP–16,591

Lyons, found east of Great Bend and the Cheyenne Bottoms Wildlife Area in Barton County, is a small town offering a minimum of services and accommodations. Sandhill cranes are legal game in a portion of this region. Within the county there are no publicly managed wildlife areas. However, 2,801 acres on 15 properties enrolled in the WIHA program are available for Rice County hunters.

UPLAND BIRDS
Pheasant, Bobwhite Quail, Greater Prairie Chicken, Mourning Dove, Sandhill Crane

WATERFOWL
Ducks & Geese

ACCOMMODATIONS
Lyons Inn, 817 West Main Street., Lyons, 67554 / 316-257-5285 / Dogs allowed / $-$$

CAMPGROUNDS AND RV PARKS
Nearest are in Great Bend (see Region 3) and Hutchinson

RESTAURANTS
Chicken Roost, 514 West Main Street, Lyons, 67554 / 316-257-3908
El Dee Grande, 802 West Main Street, Lyons, 67554 / 316-257-5340
Ranch House Restaurant, 821 West Main Street, Lyons, 67554 / 316-257-2259
Schirer's Restaurant, 700 North Grand Avenue, Lyons, 67554 / 316-257-3020

VETERINARIANS
Nearest are in Great Bend (see Region 3) and Hutchinson

SPORTING GOODS STORES
Nearest are in Great Bend (see Region 3) and Hutchinson

AUTO REPAIR
Ed's Truck & Auto Repair, 1011 West Main Street, Lyons, 67554 / 316-257-2072
Jeff's Auto Repair & Service, 210 East Commercial Street, Lyons, 67554 /
    316-257-2176

AIR SERVICE
Lyons-Rice County Airport, RR 3, Lyons, 67554 / 316-257-5002
Rice County Aviation, West Highway 56, Lyons, 67554 / 316-257-5002

MEDICAL

Hospital District No 1 Rice County, 619 South Clark Avenue, Lyons, 67554 / 316-257-5173

FOR MORE INFORMATION

Lyons Chamber of Commerce
101 West Main
Lyons, KS 67554
316-257-2842

Wichita and Sedgwick County

Population–304,017
County Population–403,562
County Area–1,000 sq. mi.

Elevation–1,397
October Temperature–58.4
Acres in WIHA–563
Acres in CRP–7,533

Wichita holds the distinction of being Kansas' most populous city. Fueled by a brisk economy in aircraft production, the city is a sprawling metropolis which can provide a multitude of services and accommodations. The Region 4 District Office of the Kansas Department of Wildlife and Parks is located here and is available for those needing information, licenses, and permits. The Cheney Reservoir touches the extreme northwestern corner of Sedgwick County. While the large flocks of snow geese that ply the state have historically traveled to the east along the Missouri River, some birds are now beginning to use the Cheney Reservoir. Snow goose hunting may improve there in the future. The 1997 Walk-In Hunting Area Atlas lists 4 enrolled properties totaling 563 acres.

UPLAND BIRDS
Pheasant, Bobwhite Quail, Greater Prairie Chicken, Mourning Dove

WATERFOWL
Ducks & Geese

ACCOMMODATIONS

Best Western Wichita Red Coach Inn, 915 East 53rd Street North, Wichita, 67219 / 316-832-9387 / Dogs allowed / $$

Comfort Inn, 4849 Laura Street, Wichita, 67216 / 316-522-1800 / Dogs allowed / $$

Econo Lodge Airport, 6245 West Kellogg Drive, Wichita, 67209 / 316-945-5261 / Dogs allowed / $$

Hampton Inn, 3800 West Kellogg Drive, Wichita, 67213 / 316-945-4100 / Dogs allowed / $$$

Harvey Hotel Wichita, 549 South Rock Road, Wichita, 67207 / 316-686-7131 / Dogs allowed / $$$

Holiday Inn–East, 7335 East Kellogg Drive, Wichita, 67207 / 316-685-1281 / Dogs allowed / $$$

Motel 6, 5736 West Kellogg Drive, Wichita, 67209 / 316-945-8440 / Dogs allowed / $-$$

Red Carpet Inn, 607 East 47th Street South, Wichita, 67216 / 316-529-4100 / Dogs allowed / $$

Sands Motel, 8401 West US Highway 54, Wichita, 67209 / 316-722-4221 / Dogs allowed / $-$$

CAMPGROUNDS AND RV PARKS

Chelsea Bar & Grill, 2949 North Rock Road, Wichita, 67226 / 316-636-1103
Denny's Restaurants, 5700 West Kellogg Drive and 8100 East Kellogg Drive, Wichita
Kansas Catfish, 2628 East 21st Street North, Wichita, 67214 / 316-687-5566
Larkspur Restaurant & Grill, 904 East Douglas Avenue, Wichita, 67202 / 316-262-5275
Magic Wok, 9504 West Central Avenue, Wichita, 67212 / 316-722-5528
Olive Tree Bistro, 2949 North Rock Road, Wichita, 67226 / 316-636-1100
Rock Island Cafe, 725 East Douglas Avenue, Wichita, 67202 / 316-263-1616
Saigon Restaurant, 1103 North Broadway Street, Wichita, 67214 / 316-262-8134
Scotch and Sirloin, 3941 East Kellogg Drive, Wichita, 67218 / 316-685-8701
Stroud's Restaurant, 3661 North Hillside Street, Wichita, 67219 / 316-838-2454

VETERINARIANS

Crestview Animal Clinic, 6011 East 21st, Wichita, 67208 / 316-684-3721
Broadway Animal Clinic, 3036 South Broadway Street, Wichita, 67216 / 316-522-6222
Chisholm Trail Animal Hospital, 1726 East 61st Street North, Wichita, 67219 / 316-744-0501
Seneca Veterinary Clinic, 435 North Seneca Street, Wichita, 67203 / 316-262-1239
Wichita Emergency Veterinary Clinic, 737 South Washington Street, Ste 4, Wichita, 67211 / 316-262-5321

SPORTING GOODS STORES

Air Capital Sporting Goods Co Inc, 791 North West Street, Wichita, 67203 / 316-942-2217
The Coleman Company Inc, 235 North Saint Francis Street, Wichita, 67202 / 316-264-0836
Dick's Sporting Goods, 11922 East Kellogg Drive, Wichita, 67207 / 316-688-5550
K-Mart Stores, 4200 West Kellogg Drive, Wichita, 67209 / 316-942-7438
K-Mart Stores, 4830 South Broadway Street, Wichita, 67216 / 316-522-4751
K-Mart Stores, 8600 East Kellogg Drive, Wichita, 67207 / 316-685-2341
RS Shooting Apparel, 913 North Colorado Street, Wichita, 67212 / 316-945-0868
Rusty's Outdoor Sports, 2487 South Seneca Street, Wichita, 67217 / 316-262-7500
Rusty's Outdoor Sports, 511 South Webb Road, Wichita, 67207 / 316-683-7851
Wal-Mart, 1618 Ohio Street, Augusta, 67010 / 316-775-2254
Wal-Mart, 2020 North Southeast Boulevard, Derby, 67037 / 316-788-9400
Wal-Mart, 3030 North Rock Road, Wichita, 67226 / 316-636-4482
Wal-Mart, 501 East Pawnee Street, Wichita, 67211 / 316-267-2400
Wal-Mart, 6110 West Kellogg Drive, Wichita, 67209 / 316-945-2800

AUTO REPAIR

Automotive Maintenance & Repair, 2425 North Broadway Street, Wichita, 67219 / 316-838-8662

Cherry Creek Automotive, 7613 East Harry Street, Wichita, 67207 / 316-684-5683

Five Star Precision Automotive, 2826 East 31st Street South, Wichita, 67216 /
316-681-2814

Kellogg Auto & Truck, 1657 South 111th Street West, Wichita, 67209 / 316-721-9066

AIR SERVICE

DOT FAA Air Traffic Control Tower, 2196 Airport Road, Wichita, 67209 / 316-946-0060

Maize Airport, 8001 West 45th Street North, Wichita, 67205 / 316-722-2690 /
Served by America West, American Airlines, Comair, Continental, Northwest,
TransWorld Airlines, United, and USAirways

MEDICAL

CSJ Health System Wichita Inc, 3720 East Bayley Street, Wichita, 67218 /
316-689-4000

Our Lady of Lourdes Rehab Hospital, 1151 North Rock Road, Wichita, 67206 /
316-634-3400

Riverside Health System, 2622 West Central Avenue, Wichita, 67203 /
316-946-5000

FOR MORE INFORMATION

Wichita Convention and Visitors Bureau
100 South Main, Suite 100
Wichita, KS 67202
316-265-2800 or 1-800-288-9424

Region 5

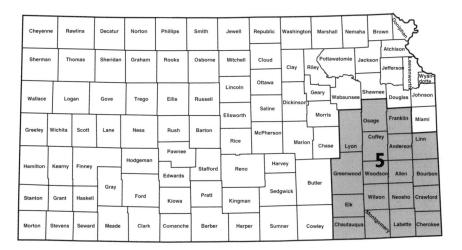

This portion of Kansas contains the area referred to as the Cherokee Lowlands. The western plains transitions at the Chautauqua Hills into a land more closely resembling the eastern portion of our continent than the Great Plains. The country is much more wooded, with heavily brushed watercourses and hardwood creek bottoms. Wildlife species foreign to Kansas are found here, such as eastern woodchucks, armadillos, and water moccasins.

The land has the look of bobwhite quail spread all over it. The land is broken up into small holdings with agricultural fields dotting the flat land creek bottoms, providing an ample food source for upland game species. It is one of the most productive bobwhite quail areas in the state. Ring-necked pheasant, however, are mostly absent; a few may be found in the northwestern part of Region 5, but as the land transitions to the southeast, ring-necked pheasants are eliminated completely. Greater prairie chickens are found in portions of the region, particularly the western and the northern, where suitable habitat exists. Mourning dove are present throughout the early gunning season, and those locating dove feedfields should experience good gunning. Like the bobwhite quail, turkeys are very much at home in this region, as the hardwood bottoms and water courses make ideal turkey habitat.

Area Hunting Guides

Hideout Hunting Lodge
Richard R. Anderson
PO Box 415
Allen, KS 66833
Business 316-528-3354
Home 785-528-4440

Collins Kansas Hunts
Michael D. Collins
105 East 10th
Altoona, KS 66710
Business & Home 316-568-5291

Robert L. Daniels
RR 2, Box 75C
Elk City, KS 67344
Business & Home 316-627-2288

Shadow Oaks
John & Pauline Doty
PO Box 37
Sedan, KS 67361
Business & Home 316-673-9791

Dudley D. Foster
RR2, Box 162 A
Sedan, KS 67361
Business & Home 316-725-3219

West Creek Hunt Club L.L.C.
Robert F. Henderson
HC1, Box 80
Hamilton, KS 66853-9749
Business & Home 316-645-2261

Black Jack Outfitters
Richard D. Hutchison
RR 1, Box 210B
Elk City, KS 67344
Business & Home 316-627-2162/5412-3

Chautauqua Hills Guide Service
Mark D. Jones
150 East Main
Sedan, KS 67361
Business 316-725-5633
Home 316-331-9221

Lil Toledo Hunting & Fishing
Ronald L. King
10600 170th Road
Chanute, KS 66720
Business 316-244-5668
Home 316-763-2494

Quail Lodge
Pierson South Morrill
RR 1, Box 3
Independence, KS 67301
Business 316-331-3706
Home 804-286-2987

Paradise Adventure
Kurtis A. Nunnenkamp
RR 1, Box 9
Altoona, KS 66710
Business & Home 316-568-2518

Mark Payne
Box 162-C
Elk City, KS 67344
Business & Home 316-627-2578

Kansas Unlimited
Wes A. Traul
11464 NW 2100 Road
Garnett, KS 66032
Business & Home 785-448-3239

Area Hunting Preserves

Flint Oak
Pete Laughlin & Ray Walton
Rt. 1
Fall River, KS 67047
316-658-4401

Show-Me Birds Hunting Resort
Kim Shira
Rt. 1, Box 134
Baxter Springs, KS 66713
316-674-8863

Lone Pine Game Birds
Mike Hamman
440 90th Road
Toronto, KS 66777
316-637-2967

Shawnee Creek Preserve
RR 2, Box 50b
Columbus, KS 66725
316-674-8563

T & C Wildlife
RR 1, Box 755
Arcadia, KS 66711
316-638-4300

Region 5
Bobwhite Quail Distribution

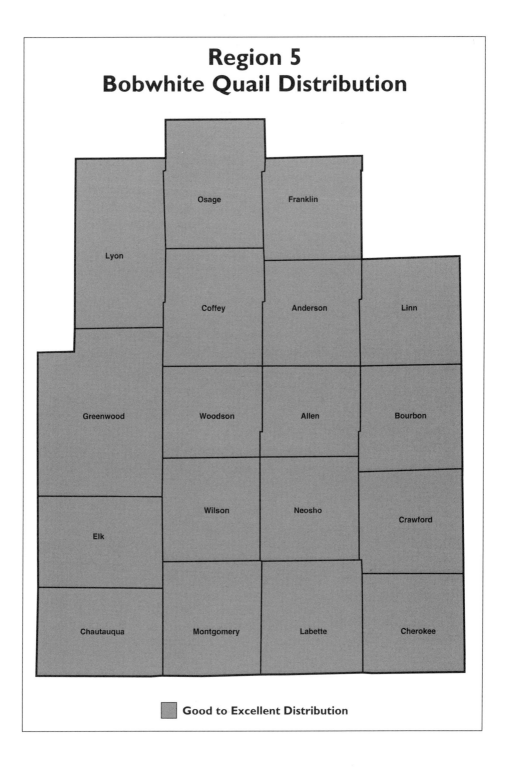

Osage

Franklin

Lyon

Coffey

Anderson

Linn

Greenwood

Woodson

Allen

Bourbon

Wilson

Neosho

Crawford

Elk

Chautauqua

Montgomery

Labette

Cherokee

Good to Excellent Distribution

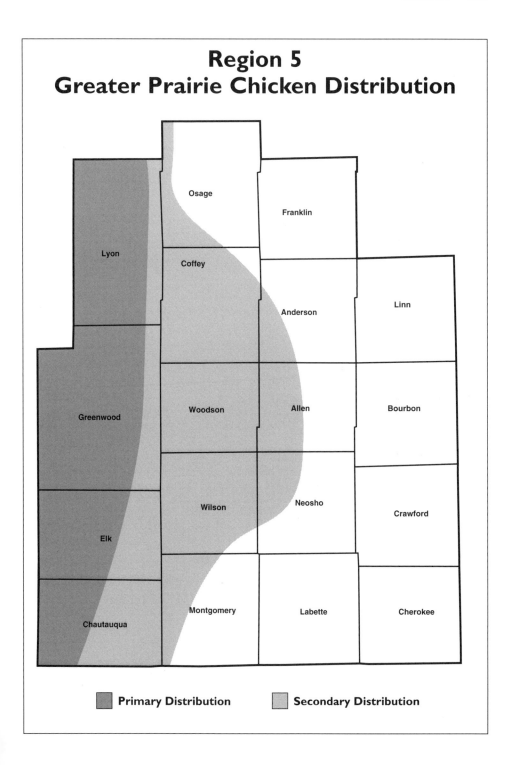

Region 5
Greater Prairie Chicken Distribution

Osage

Franklin

Lyon

Coffey

Anderson

Linn

Greenwood

Woodson

Allen

Bourbon

Wilson

Neosho

Crawford

Elk

Chautauqua

Montgomery

Labette

Cherokee

Primary Distribution   Secondary Distribution

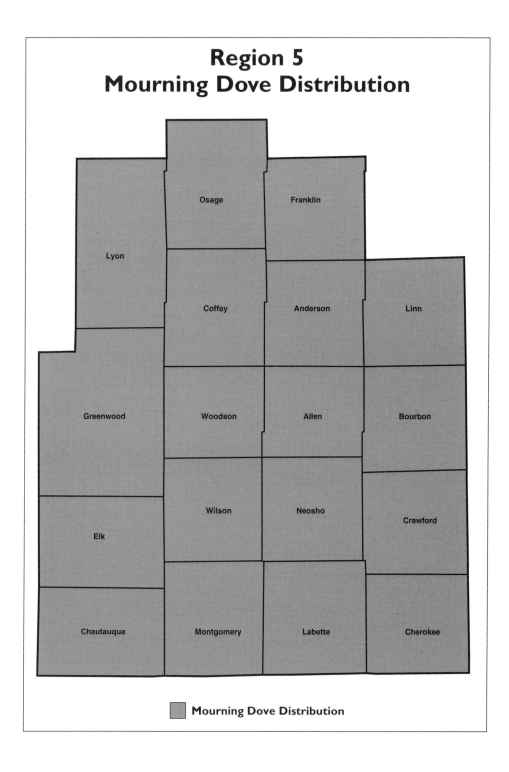

Region 5
Mourning Dove Distribution

Mourning Dove Distribution

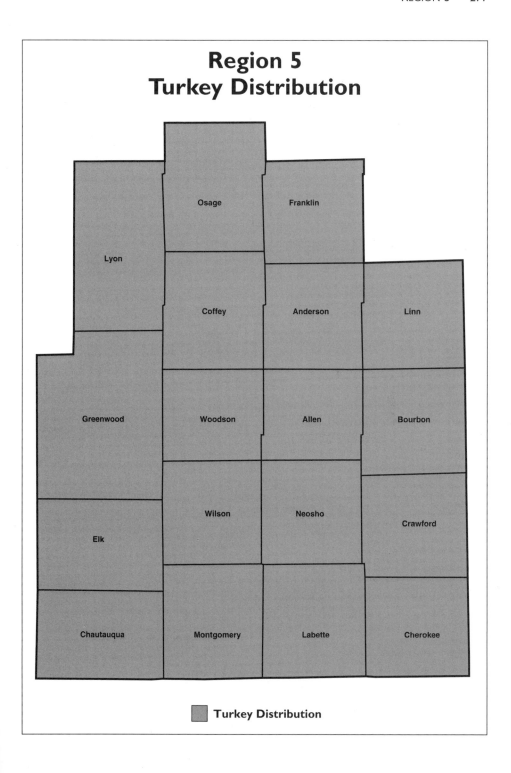

Region 5
Turkey Distribution

Turkey Distribution

Chanute and Neosho County

Population–9,488	Elevation–930
County Population–17,035	October Temperature–58.9
County Area–572 sq. mi.	Acres in WIHA–4,019
	Acres in CRP–16,259

Chanute offers a host of services and accommodations. This town is found in the geographic center of Region 5 and plays host to the Kansas Department of Wildlife and Parks Regional Office, where licenses and permits are available. The Neosho Wildlife Area, which offers public hunting, is found in the southeastern corner of Neosho County. The 1997 Walk-In Hunting Area Atlas lists 6 enrolled properties totaling 4,019 acres in Neosho County.

UPLAND BIRDS
Bobwhite Quail, Greater Prairie Chicken, Mourning Dove

WATERFOWL
Ducks & Geese

ACCOMMODATIONS
Guest House Motor Inn, 1814 South Santa Fe Street, Chanute, 66720 / 316-431-0600 / Dogs allowed / $

Holiday Park, 3030 South Santa Fe Street, Chanute, 66720 / 316-431-0850 / Dogs allowed / $-$$

Safari Inn, 35th South & Highway 169, Chanute, 66720 / 316-431-9460 / Dogs allowed / $$

CAMPGROUNDS AND RV PARKS
Nearest are in Fort Scott and Coffeyville

RESTAURANTS
Bob's Cafe, 209 West Main Street, Chanute, 66720 / 316-431-3920

Chicago Junction, 605 North Santa Fe Street, Chanute, 66720 / 316-431-4051

Elisa's Mexican Restaurant, 116 West Main Street, Chanute, 66720 / 316-431-4380

New Chicago Buffet, 605 North Santa Fe Street, Chanute, 66720 / 316-431-0675

New China Restaurant, 27 West Main Street, Chanute, 66720 / 316-431-6565

VETERINARIANS
Nearest are in Iola

SPORTING GOODS STORES
Augustin B Archery Supplies, RR 4 Box 215b, Chanute, 66720 / 316-431-4125

Wal-Mart, 2700 South Santa Fe Street, Chanute, 66720 / 316-431-3077

A pair of American widgeon.

AUTO REPAIR
North Lincoln Auto Repair, 112 North Lincoln Avenue, Chanute, 66720 / 316-431-2970

Swaney's Auto Service, 1815 South Santa Fe Street, Chanute, 66720 / 316-431-3830

AIR SERVICE
Chanute Martin Johnson Airport, Chanute

MEDICAL
Neosha Memorial Regional Medical Clinic, 629 Plummer Avenue, Chanute, 66720 / 316-431-4000

FOR MORE INFORMATION
Chanute Area Chamber of Commerce
21 North Lincoln / PO Box 747
Chanute, KS 66720
316-431-3350

Coffeyville and Montgomery County

Population–12,917	Elevation–736
County Population–38,816	October Temperature–59.2
County Area–645 sq. mi.	Acres in WIHA–0
	Acres in CRP–3,137

Coffeyville is found on the Oklahoma border in the southeastern corner of the state. A host of services and accommodations are available. Montgomery County is fortunate to contain the large Elk City Lake which is used by waterfowl during the season. Waterfowl hunting is available on the lake, at the Elk City Wildlife Area. In addition, the Copan Wildlife Area lies directly on the border, to the west of Coffeyville, and provides hunting opportunities as well. Currently in Montgomery County, no private lands are enrolled in the WIHA program.

UPLAND BIRDS
Bobwhite Quail, Mourning Dove

WATERFOWL
Ducks & Geese

ACCOMMODATIONS
Appletree Inn, 820 East 11th Street, Coffeyville, 67337 / 316-251-0002 / Dogs allowed / $$
Fountain Plaza Inn, 104 West 11th Street, Coffeyville, 67337 / 316-251-2250 / Dogs allowed / $$

CAMPGROUNDS AND RV PARKS
Walter Johnson Park, 1-800-626-3357 / 170 sites

RESTAURANTS
Bailey's Restaurant, 1103 East 5th Street, Coffeyville, 67337 / 316-251-3830
Bones Steak House, 104 East 8th Street, Coffeyville, 67337 / 918-255-6390
Cactus Grill, 602 Northeast Street, Coffeyville, 67337 / 316-251-4200
Desperado's, 2300 Woodland Avenue, Coffeyville, 67337 / 316-251-6600
Hong Kong Delight, 812 East 11th Street, Coffeyville, 67337 / 316-251-2394
Rob's BBQ, 1107 Camden Street, Coffeyville, 67337 / 316-251-9156

VETERINARIANS
Animal Health Center, 1614 Walnut Street, Coffeyville, 67337 / 316-251-9380
South Coffeyville Veterinary Clinic, 320 West 3rd Street, Coffeyville, 67337 / 918-255-6730

SPORTING GOODS STORES
Wal-Mart, 1705 West 11th Street, Coffeyville, 67337 / 316-251-2290

*Gunner comes up
on an overhead bird.*

AUTO REPAIR
A-1 Automotive, 1518 Walnut Street, Coffeyville, 67337 / 316-251-5201
Harding Auto Service, 110 East Martin Street, Coffeyville, 67337 / 316-251-3623
M & D Automotive, 1500 East 8th Street, Coffeyville, 67337 / 316-251-8634

AIR SERVICE
Coffeyville Municipal Airport, Coffeyville

MEDICAL
Coffeyville Regional Medical Center, 1400 West 4th Street, Coffeyville, 67337 /
316-251-1200

FOR MORE INFORMATION
Coffeyville Area Chamber of Commerce
807 Walnut / PO Box 457
Coffeyville, KS 67337
316-251-2550

Emporia and Lyon County

Population–25,512	Elevation–1,135
County Population–34,732	October Temperature–56.1
County Area–851 sq. mi.	Acres in WIHA–670
	Acres in CRP–21,478

Emporia is found on the Kansas Turnpike, Interstate 35. Its close proximity to the freeway system allows the visiting hunter to access many different regions of the state, using Emporia as a base camp. A multitude of services and accommodations are available. Emporia is located in the Flint Hills, which constitutes one of the last great unbroken stretches of grass prairie. For the upland bird hunter, the Flint Hills offer greater prairie chicken hunting. The Flint Hills National Wildlife Refuge is southeast of Emporia. Directly north of Flint Hills is another large public hunting area, Melvern Wildlife Area. The small Lyon State Fishing Lake and Wildlife Area is due north of Emporia. The 1997 Walk-In Hunting Area Atlas lists 1 enrolled property totaling 670 acres.

UPLAND BIRDS
Pheasant, Bobwhite Quail, Greater Prairie Chicken, Mourning Dove

WATERFOWL
Ducks & Geese

ACCOMMODATIONS

Best Western Hospitality House Motel, 3181 West US Highway 50, Emporia, 66801 / 316-342-7587 / Dogs allowed / $$

Budget Host Inn, 1830 East US Highway 50, Emporia, 66801 / 316-343-6922 / Dogs allowed / $

Comfort Inn, 2511 West 18th Avenue, Emporia, 66801 / 316-343-7750 / Dogs allowed / $$

Day's Inn, 3032 West US Highway 50, Emporia, 66801 / 316-342-1787 / Dogs allowed / $$

Holiday Inn, 2700 West 18th Avenue, Emporia, 66801 / 316-343-2200 / Dogs allowed / $$

Motel 6, 2630 West 18th Avenue, Emporia, 66801 / 316-343-1240 / Dogs allowed / $

White Rose Inn Bed & Breakfast, 901 Merchant Street, Emporia, 66801 / 316-343-6336 / $

CAMPGROUNDS AND RV PARKS

Emporia Campground, take exit 127A eastbound from US 50 and then 0.5 mile West on US 50 / 316-343-3422 / 80 sites

RESTAURANTS

The Chicken Barn, 518 East 6th Avenue, Emporia, 66801 / 316-343-2888

El Palenque Cafe, 315 Commercial Street, Emporia, 66801 / 316-342-0200

Hot Rod's Bar B-Q & Blues, 10 West 11th Avenue, Emporia, 66801 / 316-343-7979

Longhorn Restaurant, 502 Albert Street, Emporia, 66801 / 316-342-7182

McGillicutty's Restaurant & Pub, 1116 West 6th Avenue, Emporia, 66801 / 316-343-7135

New China Restaurant, 607 Merchant Street, Emporia, 66801 / 316-342-1729

VETERINARIANS

East Emporia Veterinary Clinic, 602 Exchange, Emporia, 66801 / 316-343-7682

Emporia Veterinary Hospital, 710 Anderson, Emporia, 66801 / 316-342-6515

SPORTING GOODS STORES

The Gun Den, 708 Commercial Street, Emporia, 66801 / 316-342-0711

Mike's Sporting Goods Inc, 507 Commercial Street, Emporia, 66801 / 316-343-6271

Sportsmen's Outpost Inc, 11 East 6th Avenue, Emporia, 66801 / 316-342-5200

Wal-Mart Discount Cities, 2301 Industrial Road, Emporia, 66801 / 316-343-2670

AUTO REPAIR

Hy-tech Auto Service Inc, 702 West 6th Avenue, Emporia, 66801 / 316-342-6735

Pro-care Auto Service, 616 Prairie Street, Emporia, 66801 / 316-342-4300

Quality Automotive, 702 Mechanic Street, Emporia, 66801 / 316-342-2080

Unruh Automotive, 706 Lantern Lane, Emporia, 66801 / 316-343-7063

AIR SERVICE

Emporia City of Airport, RR 4, Emporia, 66801 / 316-342-3598

MEDICAL

Newman Memorial County Hospital, 1201 West 12th Street, Emporia, 66801 / 316-343-6800

FOR MORE INFORMATION

Emporia Convention and Visitors Bureau
719 Commercial Street / PO Box 703
Emporia, KS 66801
316-342-1803 or 1-800-279-3730

Eureka and Greenwood County

Population–2,974
County Population–7,847
County Area–1,140 sq. mi.

Elevation–1,081
October Temperature–57.1
Acres in WIHA–0
Acres in CRP–4,862

Eureka sits on the western edge of Region 5. Many of the towns in this region are small, self-contained communities, and Eureka falls into this category. For a town of its size, it offers a good selection of amenities. Two public hunting areas are found in this County: the Fall River Wildlife Area at Fall River Lake, and the Toronto Wildlife Area at Toronto Lake, both located to the east of town. There are no WIHA acres enrolled in the county.

UPLAND BIRDS
Pheasant, Bobwhite Quail, Greater Prairie Chicken, Mourning Dove

WATERFOWL
Ducks & Geese

ACCOMMODATIONS
Blue Stem Lodge, 1314 East River Street, Eureka, 67045 / 316-583-5531 / Dogs allowed / $-$$
Carriage House Motel, 201 South Main Street, Eureka, 67045 / 316-583-5501

CAMPGROUNDS AND RV PARKS
Chuck Wagon RV Park, 309 South Jefferson Street, Eureka, 67045 / 316-583-6616

RESTAURANTS
City Cafe, 110 North Main Street, Eureka, 67045 / 316-583-7797
El Taco Juan, 1115 East River Street, Eureka, 67045 / 316-583-6069
Giny & Jon's Steak House & Lounge, 1201 East 7th Street, Eureka, 67045 / 316-583-5772
Paddock Restaurant, 504 North Main Street, Eureka, 67045 / 316-583-7572

VETERINARIANS
Broge Animal Health Center, 600 North Main Street, Eureka, 67045 / 316-583-7190

SPORTING GOODS STORES
D & J Sporting Goods, 210 North Main Street, Eureka, 67045 / 316-583-5211

Auto Repair
Burtin Auto Service, 219 North Oak Street, Eureka, 67045 / 316-583-5450
Fox Garage, 104 South Main Street, Eureka, 67045 / 316-583-7013

Air Service
Eureka Municipal Airport, Eureka

Medical
Greenwood County Hospital, 100 West 16th Street, Eureka, 67045 / 316-583-5909

For More Information
Eureka Chamber of Commerce
112 North Main Street
Eureka, KS 67045
316-583-5452

Fort Scott and Bourbon County

Population–8,362	Elevation–801
County Population–14,966	October Temperature–58.0
County Area–637 sq. mi.	Acres in WIHA–1,235
	Acres in CRP–20,727

Established as a military outpost in 1842 to guard the frontier, Fort Scott is located on the Missouri line in the southeastern quarter of the state. Fort Scott was once a contender with Kansas City for the honor of being the largest rail center west of the Mississippi River. During the "hay day" times of the late 1800s through the 1920s, many of the old buildings that give the town its charm were built. Present-day Fort Scott contains a wealth of amenities to meet the needs of a traveling bird shooter.

Two Department of Wildlife and Parks managed public hunting areas are found in the county: Bourbon State Fishing Lake and Wildlife Area, and Hollister Wildlife Area. There are currently 6 Walk-In Hunting Area properties, totaling 1,235 acres enrolled in the county.

UPLAND BIRDS
Bobwhite Quail, Greater Prairie Chicken, Mourning Dove

WATERFOWL
Ducks & Geese

ACCOMMODATIONS
Best Western Fort Scott Inn Motel, 101 State Street, Fort Scott, 66701 / 316-223-0100 / Dogs allowed / $$
Frontier Inn-4-Less, 2222 South Main Street, Fort Scott, 66701 / 316-223-5330 / Dogs allowed / $-$$

CAMPGROUNDS AND RV PARKS
KOA Fort Scott, 0.75 miles west on US 54 from JCT US 69 and then 0.25 miles north, 1-800-KOA-3441 / 56 sites

RESTAURANTS
Bright's Grill, 1411 East Wall Street, Fort Scott, 66701 / 316-223-4140
Cady's Chinese Restaurant, 1514 South National Avenue, Fort Scott, 66701 / 316-223-0588
Red Barn Restaurant, RR 2, Fort Scott, 66701 / 316-223-6607
Tommasi's Restaurant, 101 State Street, Fort Scott, 66701 / 316-223-0142

VETERINARIANS
Scifers Veterinary Services, Route 4, Fort Scott, 66701 / 316-223-5414

SPORTING GOODS STORES
B-B Goals, 1201 South Margrave Street, Fort Scott, 66701 / 316-223-6428
Bob's Gun & Lock Shop, 702 East Wall Street, Fort Scott, 66701 / 316-223-2530
Wal-Mart, 2400 South Main Street, Fort Scott, 66701 / 316-223-1575

AUTO REPAIR
Advance Auto Service, 207 North National Avenue, Fort Scott, 66701 / 316-223-2110
Goodtimes Auto Center, 702 North Shute Street, Fort Scott, 66701 / 316-223-1510

AIR SERVICE
Scott Fort Municipal Airport, RR 4 Box 24, Fort Scott, 66701 / 316-223-5490

MEDICAL
Mercy Hospital, 821 Burke Street, Fort Scott, 66701 / 316-223-2200

FOR MORE INFORMATION
Fort Scott Visitor Information Center
231 East Wall Street / PO Box 205
Fort Scott, KS 66701
316-223-3566 or 1-800-245-3678

Iola and Allen County

Population–6,351	Elevation–962
County Population–14,638	October Temperature–58.9
County Area–503 sq. mi.	Acres in WIHA–320
	Acres in CRP–6,377

Once centered on natural gas, the economy of Iola is now driven by agriculture and manufacturing. The town offers a moderate amount of amenities and there is a Wal-Mart. Presently, there are no state managed hunting areas in the county. The 1997 Walk-In Hunting Area Atlas lists 3 enrolled properties totaling 320 acres.

UPLAND BIRDS
Bobwhite Quail, Greater Prairie Chicken, Mourning Dove

WATERFOWL
Ducks & Geese

ACCOMMODATIONS
Best Western Inn, 1315 North State Street, Iola, 66749 / 316-365-5161 / Dogs allowed / $-$$

CAMPGROUNDS AND RV PARKS
Nearest are in Fort Scott

RESTAURANTS
China Palace, 110 North State Street, Iola, 66749 / 316-365-3723
The County Seat, 19 West Madison Street, Iola, 66749 / 316-365-8024
Ken's Pizza, 2402 North State Street, Iola, 66749 / 316-365-5315
The Greenery, North State, Iola, 66749 / 316-365-7743

VETERINARIANS
Iola Animal Clinic, North Highway 169, Iola, 66749 / 316-365-7621

SPORTING GOODS STORES
Wal-Mart, 1918 North State Street, Iola, 66749 / 316-365-6981

AUTO REPAIR
Iola Auto Body, 324 North State Street, Iola, 66749 / 316-365-3401
SS Automotive, 313 West 1st, Iola, 66749 / 316-365-8079

AIR SERVICE
National Aircraft, Allen County Airport, Iola, 66749 / 316-365-5891

Solitary hunter working thick grass.

MEDICAL
Allen County Hospital, 101 South 1st Street, Iola, 66749 / 316-365-3131

FOR MORE INFORMATION
Iola Area Chamber of Commerce
208 West Madison / PO Box 722
Iola, KS 66749
316-365-5252

Joplin, Missouri

Population–40,961	Elevation–980
County Population–97,965	County Area–640 sq. miles

While Joplin does not fall within the boundaries of the state of Kansas, it is listed here as an additional resource area for bird hunters traveling in the southeastern corner of the state. Joplin is a large city that falls just over the state line in Missouri. Southeast of Pittsburg and due east of Baxter Springs, Joplin provides a full range of services and amenities which may not be available in the more sparsely populations areas of southeastern Kansas.

ACCOMMODATIONS
Best Inns of America, 3508 South Range Line Road, Joplin, MO 64804 / 417-781-6776 / $$

Best Western Hallmark Inn, 3600 South Range Line Road, Joplin, MO 64804 / 417-624-8400 / Dogs allowed / $$

Drury Inns–Joplin Inn, 144 & US 71, Joplin, MO 64801 / 417-781-8000 / Dogs allowed / $$$

Howard Johnson Lodge, 3510 South Rangeline Road, Joplin, MO 64804 / 417-623-0000 / Dogs allowed / $$

Motel 6, 3031 South Range Line Road, Joplin, MO 64801 / 417-781-6400 / Dogs allowed / $$

Sands Inn Best Western Motel, 1611 North Range Line Road, Joplin, MO 64801 / 417-624-8300 / Dogs allowed / $$-$$$

Super 8 Motel, 2830 East 36th Street, Joplin, MO 64804 / 417-782-8765 / Dogs allowed / $$

Westwood Motel, 1700 West 30th Street, Joplin, MO 64804 / 417-782-7212 / Dogs allowed / $$

CAMPGROUNDS AND RV PARKS
KOA Kampground–Joplin, Highway I-44 & 43 South, Joplin, MO 64804 / 417-623-2246

RESTAURANTS
Casa Montez, 2324 South Range Line Road, Joplin, MO 64804 / 417-781-3610

Club 609, 609 Main, Joplin, MO 64801 / 417-623-6090

Crabby's Seafood Bar & Grill, 815 West 7th Street, Joplin, MO 64801 / 417-782-7372

Granny Shaffer's Family Restaurant, 1651 West 7th Street, Joplin, MO 64801 / 417-781-1144

Jim Bob's Steaks & Ribs, 2040 South Range Line Road, Joplin, MO 64804 / 417-781-3300

Lotus Restaurant, 804 South Range Line Road, Joplin, MO 64801 / 417-782-9342

Mike's Village Cafe, 1515 West 10th Street, Joplin, MO 64801 / 417-623-9330

The Colonel's, 842 Range Line, Joplin, MO 64801 / 417-623-7404
Travetti's Restaurante & Bar, 3010 East 20th Street, Joplin, MO 64801 / 417-781-4344
Uncle Dave's Hickory Pit, 3215 South Main Street, Joplin, MO 64804 / 417-659-9140

VETERINARIANS

Care Animal Hospital, 2 miles west of Joplin on Highway 66, Joplin, MO 64801 / 417-624-9051
Jim D Christian, Anthony A Pike, Kristy L Vanaken, and Stephanie B Watson, 2508 South Maiden Lane, Joplin, MO 64804 / 417-781-0906
Companion Animal Hospital, 34th & Main, Joplin, MO 64804 / 417-623-2032
Mark R Storey, 201 East 15th Street, Joplin, MO 64804 / 417-781-8681

SPORTING GOODS STORES

Brandon's Gun Trading Co, 321 East 20th Street, Joplin, MO 64804 / 417-623-8787
K-Mart Stores, 1717 South Range Line Road, Joplin, MO 64804 / 417-781-9900
South Town Sporting Goods, 3022 South Main Street, Joplin, MO 64804 / 417-624-4087
Wal-Mart Discount Cities, 1500 North Range Line Road, Joplin, MO 64801 / 417-624-7390
Wal-Mart Discount Cities, 15th & Range Line Road, Joplin, MO 64804 / 417-781-7005
Wal-Mart Discount Cities, 1717 West 7th Street, Joplin, MO 64801 / 417-623-3411

AUTO REPAIR

Dennis' Automotive, 2330 West 20th Street, Joplin, MO 64804 / 417-782-1200
Hatfield Automotive, 1201 East 15th Street, Joplin, MO 64804 / 417-782-5574
John & Dave's Automotive, 101 South Virginia Avenue, Joplin, MO 64801 / 417-781-6405
Sheridan Auto Service, 3046 East 7th Street, Joplin, MO 64801 / 417-781-2301

AIR SERVICE

Joplin Airport, Highway 171, Joplin, MO 64801 / Information: 417-623-5696 / Manager: 417-623-0262 / Served by TransWorld Airlines

MEDICAL

Oak Hill Hospital, 932 East 34th Street, Joplin, MO 64804 / 417-623-4640

FOR MORE INFORMATION

Joplin Area Chamber of Commerce
320 East Fourth
Joplin, MO 64802-1178
417-623-0820

Parsons and Labette County

Population–13,100	Elevation–1,200
County Population–23,693	October Temperature–57.6
County Area–649 sq. mi.	Acres in WIHA–2,630
	Acres in CRP–6,724

Parsons is a central location for several of the publicly managed hunting areas in southeastern Kansas. The town is large by area standards, and provides a full set of services and accommodations. Within the boundaries of Labette County, the Big Hill Lake Project and Wildlife Area provides hunting opportunities on both upland and waterfowl species. To the east of Parsons, across the Cherokee County line, lies the extensive holdings of the Mined Land Wildlife Area. North, in Neosho County, is the Neosho Wildlife Area, an important waterfowling site for area hunters. In addition, a large amount of WIHA land is available in Labette County. The 1997 Walk-In Hunting Area Atlas lists 7 enrolled properties totaling 2,630 acres.

UPLAND BIRDS
Bobwhite Quail, Mourning Dove

WATERFOWL
Ducks & Geese

ACCOMMODATIONS
Super 8 Motel, 229 Main Street, Parsons, 67357 / 316-421-8000 / $$
Townsman Motel, Highway 59 South, Parsons, 67357 / 316-421-6990 / Dogs allowed / $-$$

CAMPGROUNDS AND RV PARKS
Nearest are in Coffeyville and Pittsburg

RESTAURANTS
Dugout Bar & Grill, 712 Central, Parsons, 67357 / 316-449-2627
Ernesto's Mexican Food, 200 North Central Avenue, Parsons, 67357 / 316-421-2930
Grand China Restaurant, 3225 Main Street, Parsons, 67357 / 316-421-6345
The Hickory Hole, 720 Main Street, Parsons, 67357 / 316-421-9067
Peking Restaurant, 400 Main Street, Parsons, 67357 / 316-421-8487
Townsaman Restaurant, South Highway 59, Parsons, 67357 / 316-421-0932

VETERINARIANS
Crispell Veterinary Hospital, RR 2, Parsons, 67357 / 316-421-1600

Open-wing Canada goose decoys help with the wary birds.

SPORTING GOODS STORES
Wal-Mart, 300 Main Street, Parsons, 67357 / 316-421-0375

AUTO REPAIR
B & G Service, 111 South 16th Street, Parsons, 67357 / 316-421-4390
Trimble's Auto Service, 414 North 26th Street, Parsons, 67357 / 316-421-4385

AIR SERVICE
Reed Wilsonton Airport, Parsons
White Farms Airport, Galesburg

MEDICAL
Katy Clinic, 400 Katy Avenue, Parsons, 67357 / 316-421-2700
Parsons State Hospital, 2601 Gabriel Avenue, Parsons, 67357 / 316-421-6550

FOR MORE INFORMATION
Parsons Chamber of Commerce
1715 Corning / PO Box 737
Parsons, KS 67357
316-421-6500

Pittsburg and Crawford County

Population–17,789	Elevation–922
County Population–35,582	October Temperature–57.0
County Area–593 sq. mi.	Acres in WIHA–869
	Acres in CRP–11,872

Pittsburg sits on the Kansas/Missouri state line. The town has a large population, and a broad range of services and accommodations are available. Crawford County contains the scattered Mined Land Wildlife Area holdings. These sites are managed for wildlife and hunting by the Kansas Department of Wildlife and Parks. With a moderate amount of travel, Pittsburg is close to several of the better waterfowling areas in Kansas: La Cygne Wildlife Area and Marais des Cygnes Wildlife Area. These areas are found to the north in Linn County. Neosho Wildlife Area lies to the west in Neosho County. The 1997 Walk-In Hunting Area Atlas lists 5 enrolled properties totaling 869 acres.

UPLAND BIRDS
Bobwhite Quail, Mourning Dove

WATERFOWL
Ducks & Geese

ACCOMMODATIONS
Extra Inn, Highway 69 N-4023 Parkview Drive, Pittsburg, 66762 / 316-232-2800 / $$
Holiday Inn Express Pittsburg, Highway 69 N-4020 Parkview Drive, Pittsburg, 66762 / 316-231-8700 / $$$
Sunset Motel, 1159 South 220th Street, Pittsburg, 66762 / 316-231-3950 / Dogs allowed / $
Super 8 Motel, 3108 North Broadway Street, Pittsburg, 66762 / 316-232-1881 / $$

CAMPGROUNDS AND RV PARKS
Mined Land State Wildlife Area / 316-231-3173 / 30 sites

RESTAURANTS
Antonio's Mexican Restaurant, 917 West 4th Street, Pittsburg, 66762 / 316-235-1566
Bamboo Dragon, 1402 North Broadway Street, Pittsburg, 66762 / 316-231-1692
Jack's Steak House, 2912 North Broadway Street, Pittsburg, 66762 / 316-232-9787
Mel's Hickory House, 124 North Broadway Street, Pittsburg, 66762 / 316-231-9442
Nona's Ristorante, 3105 North Broadway Street, Pittsburg, 66762 / 316-235-1737
Parker's Cafe, 602 West 4th Street, Pittsburg, 66762 / 316-231-3888

VETERINARIANS
Countryside Animal Hospital, 20th & Bypass, Pittsburg, 66762 / 316-231-3430
Langdon Lane Animal Hospital, 1268 South 220th Street, Pittsburg, 66762 /
316-232-2410

SPORTING GOODS STORES
Wal-Mart Supercenter, 2710 North Broadway Street, Pittsburg, 66762 /
316-232-1593

AUTO REPAIR
The Auto Shop, 1210 East 4th Street, Pittsburg, 66762 / 316-231-8334
Darrow's Automotive, 1117 South 220th Street, Pittsburg, 66762 / 316-232-9485
Endicott Auto Repair, 111 East 10th Street, Pittsburg, 66762 / 316-231-4031

AIR SERVICE
Atkinson Municipal Airport, Pittsburg

MEDICAL
Mount Carmel Medical Center, Centennial & Rouse, Pittsburg, 66762 /
316-231-6100

FOR MORE INFORMATION
Pittsburg Area Chamber of Commerce
117 West 4th Street / PO Box 1115
Pittsburg, KS 66762
316-231-1000

Hunting the Indian Reservations of Kansas

The tribal lands in many Western states offer excellent hunting opportunities. Unfortunately, this is not the case in Kansas. There are four tribal reservations: the Potawatomi, Kickapoo, Sac and Fox, and Iowa. All four reservations are found in the northeastern corner of the state. Both the Sac and Fox and the Iowa reservations straddle the Nebraska/Kansas border, splitting their land areas about equally between both states.

All four reservations are small in size and made up of a combination of tribal and privately owned lands. The Potawatomi, Kickapoo, and Sac and Fox tribes have no standing agreements with the Kansas Department of Wildlife and Parks which would allow a successful hunter to transport game off of reservation territory. This is a problem, especially in the case of big game, where Kansas law requires that all big game be tagged (making possession of untagged big game animals a violation of the law).

The Iowa tribe does have an agreement with the state of Kansas and offers a nonresident (nontribal member) hunting program. The Iowa Indian Reservation is 12,000 acres in size. Of those 12,000 acres, 2,500 acres belong to the tribe and are open for hunting to those purchasing a tribal hunting license. Of the 2,500 acres of tribal land, approximately 2,000 are found in Kansas and the remaining 500 are north of the border in Nebraska. Half of the tribal holdings are in cultivation crops, with the remaining half in pasture and timber. The remaining private lands, included within the reservation boundaries, can only be accessed after obtaining written permission from the individual landowner.

The annual licenses are $50 and are issued to run year-round. The reservation has both ring-necked pheasants and bobwhite quail in moderate amounts. Ducks, geese, and doves are present in season in good amounts—snow and blue geese in particular.

Turkeys can be hunted with a turkey permit available from the tribe for $50. Only bearded turkeys are legal game during both the spring and fall seasons. The 1998 spring season ran from April 11th through May 17th. The 1997 fall hunt dates ran from October 10th through October 18th. Turkey tag numbers are limited and sold on a first come, first served basis. Turkey tags sell out quickly each season.

For More Information
The Iowa Tribe of Kansas and Nebraska
Route 1, Box 58A
White Cloud, KS 66094
785-595-6614, 785-595-3258

Cimarron National Grasslands

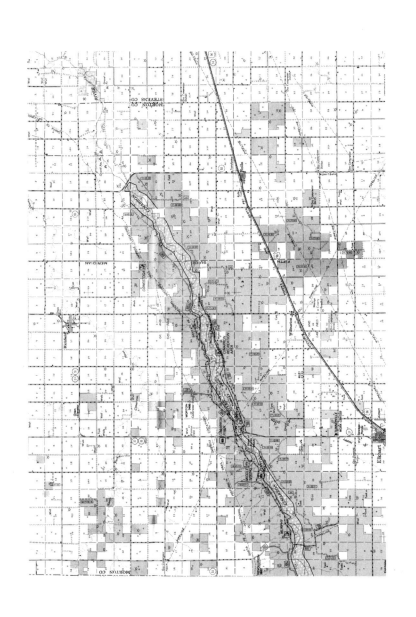

Cimarron National Grasslands

It is a bit of an irony that in Kansas, a mostly treeless plains state, the largest public hunting area is managed by the U.S. Forest Service.

The Cimarron National Grasslands is located in the extreme southwestern corner of the state, in Morton and Stevens counties. The Grasslands are a mostly contiguous unit of 108,175 acres of former sand sage prairie. The dry Cimarron River bottom dissects the Grasslands running northeast to southwest. South of the Cimarron river, the prairie rolls up in a gentle arch of grass interspersed with stands of sand sage. The lands to the north of the river are short grass steps. The river bottom is shaded with a quarter- to half-mile wide band of trees and brush that make ideal habitat for bobwhite quail, the principal game bird taken on the grasslands. A second species of quail, scaled quail, is found in the open grass south of the river.

Cimarron Grasslands are famous for their premier, seldom-taken, game bird, the lesser prairie chicken. Lessers are found south of the river, near the remaining stands of sand sage. Mourning dove and waterfowl are seasonal migrants that utilize the Grasslands' limited water. Ring-necked pheasants are present in limited numbers on adjacent cultivated lands.

Cimarron Grasslands is a few miles north of Elkhart, Kansas, and visiting hunters can find accommodations, restaurants and the Cimarron Grasslands Headquarters office there. Camping is available on the Grasslands.

For More Information
Cimarron National Grasslands
242 Highway 56 East, P.O. Box J
Elkhart, KS 67950
316-697-4621

Fort Riley
Military Reservation

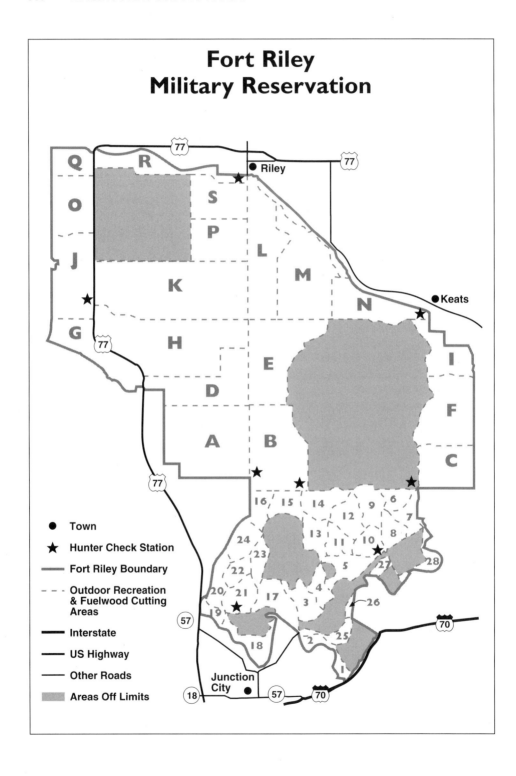

Town

Hunter Check Station

Fort Riley Boundary

Outdoor Recreation
& Fuelwood Cutting
Areas

Interstate

US Highway

Other Roads

Areas Off Limits

Fort Riley Military Reservation

Fort Riley weighs in as Kansas's second-largest public hunting area. The fort is an active duty military training base that was first established in 1853 to protect travelers on the Oregon and Santa Fe trails. The fort has a total land mass of 101,000 acres. Public hunting is made available through the post's Conservation Division Office.

The fort is composed of classic Kansas Flint Hills country. Vast sweeps of open grass hills are veined with hardwood lined drainages. On the post's western border is the 44,231-acre Milford Lake project which contains the 18,873-acre Milford Wildlife Area. This area offers bobwhite quail, pheasant, dove, greater prairie chicken, and waterfowl. To the northeast lies the 33,400-acre Tuttle Creek Lake Project, which contains the 12,200-acre Tuttle Creek Wildlife Area. Tuttle Creek hosts bobwhite quail, pheasant, greater prairie chicken, mourning dove, turkey, and waterfowl.

The fort itself offers good bird hunting to a visiting hunter. Available species are bobwhite quail, pheasant, greater prairie chicken, mourning dove, and wild turkey. Ducks may be seasonally present on the base's small ponds.

The cities of Manhattan, Junction City, and Clay Center are found in close proximity to Fort Riley and provide ample amenities.

Hunters must be in possession of a Fort Riley hunting permit in addition to a valid Kansas state hunting license. Base hunting permits are sold at the post's Outdoor Recreation Center. Permits are $10 and issued on an annual basis. The licensing period runs year-round. All state and federal requirements apply.

A hunter check in/out procedure is required for those hunting on the post. Before going into the field in the morning, each day, persons are required to physically sign in at one of the post's 9 check stations. While there, the hunter will fill out a two-part form and put part one of the form into a deposit box. Part two of the form is kept in the hunter's possession throughout the day; at the completion of the day's hunting, it is filled out and returned to one of the post's check stations. A white Natural Resources vehicle marker form must be displayed in the front windshield of a hunter's vehicle while on the post.

Each day a map board is updated showing which of the post's many management areas are being used for training purposes and are therefore off-limits to public access and hunting. Specific areas on the base, or even the entire facility, may be closed at any time. Hunters must check in and out daily. Nine base check stations allow a hunter to check in before the hunt and check a copy of the area closure map to be sure his preferred site is available for that day. In addition, a 24-hour message phone number allows hunters off post to call in and check on hunt area availability.

Being a military installation, certain registration requirements exist for firearms possession. Personnel assigned to or stationed at Fort Riley "must register their privately-owned firearms and the firearms of their family members and guests with their unit commander, before bringing the firearm onto Fort Riley."

Private citizens and unattached military personnel are exempted from the registration requirement: "Hunting firearms in the possession of licensed hunters on-post during hunting season will be considered properly registered provided the hunter is a military member not assigned to, attached to, or temporarily stationed at Fort Riley or a civilian…All privately-owned firearms transported in vehicles on Fort Riley must be locked in the vehicle's trunk. If the vehicle has no trunk, they must be transported in such a way as to not be readily accessible to the vehicle's occupants."

Turkey hunting is available on the base. A turkey permit is $10 and sold through the Outdoor Recreation Center.

For more Information
U.S. Department of the Army
Director of Enviroment & Safety
Natural Resources Bldg.
Fort Riley, Kansas 66442
913-239-6211, 913-239-6669

National Wildlife Refuges and Federal Areas

Flint Hills National Wildlife Refuge

- 7,500 acres
- 15 miles southeast of Emporia
- Region 5
- Waterfowl, bobwhite quail, greater prairie chicken, mourning dove, and turkey

The Flint Hills National Wildlife Refuge/John Redmond Reservoir is an important snow goose holding area. Located near Emporia, the area is a popular hunting destination for resident waterfowlers.

The refuge property follows the Neosho river drainage to the northwest of the reservoir. Open water, flooded sloughs, shallow marsh, hardwood timber, agricultural land, and Flint Hills uplands are all contained within the Refuge's boundaries.

For More Information
Refuge Manager
Flint Hills National Wildlife Refuge
P.O. Box 128
Hartford, KS 66854
316-392-5553

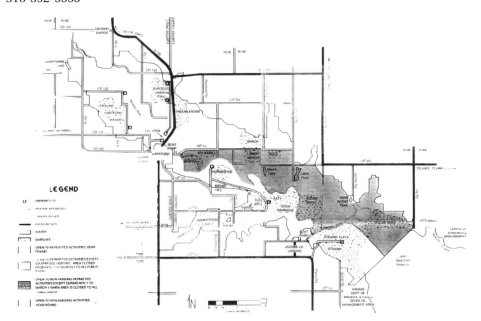

Kanopolis Reservoir

- 12,500 acres. 12 miles southeast of Ellsworth
- Region 1
- Waterfowl, pheasant, bobwhite quail, mourning dove, greater prairie chicken, and turkey

Kanopolis Reservoir is operated by the U.S. Army Corps of Engineers and managed for wildlife and hunting through an agreement with the Kansas Department of Wildlife and Parks. Hunting is permitted on 12,500 acres of the project's total holdings of 18,000 acres. A goose refuge exists on the northwestern portion of the reservoir, established to offer geese a sanctuary and hold birds in the area. The upper western reaches of the area are managed as a Wildlife Area by the Kansas Department of Wildlife and Parks. In addition to waterfowl, there are huntable populations of upland game birds and turkey.

Camping, as well as a full service marina, is available on the project at Kanopolis State Park. The nearest amenities are in Ellsworth.

For More Information

U.S. Army Corps of Engineers
Kanopolis Project Office
105 Riverside Dr.
Marquette, KS 67464
913-546-2294

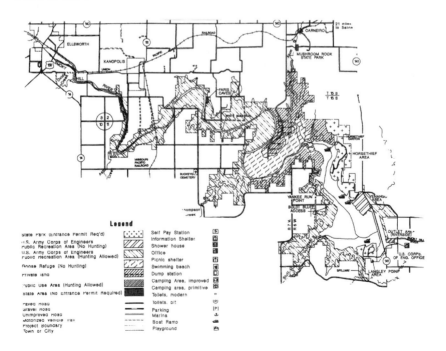

Kirwin National Wildlife Refuge

- 3,700 acres. 15 miles southeast of Phillipsburg
- Region 1
- Waterfowl, pheasant, bobwhite quail, mourning dove and turkey

Kirwin National Wildlife Refuge was established in 1954 as a feeding and resting area for returning waterfowl during their northward spring migration. Hunting is allowed on 3,700 acres of the 10,778-acre refuge. Kirwin Reservoir contains both open water resting areas and marsh. Canada geese are a popular game species on the refuge. In certain zones, hunters are restricted to a daily maximum of three shells per Canada goose by bag limit.

Camping is allowed in campsites and designated areas. Food and lodging is available in the town of Phillipsburg.

For More Information
Refuge Manager
Kirwin National Wildlife Refuge
RR 1, Box 103
Kirwin, KS 67644
913-543-6673

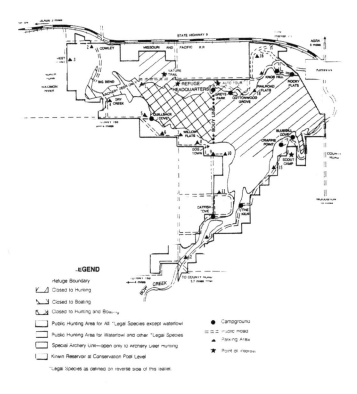

Pomona Reservoir

- 3,600 acres. 17 miles west of Ottawa
- Region 5
- Waterfowl, bobwhite quail and mourning dove

Portions of Pomona Reservoir are managed for controlled hunting under an agreement with the Kansas Department of Wildlife and Parks. The site is an Army Corps of Engineers project designated as a state park. The Reservoir is one of the large open water roosting sites currently being used by migrating snow geese and other waterfowl species. The upper reaches of the reservoir encompass the Pomona Wildlife Area and are open to hunting.

For camping and R.V. enthusiasts, the state park offers 156 utility campsites and over 160 primitive sites.

For More Information

U.S. Army Corps of Engineers
Pomona Project Office
5260 Pomona Dam Rd.
Vassar, KS 66543
913-453-2202

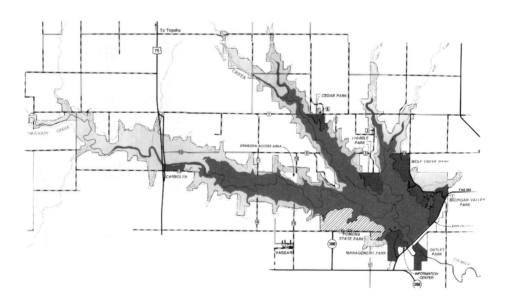

Quivira National Wildlife Refuge

- 8,000 acres. 13 miles north of Stafford
- Region 3
- Waterfowl, pheasant, and bobwhite quail

Quivira National Wildlife Refuge is known for the sandhill and whooping cranes stopping there on their southern migrations to the Texas coast. As a result of the whooper's endangered status, crane hunting is not permitted within the refuge boundaries. However, when the whoopers are not present, waterfowl hunting is allowed on 8,000 of the refuge's 21,820 acres. The private farmlands surrounding Quivira provide excellent goose and crane hunting.

Overnight camping is forbidden on the refuge, but amenities are available locally in the towns of Stafford, Great Bend, and Hutchinson.

For More Information

Refuge Manager
Quivira National Wildlife Refuge
RR 3, Box 48A
Stafford, KS 67578
316-486-2393

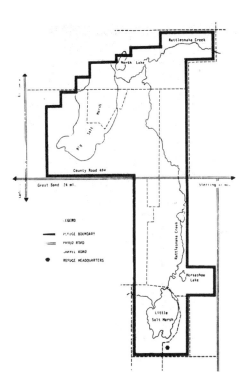

State Wildlife Areas

Kansas has much in the way of public hunting opportunities. The state manages 91 wildlife areas which encompass a combined total of 292,054 huntable acres. When taken with the 148,672 huntable acres of federal areas, Kansas hunters enjoy a total of 440,726 huntable acres of publicly owned lands within the state.

Holdings are found statewide and encompass many diverse habitats and huntable species. The Department of Wildlife and Parks has done an exemplary job of assisting the public in accessing these lands. They publish a booklet entitled *Guide to Kansas Public Hunting* which contains maps that show state wildlife area placements by region. The publication is available through the Department free of charge.

A visual index to the locations of both the state and federal wildlife areas and parks listed in this book follows this section.

Contact

Operations Office
512 SE 25th Avenue
Pratt, KS 67124-8174
316-672-5911.

BERENTZ/DICK WILDLIFE AREA (BUFFALO RANCH)

- 1360 acres
- Region 5
- 2 miles west, 2 miles south and 10.5 miles west of Independence.
- 3 day per week hunting on Tuesday, Thursday, and Saturday: shotgun and archery only.
- Upland Birds: Bobwhite quail

Located in the southeastern corner of the state, and composed of primarily hardwood lowlands, this wildlife area is situated in one of the most productive bobwhite quail areas in Kansas. This area is managed primarily for deer and turkey hunting.

BIG HILL WILDLIFE AREA

- 1,320 acres
- Region 5
- 8 miles west, 4 south of Parsons.
- Upland Birds: Bobwhite quail
- Waterfowl: Ducks and geese

Big Hill Wildlife Area is found southeast of the Army Corps of Engineer's Big Lake Project. Canada goose hunting is available with a Southeast Unit permit. The area provides good hunting for bobwhite quail and turkey.

BYRON WALKER WILDLIFE AREA

- 4,462 acres
- Region 4
- 7 miles west of Kingman
- Upland Birds: Pheasant, bobwhite quail, mourning dove
- Waterfowl: Ducks and geese

Byron Walker Wildlife Area is directly west of Kingman State Fishing Lake. Hunting for upland bird species predominate, with bobwhite quail leading the bag. Public camping is available on the wildlife area.

Cedar Bluff State Park & Wildlife Area

- 10,279 acres
- Region 1
- 16 miles south of WaKeeney
- Upland Birds: Pheasant, bobwhite quail, mourning dove
- Waterfowl: Ducks and geese

Cedar Bluff Wildlife Area is located southwest of Hays on the western high plains. The large Cedar Bluff Reservoir is the centerpiece of the wildlife area. Upland bird hunting for pheasant, quail, and dove is available on the hills surrounding the reservoir; waterfowl hunting is available on the western arm of the reservoir. Cedar Bluff State Park sits on the southeastern shore and is available for campers and RV enthusiasts.

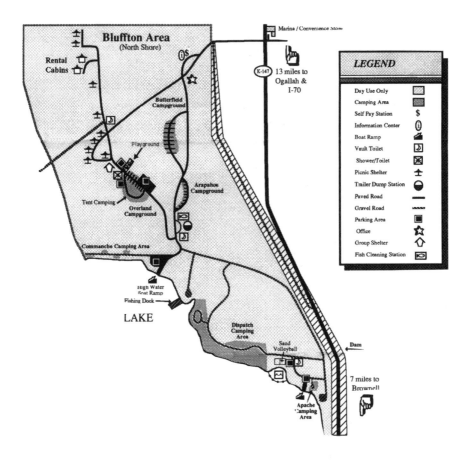

CHENEY WILDLIFE AREA

- 17,308 acres
- Region 4
- 7 miles east of Pretty Prairie
- Upland Birds: Pheasant, bobwhite quail, mourning dove
- Waterfowl: Ducks and geese

Cheney Wildlife Area is west of Wichita, Kansas' most populous city, and thereby an important hunting resource. The public lands surrounding the Cheney Reservoir are designated as a Wildlife Area to the north and a state park to the south; a map is available that delineates these sections. While historically the large flocks of snow geese have migrated to the east of Cheney along the Missouri/Kansas border, migrating geese have recently begun utilizing the reservoir as a stop-off point. With the extended conservation season being proposed, Cheney may mark the most westerly point for snow geese hunting in Kansas. Cheney State Park includes 185 electric hook-up sites with water and other amenities. Camping is permitted in designated areas.

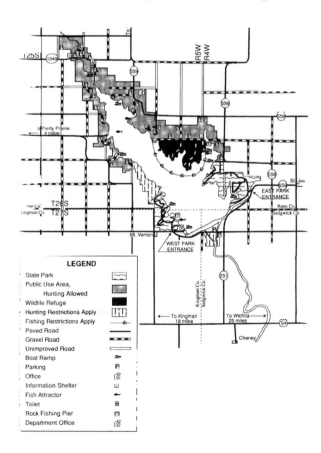

LEGEND

State Park	
Public Use Area, Hunting Allowed	
Wildlife Refuge	
Hunting Restrictions Apply	
Fishing Restrictions Apply	
Paved Road	
Gravel Road	
Unimproved Road	
Boat Ramp	
Parking	
Office	
Information Shelter	
Fish Attractor	
Toilet	
Rock Fishing Pier	
Department Office	

CHEYENNE BOTTOMS WILDLIFE AREA

- 13,280 acres
- Region 3
- 5 miles north, 5 east of Great Bend
- Upland Birds: Pheasant, mourning dove
- Waterfowl: Ducks and geese

To Central Flyway waterfowlers, Cheyenne Bottoms is a sacred place. The "Bottoms" is one of North America's great waterfowl staging areas. The area is divided into five pools with hunting access varying according to the area. Pools 1 and 5 are a refuge area closed to all activities. Marsh hunting is allowed in Pools 2, 3, and 4 with a daily permit for the 167 concrete blinds in the area. Permits are issued on a first come, first served basis, and they are free of charge. After a blind is assigned, hunters exchange their hunting license for the permit. At the conclusion of the hunt, hunting licenses are returned in exchange for blind permits. Refuge personnel inspect the daily bag of birds upon departure.

Hunting is allowed without permit along the perimeter areas of Pools 2, 3, and 4 for those willing to walk. In addition, a goose hunting zone is available on the south border of the refuge area. Access for the goose hunting zone is controlled and permits are required on Friday, Saturdays, Sundays, and state holidays. Occasionally whooping cranes stray over from Quivira Refuge and can cause closures on the wildlife area.

A primitive camping area is available on the wildlife area. Food and lodging can be found in Great Bend.

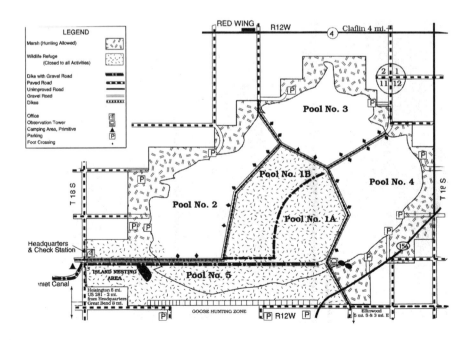

CLINTON WILDLIFE AREA

- 8,700 acres
- Region 2
- 8 miles southwest of Lawrence
- Upland Birds: Bobwhite quail, mourning dove
- Waterfowl: Ducks and geese

Clinton Wildlife Area and State Park surrounds the large, sprawling 7,000-surface acre Clinton Reservoir. Public hunting is allowed in the three westerly arms that radiate off the main body of the reservoir. Hunting for bobwhite quail and dove is found in the upland portions of the wildlife area. Clinton is an important waterfowl area, and large congregations of geese often amass late in the season. Snow geese are present in good numbers.

There are numerous boat ramps, and Clinton State Park offers 375 campsites.

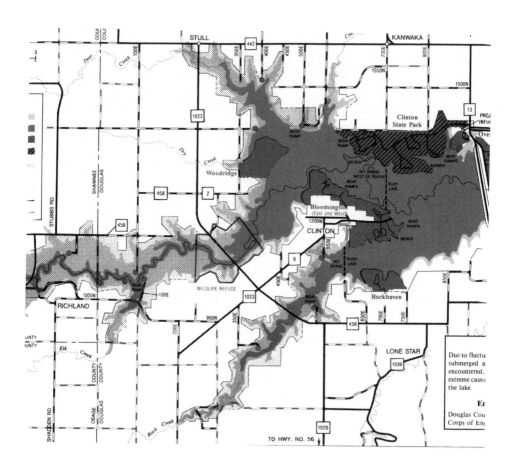

COPAN WILDLIFE AREA

- 2,360 acres
- Region 5
- 0.5 miles west of Caney
- Upland Birds: Bobwhite quail, mourning dove
- Waterfowl: Ducks and geese

Copan Wildlife Area sits directly on the Oklahoma border, in the southeastern corner of the state. The area contains an extensive wet marsh. Dry portions of the wildlife area are covered with trees (deer and turkey habitat).

Bobwhite quail is the principal game bird available. Southeastern Kansas is considered to be one of the most productive quail hunting areas in the state.

COUNCIL GROVE WILDLIFE AREA

- 5,873 acres
- Region 4
- 5 miles northwest of Council Grove
- Upland Birds: Pheasant, bobwhite quail, greater prairie chicken, mourning dove
- Waterfowl: Ducks and geese

Council Grove's Lake Project is managed by the U.S. Army Corps of Engineers. The construction of Council Grove Reservoir was begun in 1960 and came to full operation in 1964. The water area splits into two separate bodies just north of the dam.

The Kansas Department of Wildlife and Parks manages the area for public hunting and wildlife. The wildlife area extends around the shoreline and up the drainage on both arms of the reservoir. Bobwhite quail and ring-necked pheasant are available for upland shooters. Waterfowl hunting is available in season. Services are available for camping and RV enthusiasts, including campsites, boat ramps, water, and sanitary facilities.

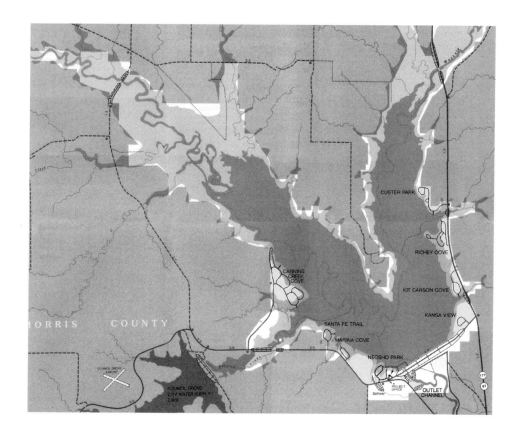

EL DORADO STATE PARK & WILDLIFE AREA

- 13,000 acres
- Region 4
- 2 miles east, 1 north of El Dorado
- Upland Birds: Pheasant, bobwhite quail, greater prairie chicken, mourning dove
- Waterfowl: Ducks and geese

El Dorado State Park and Wildlife Area is a sprawling expanse of flooded trees and water. The area contains good-looking waterfowl habitat. The reservoir holds good numbers of Canada geese in season. Located in the Flint Hills, the surrounding hillsides are rolling grass and provide habitat for bobwhite quail, dove, and greater prairie chicken. Turkey hunting is available in the timbered areas. Nearly 1,100 campsites are available; both primitive camping and full-service for RVs are found on this site. A boat marina and launch ramps are available.

El Dorado is northeast of Wichita and the city of El Dorado, where ample amenities are available.

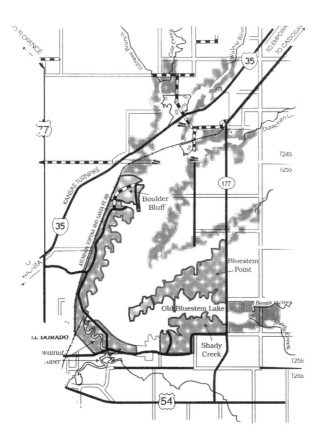

ELK CITY WILDLIFE AREA

- 12,240 acres
- Region 5
- 3 miles west of Independence
- Upland Birds: Bobwhite quail, mourning dove
- Waterfowl: Ducks and geese

Elk City Lake Project is managed by the U.S. Army Corps of Engineers. Through agreement, the Kansas Department of Wildlife and Parks manages the Elk City Wildlife Area for hunting and the State Park for recreation. Elk City is an important waterfowling area for Kansas hunters: large flocks of migrating snow geese frequent the area and duck hunting can be superior in the shallow water areas of the reservoir. In addition, bobwhite quail and turkey are available, and greater prairie chickens are found in very limited numbers. Extensive camping and RV sites are offered in the state park. Independence is found to the east, where food, lodging, and other amenities are available.

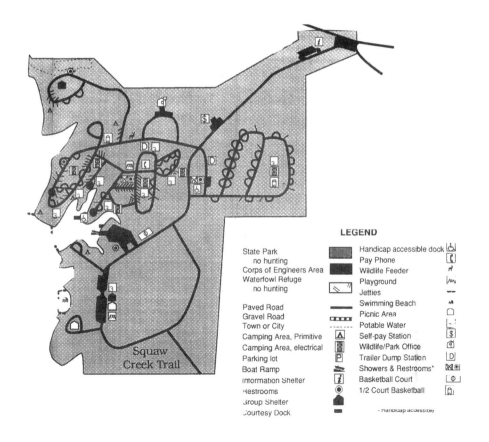

LEGEND

State Park		Handicap accessible dock	🚻
no hunting		Pay Phone	☎
Corps of Engineers Area		Wildlife Feeder	⚲
Waterfowl Refuge		Playground	
no hunting		Jetties	
Paved Road		Swimming Beach	
Gravel Road		Picnic Area	□
Town or City		Potable Water	
Camping Area, Primitive	▲	Self-pay Station	$
Camping Area, electrical		Wildlife/Park Office	
Parking lot	P	Trailer Dump Station	D
Boat Ramp		Showers & Restrooms*	
Information Shelter	i	Basketball Court	
Restrooms	◉	1/2 Court Basketball	
Group Shelter			
Courtesy Dock	▬	*- Handicap accessible	

Fall River Wildlife Area

- 8,392 acres
- Region 5
- 10 southeast of Eureka
- Upland Birds: Bobwhite quail, greater prairie chicken, mourning dove
- Waterfowl: Ducks and geese

Fall River Lake Project is another of the large reservoir projects run by the Army Corps of Engineers. Through agreement, the Kansas Department of Wildlife and Parks manages the area as a State Park and Wildlife Area. Habitat is managed to propagate wildlife species and to attract and hold game birds and waterfowl. Bobwhite quail and dove top the list of bagged birds. Waterfowl habitat is extensive and affords ample opportunities for duck and goose hunters.

The state park is found on the southern shore of the reservoir, with both improved and primitive camping. The large city of Wichita lies to the west, while the small town of Eureka is close at hand at the northeast edge of the wildlife area.

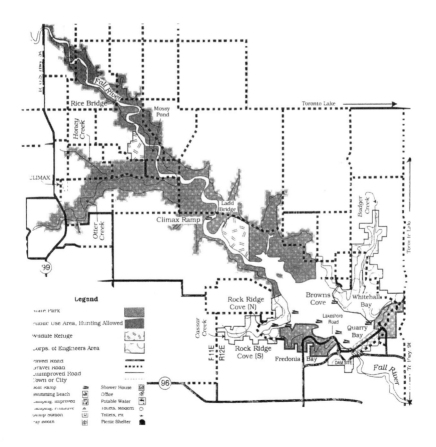

GLEN ELDER STATE PARK & WILDLIFE AREA

- 11,314 acres
- Region 1
- Tracts immediately surrounding Cawker City
- Upland Birds: Pheasant, bobwhite quail, mourning dove
- Waterfowl: Ducks and geese

Glen Elder Wildlife Area and State Park encompass the lands surrounding the sprawling Waconda Reservoir. Hunting areas are along the southern and western arms of the Reservoir. Upland bird species include pheasant, quail, and dove. Waterfowl use the protection of the reservoir during migration.

Camping is available on both primitive and developed sites in the state park area. Amenities may be found in the city of Beloit to the east, and Downs, Cawker City, and Glen Elder on the northern perimeter of the area.

HILLSDALE WILDLIFE AREA

- 12,720 acres
- Region 2
- 3 miles northwest of Paola
- Upland Birds: Bobwhite quail, mourning dove
- Waterfowl: Ducks and geese

Hillsdale Lake Project is another of the large water impoundment areas managed by the U.S. Army Corps of Engineers. The area is managed by the Kansas Department of Wildlife and Parks for uses as both a Wildlife Area and State Park. Large bodies of water such as this, which lie close to the Missouri border, are used heavily by migrating waterfowl—snow geese in particular. Bobwhite quail and dove are available for upland shooters. 200 campsites are available for public use in the state park area; 140 of the sites have electrical and water hook-ups. The Greater Kansas City Area lies to the north, and is a source for amenities. Hillsdale Lake is surrounded by the small towns of Gardner, Wellsville, Springhill, and Paola in which amenities may also be found.

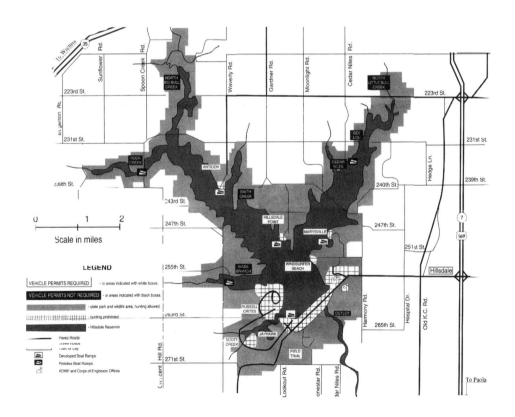

HOLLISTER WILDLIFE AREA

- 2,432 acres
- Region 5
- 6 miles west
- 2 south of Fort Scott
- Upland Birds: Bobwhite quail, greater prairie chicken, mourning dove, turkey

Hollister Wildlife Area is located at the northern edge of the Cherokee Lowlands region of Kansas, on the Missouri border. The wildlife area has no large bodies of water, and huntable populations are restricted to upland species. Camping is available. The city of Fort Scott lies to the northeast and offers amenities.

JAMESTOWN WILDLIFE AREA

- 3,239 acres
- Region 1
- 3.5 miles north, 2 west of Jamestown
- Upland Birds: Pheasant, mourning dove
- Waterfowl: Ducks and geese

Salt Lake and Sportsman's Lake are the nucleus of the Jamestown Wildlife Area. Uplands surrounding the lake hold pheasant and mourning dove in limited numbers. Waterfowl hunting is a productive endeavor depending upon the availability of migrating waterfowl. Camping is available on-site. The city of Concordia, with its full host of services, sits to the southwest.

JEFFREY ENERGY CENTER–HANZLICK WILDLIFE AREA

- 6,900 acres
- Region 2
- 5 miles north, 3 west of St. Mary's
- Special Permit required some areas, contact office on site, 913-456-6153.
- Upland Birds: Pheasant, bobwhite quail, greater prairie chicken, mourning dove
- Waterfowl: Ducks and geese

The 10,500-acre Jeffrey Energy Center sits just north of the Kansas river near the town of St. Mary's. The site is a coal burning, electric power plant. In a cooperative effort between the managing company, Western Resources, and the Kansas Department of Wildlife and Parks, the property is managed for the benefit of wildlife populations and public hunting.

Jeffrey is divided into four wildlife areas. Wildlife areas 1 and 2 are open to public hunting. Area 1, which consists of 1,385 acres, sits outside of the facility site and is open for unlimited hunting-only access. The 5,600 acres of Area 2 are available for hunting only through a check-in and -out procedure at the front gate. Hunters are issued badges color-coded according to the types of hunting in which they are engaging. Area 2 is a limited access area and entry permits are issued on a first come, first served basis.

Area 3 is closed to entry and maintained as a wildlife refuge. As a result of the plant's cooling requirements, open water is found on the site after freeze-up, and consequently waterfowl congregate in good numbers. Area 4, the Oregon Nature Trail and Public Education Center, is set aside as a public park.

Amenities are available in the adjacent town of St. Mary's.

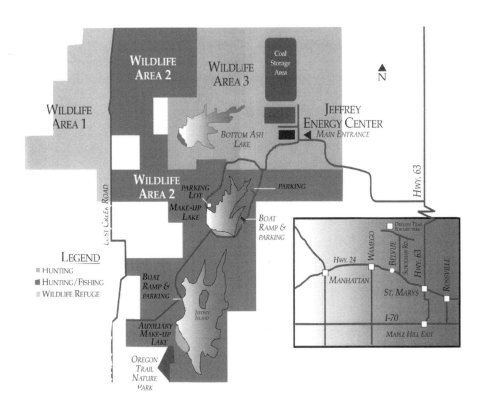

JOHN REDMOND WILDLIFE AREA
(OTTER CREEK ARM)

- 1,472 acres
- Region 5
- 4 miles west, 2 north of Burlington
- Upland Birds: Bobwhite quail, mourning dove
- Waterfowl: Ducks and geese

The John Redmond Wildlife Area sits due south of the Flint Hills National Wildlife Refuge, on the sprawling John Redmond Reservoir. The reservoir project site is managed by the U.S. Army Corps of Engineers. Through a cooperative agreement, the Otter Creek arm of the reservoir is managed as a Wildlife Area by the Kansas Department of Wildlife and Parks.

John Redmond is famous among local gunners as a waterfowling site. Large concentrations of birds, including big flocks of snow geese, are found in the area. Bobwhite quail, mourning dove and turkey hunting is also available.

Camping and RV sites are available adjacent to the wildlife area on the southeast end of the reservoir, near the dam. The city of Emporia sits to the northwest, where amenities may be found.

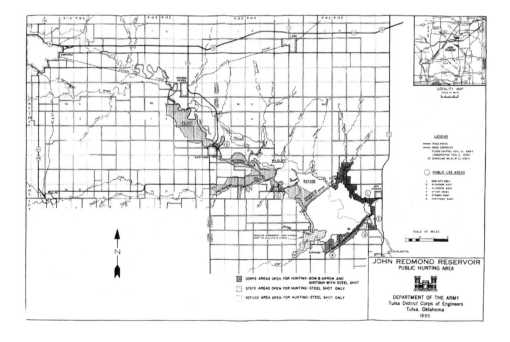

KAW WILDLIFE AREA

- 4,341 acres
- Region 4
- 1 mile southeast of Arkansas City
- Upland Birds: Bobwhite quail, mourning dove
- Waterfowl: Ducks and geese

Kaw Wildlife Area is owned by the U.S. Army Corps of Engineers and managed by the Kansas Department of Wildlife and Parks. The site is found on the Oklahoma border, in the southeastern edge of Kansas. The wildlife area follows a stretch of the Arkansas River and contains both wetlands and hardwood uplands. The site is managed as wildlife habitat and the entire acreage is open to hunting. One quarter of the wildlife area is farmed on a sharecrop basis, with a portion of the harvest left in the fields to provide wildlife food.

Kaw is known as an important snow goose hunting area. Waterfowling is the principal type of hunting done on the area. Hunting for bobwhites, mourning dove, and turkey is also available. Primitive camping is permitted in designated areas. Services are available in Arkansas City.

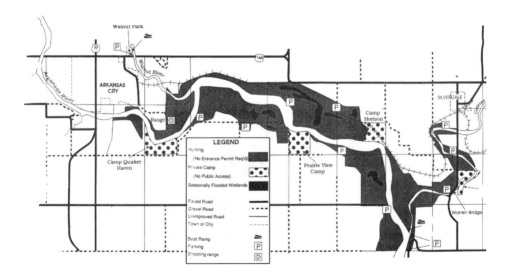

LA CYGNE LAKE & WILDLIFE AREA

- 4,600 acres
- Region 5
- 5 miles east of La Cygne
- Firearms restricted to shotguns and .22 caliber rifles; no high-powered rifles allowed.
- Upland Birds: Bobwhite quail, mourning dove
- Waterfowl: Ducks and geese

La Cygne Lake is owned by the Kansas City Power and Light Company, which operates a coal-fueled generating facility on the lake's lower end. Warm discharged water raises the ambient temperature of the lake and maintains an ice-free area, allowing waterfowl to congregate when other available loafing areas become closed due to ice. This condition generates hunting opportunities when weather conditions turn severe.

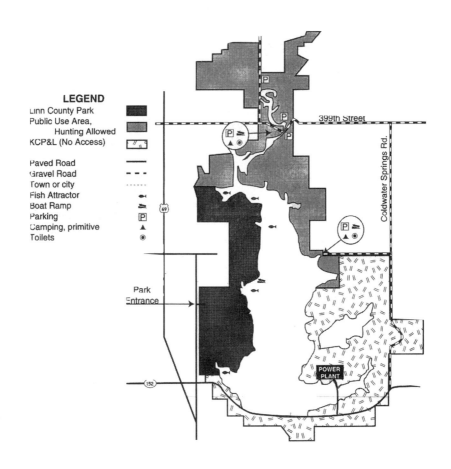

Waterfowl hunting is generally good all along the Missouri border where the lake is located. Large flocks of snows and blues will congregate on both La Cygne Lake and Marais des Cygnes Wildlilfe Area, a short distance to the south. Other hunting is available for bobwhite quail and mourning dove.

While no structured camping facilities are available, primitive camping is allowed in designated areas. Boat ramps and public toilets are available on the wildlife area. No large towns are in the immediate area.

LOVEWELL STATE PARK & WILDLIFE AREA

- 5,215 acres
- Region 1
- 5 miles east, 9 north of Mankato
- Upland Birds: Pheasant, bobwhite quail, mourning dove
- Waterfowl: Ducks and geese

Lovewell Reservoir is owned by the U.S. Bureau of Reclamation and leased by the Kansas Department of Wildlife and Parks to be managed as a State Park and Wildlife Area. The water impoundment was constructed to provide flood control relief and irrigation water. Lovewell is located on the Nebraska border, in the extreme north-central part of the state.

Uplands are managed for pheasant and bobwhite quail, and hunting for these species has been rated as good. The principal beneficiaries of the Department of Wildlife and Parks' efforts are the many ducks and geese utilizing the area. Large numbers of migrating birds stop at the reservoir during their fall and spring migrations. Hunting is allowed on the majority of the reservoir, which is contained in the wildlife area. A flock of up to a thousand Canada geese winter over on the reservoir.

Camping is available at both the state park and the wildlife area. For RV enthusiasts, the park offers 36 utility hook-ups. The closest services are available in Mankato.

MARAIS DES CYGNES WILDLIFE AREA

- 6,699 acres
- Region 5
- 5 miles north of Pleasanton
- Upland Birds: Bobwhite quail, mourning dove
- Waterfowl: Ducks and geese

Marais des Cygnes is a large expanse of waterfowl habitat at the southeastern edge of Kansas on the Missouri border. It is one of the state's most productive waterfowl areas and attracts large flocks of snows and blues.

The Wildlife Area is broken up into multiple units and waterfowl hunters are required to register and obtain a permit prior to hunting. At the conclusion of the hunt, waterfowlers are required to report their daily harvest. Permits are free of charge and available after 5 am at the area headquarters. There are no assigned hunt areas for permittees, and choice of hunt location is given on a first come, first served basis. Nontoxic shot is required for all species area-wide.

Some special closures apply, so be sure to familiarize yourself with the area. A hunting information phone number with a recorded message is available. This provides an easy way to access information on Marais des Cygnes Wildlife Area's hunting conditions and current success rates. The number is 913-352-8941 and is accessible throughout most of the season.

Primitive camping is available in designated areas on the Wildlife Area. The nearest large towns are Fort Scott and Paola.

MARION WILDLIFE AREA

- 9,560 acres
- Region 4
- 15 miles west of Marion
- Upland Birds: Pheasant, mourning dove
- Waterfowl: Ducks and geese

Marion Reservoir Project is a large water impoundment constructed and operated by the U.S. Army Corps of Engineers. Through a cooperative agreement, the Kansas Department of Wildlife and Parks manages the reservoir for geese and as a Wildlife Area open to hunting. A 500-acre waterfowl refuge has been established on the south central shore of the lake to provide a sanctuary that will hold bird numbers on the reservoir. Along with waterfowl, pheasants and mourning dove are also in good supply. Bobwhites are also found on the area.

Campsites and boat ramps are available. The nearest services are in Marion, 15 miles to the east, and Hillsboro, 20 miles to the west.

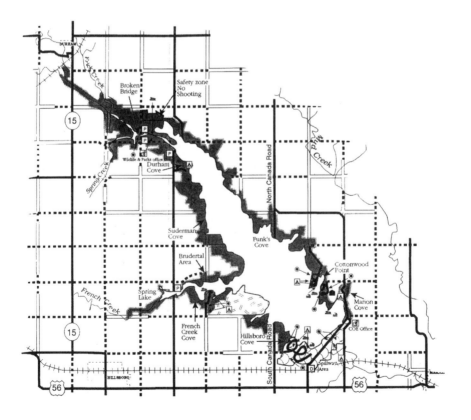

McPherson Wetlands Wildlife Area

- 1,543 acres
- Region 4
- 2 miles north, 1 east of Conway
- Subject to change; call for current regulations, 316-241-7669.
- Upland Birds: Pheasant, mourning dove
- Waterfowl: Ducks and geese

Located near the town of McPherson, the McPherson Wetlands are a remnant of the vast wetlands that existed there prior to 1900. The wetlands are managed for waterfowl. Snipe and rail ply the shallow waters. Pheasant and mourning dove are also available. Nontoxic shot is required for all shotgun hunting.

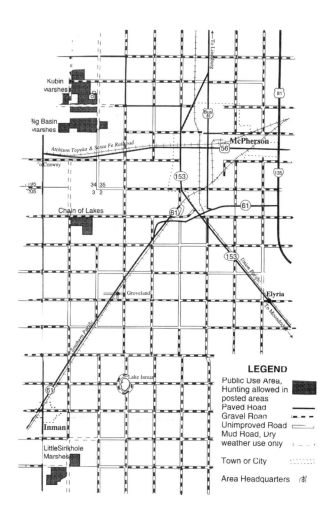

LEGEND

Public Use Area,
Hunting allowed in
posted areas
Paved Road
Gravel Road
Unimproved Road
Mud Road, Dry
weather use only

Town or City

Area Headquarters

MELVERN WILDLIFE AREA

- 9,407 acres
- Region 5
- 4 miles north of Lebo
- Refuge portion closed October 1–January 15.
- Upland Birds: Bobwhite quail, mourning dove
- Waterfowl: Ducks and geese

Due north of the John Redmond Reservoir, the Melvern Lake is another large-scale reservoir project constructed and operated by the U.S. Army Corps of Engineers. The project lies on the eastern edge of the Flint Hills and is formed in the channel of the Marais des Cygnes River. Managed by the Department of Wildlife and Parks, the area contains a Wildlife Area which allows hunting. Adjacent parks have complete facilities for campers and RV enthusiasts. Available species include bobwhite quail, mourning dove, and turkey. The reservoir sits in an important waterfowl area and is a magnet for traveling birds. Waterfowl hunting could be very good in season, depending on bird numbers.

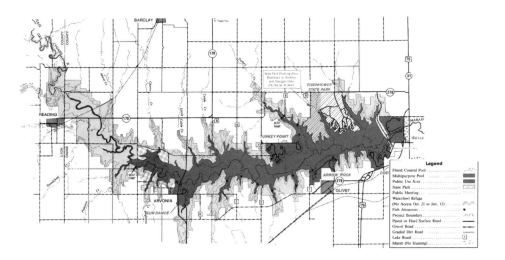

MILFORD WILDLIFE AREA

- 18,873 acres
- Region 2
- 5 miles northwest of Junction City
- Upland Birds: Pheasant, bobwhite quail, greater prairie chicken, mourning dove
- Waterfowl: Ducks and geese

The Milford Lake Project is a U.S. Army Corps of Engineer's impoundment on the Republican River. The site encompasses a total of 44,231 acres. Hunting is allowed on the 18,873 Milford Wildlife Area. Fort Riley Military Reservation, the second largest public hunting area in the state, sits on the eastern border of the reservoir and provides additional hunting opportunities. Upland species include bobwhite quail, pheasant, mourning dove, greater prairie chicken, and turkey. Waterfowl habitat adds ducks and geese to the bag. A 1,103 acre wildlife refuge provides an important sanctuary for area waterfowl.

State park facilities provide a range of services from primitive camping sites to full service RV hook-ups. Clay Center sits north of the area, and Junction City sits to the south.

MINED LAND WILDLIFE AREA

- 14,500 acres
- Region 5
- Scattered tracts throughout Crawford, Cherokee, and Labette Counties
- Upland Birds: Bobwhite quail, mourning dove
- Waterfowl: Ducks and geese

The Mined Lands Wildlife Area is one of those Cinderella stories: former strip mined lands were rehabilitated and donated to the Department of Wildlife and Parks as a wildlife habitat and public use area. Assorted tracts of land are scattered over three counties. The Mined Lands unit is located in the extreme southeastern corner of the state, in an area called the Cherokee Lowlands. This habitat type is characterized by heavily brushed and forested oak- and hickory-lined watercourses with small grass openings. The area is prime white-tailed deer and turkey habitat. Bobwhite quail and dove do well on the portions of the wildlife area managed for them. There are a multitude of small bodies of water left over from former mining activities, and these impoundments furnish opportunities for waterfowl hunters.

Provisions are made for those interested in camping or RV's. The towns of Pittsburg, Columbus, and Oswego can provide any required amenities.

NEOSHO WILDLIFE AREA

- 2,246 acres
- Region 5
- 1 mile east of St. Paul
- Upland Birds: Bobwhite quail, mourning dove
- Waterfowl: Ducks and geese

The Neosho Wildlife Area is a manmade marsh project originally constructed with funding provided by Pittman-Robertson Federal Aid funds and the Kansas Department of Wildlife and Parks. It opened to the public in 1962. In 1988, the area was expanded through a cost-sharing agreement with Ducks Unlimited. The area is managed principally for waterfowl hunting. Bobwhite quail and turkey are also found in good numbers in the area. The unit is divided into pools and flooded at an approximate depth of two feet. Corn, milo, and millet are planted on the wildlife area to provide food for wildlife species.

A permitting system is in place, and area hunters must check in at the check station prior to the start of their hunt and return a completed permit form at the end of their hunt.

Primitive camping is permitted on the wildlife area. Consult with area personnel for additional information on rules and regulations governing the use of the area. Amenities are found in the surrounding towns of Erie, Girard, and Parsons.

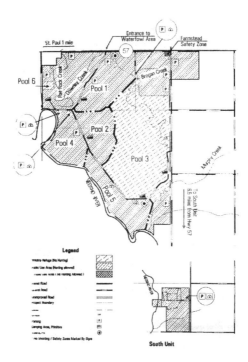

NORTON WILDLIFE AREA

- 6,421 acres
- Region 1
- 5 miles west, 2 south of Norton
- Upland Birds: Pheasant, bobwhite quail, mourning dove
- Waterfowl: Ducks and geese

Norton Public Lands sits tucked directly under the Nebraska border, on the high plains of northwestern Kansas. The Public Lands consist of land surrounding the Keith Sebelius Reservoir. The Norton Public Lands area is split into two types of management: Norton Wildlife Area and Prairie Dog State Park.

The Wildlife Area is managed for public hunting, and ring-necked pheasants are present in good numbers. Small populations of bobwhite quail, greater prairie chickens, and turkeys also provide a hunting opportunity in the area. Agricultural fields concentrate doves during their early season and do provide shooting. The central section of the reservoir, bordering Prairie Dog State Park, is set aside as a Waterfowl Refuge; all other portions of the wildlife area are open to waterfowl hunting. Numbers of ducks and geese fluctuate according to weather and migration patterns, but the area can provide good waterfowl shooting.

Camping is found in Prairie Dog State Park. For RV enthusiasts, there are 42 electrical hook-ups, 30 with water. The nearest amenities are in the town of Norton.

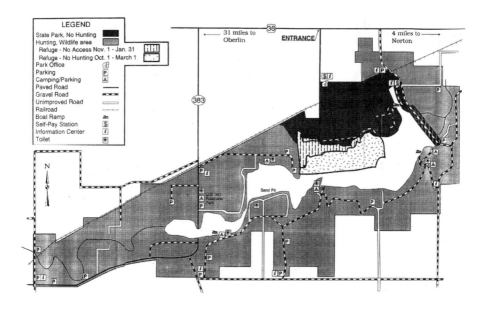

PERRY WILDLIFE AREA

- 10,984 acres
- Region 2
- 1.5 miles north, 1 west of Valley Falls
- Upland Birds: Pheasant, bobwhite quail, mourning dove
- Waterfowl: Ducks and geese

The Perry Lake Project is an impoundment on the Delaware River, managed by the U.S. Army Corps of Engineers. It is one of the largest impoundments in the state, and sits in close proximity to one of the largest cities in the state, the state capital, Topeka. Through agreement, the Kansas Department of Wildlife and Parks operates the Perry Wildlife Area on the northern half of the Project. The Department also operates numerous park facilities at the southern end of the reservoir. The large open water and marsh areas serve as a draw for migrating waterfowl. Pheasant, bobwhite quail, and turkey are also available to Perry Wildlife Area hunters.

A full range of facilities are available at the southern end of the reservoir for campers and RV owners. The cities of Topeka and Lawrence sit to the southwest and the southeast of the reservoir, respectively.

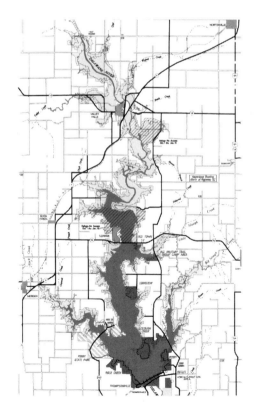

Pratt Sandhills Wildlife Area

- 4,757 acres
- Region 3
- 5 miles west, 6 north of Cullison
- Upland Birds: Pheasant, bobwhite quail, lesser prairie chicken, mourning dove

Pratt Sandhills Wildlife Area is known as one of only two public areas where lesser prairie chickens are available for hunting. The area consists of grasslands with some stretches of tree windbreaks. The principal game available on the wildlife area is bobwhite quail, and the topography is ideally suited for the running of bird dogs. The area also contains limited populations of ring-necked pheasant. During early season, mourning doves frequent the grasslands and are generally hunted on the water at area windmills. Turkey hunting is also available. Having traveled the roads there personally, I can tell you that the sand gets a little dicey in places.

Amenities can be found in the nearby town of Pratt.

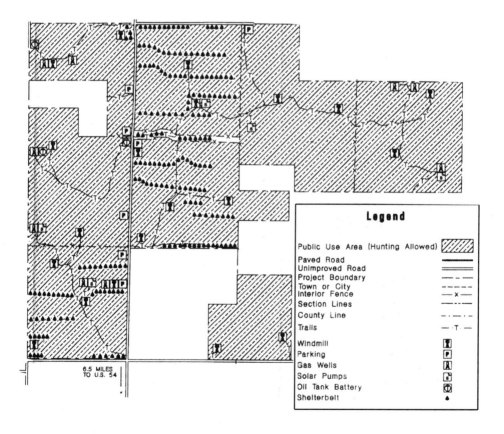

SHERMAN STATE FISHING LAKE & WILDLIFE AREA

- 1,547 acres
- Region 1
- 10 miles south, 2 west of Goodland
- Upland Birds: Pheasant, mourning dove

Sherman State Fishing Lake and Wildlife Area is located south of Goodland, on the high plains near the western border of Kansas and very close to Colorado. Available species include pheasant and dove. Camping is available on-site.

SOUTH FORK WILDLIFE AREA

- 1,000 acres
- Region 1
- 12.5 miles northeast of St. Francis
- Upland Birds: Pheasant, bobwhite quail, mourning dove
- Waterfowl: Ducks and geese

South Fork Wildlife Area is managed by the Department of Wildlife and Parks. Available species include bobwhite quail, pheasant, dove, turkey, and waterfowl. Amenities may be found in the town of St. Francis.

TEXAS LAKE WILDLIFE AREA

- 1,040 acres
- Region 3
- 4 miles west, 1 north of Cullison
- Upland Birds: Pheasant, bobwhite quail, mourning dove
- Waterfowl: Ducks and geese

Texas Lake Wildlife Area is found west of Pratt, where amenities may be found. The small site offers opportunities for waterfowl. In addition, bobwhite quail, dove, and pheasants are found on the Wildlife Area.

TORONTO WILDLIFE AREA

- 4,766 acres
- Region 5
- 3 miles northwest of Toronto
- Upland Birds: Bobwhite quail, greater prairie chicken, mourning dove
- Waterfowl: Ducks and geese

The Toronto Lake Project is run by the U.S. Army Corps of Engineers. The site includes a State Park near the dam, at the southern end of the impoundment, and an extensive Wildlife Area on the northern extremities of Project lands. The unit is an important waterfowling area. In addition, bobwhite quail, mourning dove, greater prairie chickens, and turkeys are available for hunting.

Facilities for camping and RV's and boat launching are available at the southern end of the reservoir. The town Yates Center is found to the northeast.

TUTTLE CREEK WILDLIFE AREA

- 12,200 acres
- Region 2
- Extending upriver from Randolph to Blue Rapids
- Upland Birds: Pheasant, bobwhite quail, greater prairie chicken, mourning dove
- Waterfowl: Ducks and geese

Tuttle Creek Lake Project is an impoundment on the Big Blue River, just north of Manhattan. This body of water is the second largest lake in the state. The Project is operated by the U.S. Army Corps of Engineers. Through a cooperative agreement with the Kansas Department of Wildlife and Parks, Tuttle Creek Wildlife Area is open to public hunting. In addition, the Department operates numerous park facilities, including boat ramps and camping areas on the southern end of the lake. The town of Manhattan, due south of the reservoir, can provide needed amenities.

Tuttle Creek is a popular waterfowling area, and in season, migrating waterfowl use the site as a resting and feeding area. The area falls within the Flint Hills region of Kansas. The large, rolling grass hills surrounding the reservoir contain bobwhite quail, ring-necked pheasant, and greater prairie chicken.

WEBSTER WILDLIFE AREA

- 5,000 acres
- Region 1
- 8 miles west of Stockton
- Upland Birds: Pheasant, mourning dove
- Waterfowl: Ducks and geese

Webster Wildlife Area sits at the south end of the Webster Reservoir near the town of Stockton. Hunting is allowed on site and opportunities exist for pheasant, mourning dove, and waterfowl.

Campsites and boat launching ramps exist in several areas of the facility. The nearest services can be found in Stockton.

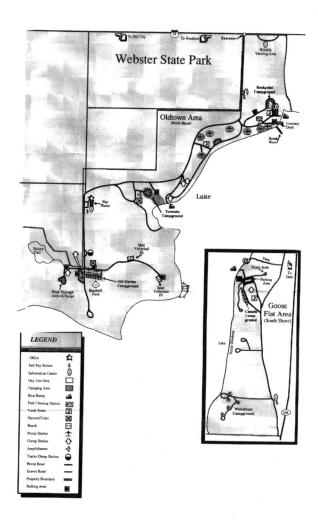

WILSON STATE PARK & WILDLIFE AREA

- 8,039 acres
- Region 1
- 7 miles north of Bunker Hill
- Upland Birds: Pheasant, bobwhite quail, mourning dove

Wilson Lake Project is a site constructed and operated by the U.S. Army Corps of Engineers. The site is managed for public hunting and as a State Park access by the Kansas Department of Wildlife and Parks. The western end of Wilson Lake is incorporated into the Wilson Wildlife Area. Available game birds include ring-necked pheasant, bobwhite quail, mourning dove, and turkey. Waterfowl hunting is available in season.

Numerous campsites and boat launches line the shore of this large water impoundment. Amenities can be found in Russell, the nearest large town, found to the west of the Project.

WOODSON STATE FISHING LAKE & WILDLIFE AREA

- 3,065 acres
- Region 5
- 5 miles east of Toronto
- Upland Birds: Bobwhite quail, greater prairie chicken, mourning dove
- Waterfowl: Ducks and geese

Woodson State Fishing Lake and Wildlife Area sits above Toronto Lake and Fall River Lake. Waterfowl hunting is available on the lake portion of the site. The surrounding hillsides exemplify the rolling grass of Kansas' Flint Hills. Upland species include bobwhite quail, mourning dove, greater prairie chicken, and turkey.

Campsites and a boat launch are available on-site. The town of Yates Center sits to the northeast and can provide any needed services.

SMALLER WILDLIFE AREAS

Almena Diversion Wildlife Area
- 111 acres
- Region 1
- 2.5 miles southwest of Almena
- Upland Birds: Pheasant, bobwhite quail, mourning dove

Atchison State Fishing Lake & Wildlife Area
- 202 acres
- Region 2
- 3 miles north, 2 west, 0.5 north of Atchison
- Upland Birds: Pheasant, bobwhite quail, mourning dove

Barber State Fishing Lake & Wildlife Area
- 80 acres
- Region 3
- 0.25 miles north of Medicine Lodge
- Upland Birds: Pheasant, bobwhite quail, mourning dove

Bolton Wildlife Area
- 640 acres
- Region 2
- 2 miles north, 1.5 west of Paxico
- Upland Birds: Bobwhite quail, mourning dove

Bourbon State Fishing Lake & Wildlife Area
- 210 acres
- Region 5
- 4.5 miles east of Elsmore
- Upland Birds: Bobwhite quail, mourning dove
- Waterfowl: Ducks and geese

Brown State Fishing Lake & Wildlife Area
- 189 acres
- Region 2
- 8 miles east, 0.5 south of Hiawatha
- Special regulations; phone Perry Office, 913-945-6615.
- Upland Birds: Pheasant, bobwhite quail, mourning dove
- Waterfowl: Ducks and geese

Brzon Wildlife Area
- 320 acres
- Region 1
- 7 miles west, 4 north of Belleville
- Special only: permits for upland game. Phone 913-753-4971.
- Upland Birds: Pheasant, bobwhite quail, mourning dove

Butler State Fishing Lake & Wildlife Area
- 320 acres
- Region 4
- 3 miles west, 1 north of Latham
- Upland Birds: Bobwhite quail, greater prairie chicken, mourning dove
- Waterfowl: Ducks and geese

Chase State Fishing Lake & Wildlife Area
- 469 acres
- Region 4
- 1.5 miles west of Cottonwood Falls
- Upland Birds: Bobwhite quail, greater prairie chicken, mourning dove
- Waterfowl: Ducks and geese

Clark State Fishing Lake & Wildlife Area
- 700 acres
- Region 3
- 9 miles south, 1 west of Kingdown
- Upland Birds: Bobwhite quail, mourning dove

Concannon Wildlife Area
- 800 acres
- Region 3
- 15 miles northeast of Garden City
- Upland Birds: Pheasant, mourning dove,
- Waterfowl: Ducks and geese

Cowley State Fishing Lake & Wildlife Area
- 197 acres
- Region 4
- 16 miles east of Arkansas City
- Upland Birds: Bobwhite quail, mourning dove
- Waterfowl: Ducks and geese

Crawford Wildlife Area
- 510 acres
- Region 5
- 4 miles north, 1 east of Pittsburg
- Upland Birds: Bobwhite quail, mourning dove
- Waterfowl: Ducks and geese

Douglas State Fishing Lake & Wildlife Area
- 538 acres
- Region 2
- 1 mile north, 3 east of Baldwin
- Upland Birds: Bobwhite quail, mourning dove
- Waterfowl: Ducks and geese

Dove Flats Wildlife Area
- 206 acres
- Region 5
- 2.5 miles east, 1 mile north of Elk City
- Upland Birds: Bobwhite quail, mourning dove
- Waterfowl: Ducks and geese

Duck Creek Wildlife Area
- 246 acres
- Region 5
- 1.5 miles east, 3.3 miles north of Elk City
- Upland Birds: Bobwhite quail, mourning dove
- Waterfowl: Ducks and geese

Finney Game Refuge
- 670 acres
- Region 3
- 0.5 miles south of Garden City
- Portions open at certain times. Phone 316-276-8886 for more information.
- No prairie chicken hunts.
- Upland Birds: Pheasant, mourning dove

Finney State Fishing Lake & Wildlife Area
- 863 acres
- Region 3
- 8 miles north, 3 west of Kalvesta
- Upland Birds: Pheasant, mourning dove
- Waterfowl: Ducks and geese

Geary State Fishing Lake & Wildlife Area
- 185 acres
- Region 2
- 8.5 miles south, 1 west of Junction City
- Upland Birds: Pheasant, bobwhite quail, mourning dove
- Waterfowl: Ducks and geese

Goodman Wildlife Area
- 265 acres
- Region 3
- 5 miles east of Ness City
- Upland Birds: Pheasant, bobwhite quail, mourning dove
- Waterfowl: Ducks and geese

Gove Public Domain Lands
- 160 acres
- Region 1
- 22 miles south, 1 west of Quinter
- Upland Birds: Bobwhite quail, mourning dove

Greeley County Wildlife Area
- 900 acres
- Region 3
- 10 miles north, 5 east of Tribune
- Upland Birds: Pheasant, mourning dove

Hain State Fishing Lake & Wildlife Area
- 53 acres
- Region 3
- 5 miles west of Spearville
- Open to migratory bird hunting.
- Upland Birds: Mourning dove
- Waterfowl: Ducks and geese

Hamilton State Fishing Lake & Wildlife Area
- 666 acres
- Region 3
- 3 miles west, 2 north of Syracuse
- Upland Birds: Pheasant, mourning dove
- Waterfowl: Ducks and geese

Harmon Wildlife Area
- 102 acres
- Region 5
- 1 mile north, 1 east of Chetopa
- Upland Birds: Bobwhite quail, mourning dove
- Waterfowl: Ducks and geese

Hodgeman State Fishing Lake & Wildlife Area
- 254 acres
- Region 3
- 4 miles east, 2 south of Jetmore
- Upland Birds: Pheasant, bobwhite quail, mourning dove

Hulah Wildlife Area
- 844 acres
- Region 5
- Scattered tracts east and west of Elgin
- Upland Birds: Bobwhite quail, mourning dove

Isabel Wildlife Area
- 200 acres
- Region 3
- 1 mile east, 2 miles north of Isabel
- Upland Birds: Pheasant, bobwhite quail, mourning dove
- Waterfowl: Ducks and geese

Jewell State Fishing Lake &Wildlife Area
- 165 acres
- Region 1
- 6 miles south, 3 west of Manakato
- Upland Birds: Pheasant, mourning dove

Leavenworth State Fishing Lake & Wildlife Area
- 200 acres
- Region 2
- 3 miles north, 2 west of Tonganoxie
- Upland Birds: Bobwhite quail, mourning dove
- Waterfowl: Ducks and geese

Logan State Fishing Lake & Wildlife Area
- 271 acres
- Region 1
- 9 miles south of Winona
- Upland Birds: Pheasant, mourning dove
- Waterfowl: Ducks and geese

Louisburg-Middle Creek State Fishing Lake
- 511 acres
- Region 2
- 7 miles south of Louisburg
- Upland Birds: Bobwhite quail, mourning dove
- Waterfowl: Ducks and geese

Lyon State Fishing Lake & Wildlife Area
- 562 acres
- Region 5
- 5 miles west, 1 north of Reading
- Upland Birds: Bobwhite quail, mourning dove
- Waterfowl: Ducks and geese

Meade State Fishing Lake & Wildlife Area
- 420 acres
- Region 3
- 8 miles south, 5 west of Meade
- Archery or muzzleloader only for deer.
- Upland Birds: Pheasant, bobwhite quail, scaled quail, mourning dove
- Waterfowl: Ducks and geese

Miami State Fishing Lake & Wildlife Area
- 267 acres
- Region 2
- 8 miles east, 6 south of Osawatomie
- Upland Birds: Bobwhite quail, mourning dove
- Waterfowl: Ducks and geese

Nebo State Fishing Lake & Wildlife Area
- 75 acres
- Region 2
- 8 miles east of Holton
- Upland Birds: Pheasant, bobwhite quail, mourning dove
- Waterfowl: Ducks and geese

Nemaha Wildlife Area
- 710 acres
- Region 2
- 1 mile east, 4 south of Seneca
- Upland Birds: Pheasant, bobwhite quail, mourning dove

Osage State Fishing Lake
- 480 acres
- Region 5
- 3 miles south of Carbondale
- Special Restrictions.
- Upland Birds: Bobwhite quail, mourning dove
- Waterfowl: Ducks and geese

Ottawa State Fishing Lake & Wildlife Area
- 611 acres
- Region 1
- 6 miles east of Minneapolis
- Shotgun and archery only, November 1–March 31.
- Upland Birds: Pheasant, bobwhite quail, mourning dove

Pottawatomie No. 1 State Fishing Lake & Wildlife Area
- 190 acres
- Region 2
- 4.5 miles north of Westmoreland
- Upland Birds: Bobwhite quail, mourning dove

Rooks State Fishing Lake & Wildlife Area
- 243 acres
- Region 1
- 1.5 miles south, 2 west of Stockton
- Upland Birds: Pheasant, bobwhite quail, mourning dove
- Waterfowl: Ducks and geese

Rutlader Wildlife Area
- 108 acres
- Region 2
- 0.5 miles north of Louisburg-Middle Creek State Fishing Lake, 355 st. and Metcalf
- Upland Birds: Bobwhite quail, mourning dove

Sand Hills State Park
- 800 acres
- Region 4
- 3 miles northeast of Hutchinson
- Hunting only by special permit; call 316-542-3664.
- Upland Birds: Pheasant, bobwhite quail, mourning dove

Scott Wildlife Area
- 160 acres
- Region 3
- 15 miles north of Scott City
- Upland Birds: Bobwhite quail, mourning dove

Shawnee State Fishing Lake
- 680 acres
- Region 2
- 7.5 miles north of Silver Lake
- Contact Clinton Office for special regulations, 913- 887-6882.
- Upland Birds: Pheasant, bobwhite quail, greater prairie chicken, mourning dove

Sheridan Wildlife Area
- 458 acres
- Region 1
- 2 miles east, 4 north of Quinter
- Upland Birds: Pheasant, mourning dove
- Waterfowl: Ducks and geese

Slate Creek Wildlife Area
- 667 acres
- Region 4
- 6 miles south, 1.5 west of Oxford
- Special Restrictions; call 316-321-7180.
- Upland Birds: Pheasant, bobwhite quail, mourning dove

Spring River Wildlife Area
- 424 acres
- Region 5
- 3 miles east, 0.25 north of Crestline
- Upland Birds: Bobwhite quail, mourning dove
- Waterfowl: Ducks and geese

St. Francis Wildlife Area
- 480 acres
- Region 1
- 2 miles south, 2.5 west of St. Francis
- Upland Birds: Pheasant, bobwhite quail, mourning dove
- Waterfowl: Ducks and geese

Washington State Fishing Lake & Wildlife Area
- 442 acres
- Region 2
- 7 miles north, 3 west of Washington
- Upland Birds: Pheasant, bobwhite quail, mourning dove
- Waterfowl: Ducks and geese

Wilson State Fishing Lake & Wildlife Area
- 90 acres
- Region 5
- 1 mile south of Buffalo
- Upland Birds: Bobwhite quail, mourning dove

Woodston Diversion Wildlife Area
- 210 acres
- Region 1
- 8 miles east of Stockton
- Upland Birds: Pheasant, bobwhite quail, mourning dove

Kansas Public Hunting Areas

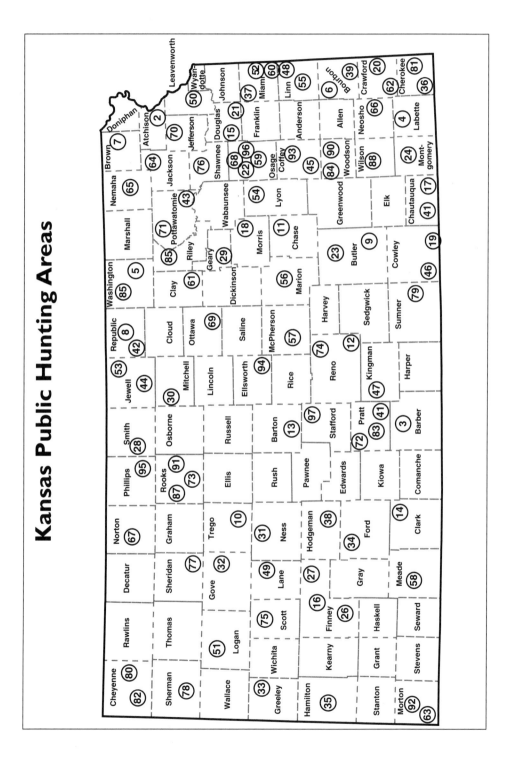

Visual Index to Public Hunting Areas

State Areas

Area Name	Acres	Location
1. Almena Diversion Wildlife Area	111	2½ miles SW of Almena
2. Atchison State Fishing Lake and Wildlife Area	202	3 miles N, 2 W, ½ N of Atchison
3. Barber State Fishing Lake and Wildlife Area	202	¼ mile N of Medicine Lodge
4. Big Hill Wildlife Area	1,320	8 miles W, 4 S of Parsons
5. Blue River Wildlife Area	35	7 miles E, 1 S of Washington
6. Bourbon State Fishing Lake and Wildlife Area	210	4½ miles E of Elsmore
7. Brown State Fishing Lake and Wildlife Area	189	8 miles E, ½ S of Hiawatha **Special:** Phone Perry Unit Office
8. Brzon Wildlife Area	320	7 miles W, 4 N of Belleville **Special:** Permits for upland game
9. Butler State Fishing Lake and Wildlife Area	320	3 miles W, 1 N of Latham
10. Cedar Bluff Wildlife Area	12,000	16 miles S of WaKeeney
11. Chase State Fishing Lake and Wildlife Area	469	1½ miles W of Cottonwood Falls
12. Cheney Wildlife Area	17,308	7 miles E of Pretty Prairie
13. Cheyenne Bottoms Wildlife Area	13,280	5 miles N, 5 E of Great Bend
14. Clark State Fishing Lake and Wildlife Area	400	9 miles S, 1 W of Kingstown No migratory waterfowl hunting
15. Clinton Wildlife Area	8,700	8 miles SW of Lawrence
16. Concannon Wildlife Area	800	15 miles NE of Garden City
17. Copan Wildlife Area	2,360	½ mile W of Caney
18. Council Grove Wildlife Area	5,873	5 miles NW of Council Grove
19. Cowley State Fishing Lake and Wildlife Area	197	16 miles E of Arkansas City
20. Crawford Wildlife Area	70	4 miles N, 1 E of Pittsburg

Area Name	Acres	Location
21. Douglas State Fishing Lake and Wildlife Area	538	1 mile N, 3 E of Baldwin
22. Eisenhower State Park	620	5 miles S, 3 W of Lyndon Archery and shotgun only, October 16–March 31
23. El Dorado State Park and Wildlife Area	13,000	2 miles E, 1 N of El Dorad0
24. Elk City Wildlife Area	12,240	3 miles W of Independence
25. Fall River Wildlife Area	8,392	10 miles SE of Eureka
26. Finney Buffalo Refuge	3,800	½ mile S of Garden City Portions open at certain times of year; call 316-276-8886 for more information
27. Finney State Fishing Lake and Wildlife Area	863	8 miles N, 3 W of Kalvesta
28. Francis Wach Wildlife Area	800	10 miles E, 1 N of Agra
29. Geary State Fishing Lake and Wildlife Area	185	8½ miles S, 1 W of Junction City
30. Glen Elder Wildlife Area	11,314	Tracts immediately surrounding Cawker City
31. Goodman Wildlife Area	265	5 miles E of Ness City
32. Gove Public Domain Lands	160	22 miles S, 1 W of Quinter
33. Greeley County Wildlife Area	900	10 miles N, 5 E of Tribune
34. Hain State Fishing Lake and Wildlife Area	53	5 miles W of Spearville Migratory bird hunting only
35. Hamilton State Fishing Lake and Wildlife Area	592	3 miles W, 2 N of Syracuse
36. Harmon Wildlife Area	102	1 mile N, 1 E of Chetopa
37. Hillsdale Reservoir	12,720	3 miles NW of Paola
38. Hodgeman State Fishing Lake and Wildlife Area	254	4 miles E, 2 S of Jetmore
39. Hollister Wildlife Area	2,432	6 miles W, 2 S of Fort Scott
40. Hulah Wildlife Area	844	Scattered tracts E and W of Elgin
41. Isabel Wildlife Area	200	1 mile E, 2 N of Isabel
42. Jamestown Wildlife Area	3,239	3½ miles N, 2 W of Jamestown

Area Name	Acres	Location
43. Jeffrey Energy Center/ Hanzlick Wildlife Area	6,900	5 miles N, 3 W of St. Marys Special permit required for some areas; contact office on site
44. Jewell State Fishing Lake and Wildlife Area	165	6 mile S, 3 E of Mankato
45. John Redmond Wildlife Area (Otter Creek Arm)	1,472	4 miles W, 2 N of Burlington
46. Kaw Wildlife Area	4,341	1 mile SE of Arkansas City
47. Kingman State Fishing Lake and Byron Walker Wildlife Area	4,043	7 miles W of Kingman
48. La Cygne Lake and Wildlife Area	4,600	5 miles E of La Cygne Firearms restricted to shotguns and .22 caliber rifles; no high-powered rifles allowed
49. Lane Wildlife Area	42	3 miles E, 6½ N of Dighton
50. Leavenworth State Fishing Lake and Wildlife Area	200	3 miles N, 2 W of Tonganoxie
51. Logan State Fishing Lake and Wildlife Area	271	9 miles S of Winona
52. Louisburg-Middle Creek State Fishing Lake	511	7 miles S of Louisburg
53. Lovewell Wildlife Area	5,215	5 miles E, 9 N of Mankato
54. Lyon State Fishing Lake and Wildlife Area	562	5 miles W, 1 N of Reading
55. Marais des Cygnes Wildlife Area	6,699	5 miles N of Pleasanton
56. Marion Wildlife Area	9,560	2 miles S, 2 E of Durham
57. McPherson Wetlands Wildlife Area	1,470	2 miles N, 1 E of Conway Subject to change
58. Meade State Fishing Lake and Wildlife Area	420	8 miles S, 5 W of Meade
59. Melvern Wildlife Area	9,407	Vicinity of Olivet and west to near Reading Refuge closed Oct. 21–Jan. 15
60. Miami State Fishing Lake and Wildlife Area	267	8 miles E, 6 S of Osawatomie

Area Name	Acres	Location
61. Milford Wildlife Area	17,773	Tract from the SW side of Milford Dam extending up the lake to 8 miles N of Wakefield
62. Mined Land Wildlife Area	14,500	Scattered tracts throughout Crawford, Cherokee, and Labette Counties
63. Morton Wildlife Area	533	7 miles N of Elkhart (located within Cimarron National Grasslands)
64. Nebo State Fishing Lake and Wildlife Area	75	8 miles E of Holton
65. Nemaha Wildlife Area	710	1 mile E, 4 S of Seneca
66. Neosho Wildlife Area	2,246	1 mile E of St. Paul
67. Norton Wildlife Area	6,421	5 miles W, 2 S of Norton
68. Osage State Fishing Lake	480	3 miles S of Carbondale Special restrictions
69. Ottawa State Fishing Lake and Wildlife Area	611	6 miles E of Minneapolis Shotgun and archery only, Nov. 1–Mar. 31
70. Perry Wildlife Area	10,984	1½ miles S, 2 W of Stockton
71. Pottawatomie No. 1 State Fishing Lake and Wildlife Area	190	4½ miles N of Westmoreland
72. Pratt Sandhills Wildlife Area	4,757	5 miles W, 6 N of Cullison
73. Rooks State Fishing Lake and Wildlife Area	243	1½ miles S, 2 W of Stockton
74. Sand Hills State Park	800	3 miles NE of Hutchinson Hunting only by special permit
75. Scott Wildlife Area	160	15 miles N of Scott City
76. Shawnee State Fishing Lake	680	7½ miles N of Silver Lake Contact Perry Unit for special regulations
77. Sheridan Wildlife Area	458	2 miles E, 4 N of Quinter
78. Sherman State Fishing Lake and Wildlife Area	1,547	10 miles S, 2 W of Goodland No waterfowl hunting
79. Slate Creek Wildlife Area	667	6 miles S, 1½ W of Oxford

Area Name	Acres	Location
80. South Fork Wildlife Area	1,000	12½ miles NE of St. Francis May be refuge—contact Region 1 office
81. Spring River Wildlife Area	424	3 miles E, ¼ N of Crestline
82. St. Francis Wildlife Area	480	2 miles S, 2½ W of St. Francis
83. Texas Lake Wildlife Area	1,040	4 miles W, 1 N of Cullison
84. Toronto Wildlife Area	4,766	3 miles NW of Toronto
85. Tuttle Creek Wildlife Area	12,200	Extending upriver from Randolph to Blue Rapids
86. Washington State Fishing Lake and Wildlife Area	442	7 miles N, 3 W of Washington
87. Webster Wildlife Area	8,018	8 miles W of Stockton
88. Wilson State Fishing Lake and Wildlife Area	90	1 mile S of Buffalo
89. Wilson Wildlife Area	8,039	7 miles N of Bunker Hill
90. Woodson State Fishing Lake and Wildlife Area	3,065	5 miles E of Toronto
91. Woodston Diversion Wildlife Area	210	8 miles E of Stockton

Federal Areas

Area Name	Acres	Location
92. Cimmarron National Grasslands	108,000	Contact Resident Manager, U.S. Forest Service, Elkhart, KS
93. John Redmond Reservoir	8,972	Contact Resident Manager, Flint Hills National Wildlife Refuge, Hartford, KS, or Resident Engineer, Corps of Engineers, New Straw, KS (office at dam)
94. Kanopolis Reservoir	13,500	(11,580 acres from Oct. 1–Jan. 20) Contact Resident Engineer, Corps of Engineers, Marquette, KS (office at dam)
95. Kirwin National Wildlife Refuge	5,700	(1,751 archery only; 3,372 all species; 619 no waterfowl; no special goose hunt) Contact U.S. Fish and Wildlife Service, Kirwin National Wildlife Refuge, Kirwin, KS (office at dam)

Area Name	Acres	Location
96. Pomona Reservoir	4,500	Contact Project Manager, Corps of Engineers, Vassar, KS (office at dam)
97. Quivira National Wildlife Refuge	8,000 open to hunting	13 miles NE of Stafford. Contact Resident Manager, Quivira National Wildlife Refuge, Stafford, KS (headquarters on south side of refuge). No deer, turkey, or furbearer hunting.

* Areas with notations for special restrictions may mean restrictions on seasons, equipment, species, bag limits, special permits, or other conditions. Contact the area or unit office for more information.

Walk-In Hunting Areas

The Kansas WIHA (Walk-In Hunting Area) program began in 1995 and was modeled after a successful South Dakota walk-in hunter access program. At the onset of the program, many of the enrolled lands came from the CRP program.

Interested private land owners contact the department and propose their land for entry in the program. The land is evaluated for its wildlife habitat and hunting potential, and if found desirable the land is enrolled on an annual basis. Landowners are compensated monetarily and held safe from liability concerns by state law. Tracts must be eighty acres or larger to qualify for entry into the program. Access is available only for designated months during the hunting season. The Department provides patrols and signs for enrolled areas.

WIHA lands are restricted to foot access only. In the case of very large tracts of land, vehicles may travel on trails designated by the land owner.

The Kansas Department of Wildlife and Parks publishes an annual directory that catalogs all enrolled lands by county, complete with acreage listings and county maps. The state's 1996 directory lists 183,906 acres enrolled in the program. Currently, enrolled lands are extensive and found in most counties, statewide.

A breakdown of WIHA and Conservation Reserve Program (CRP) acres by county follows.

For More Information
Kansas Department of Wildlife and Parks
Operations Office
512 SE 25th Ave
Pratt, KS 67124-8174
316-672-5911

County	CRP Acres	WIHA Acres	No. of Landowners in WIHA program
Allen	6,377	320	3
Anderson	8,670	2,585	15
Atchison	6,061	598	2
Barber	26,837	1,302	5
Barton	25,975	2,640	8
Bourbon	20,727	1,235	6
Brown	9,337	2,080	13
Butler	6,483	1,396	7
Chase	1,512	0	0
Chautauqua	4,302	0	0
Cherokee	4,677	343	2
Cheyenne	45,090	8,340	13
Clark	44,991	160	1
Clay	23,189	1,480	7
Cloud	16,464	2,370	11
Coffey	11,099	1,535	9
Comanche	40,923	11,735	16
Cowley	7,387	0	0
Crawford	11,872	869	5
Decatur	8,329	2,660	8
Dickinson	24,964	3,467	19
Doniphan	10,900	815	4
Douglas	5,492	0	0
Edwards	47,673	4,536	16
Elk	7,746	0	0
Ellis	33,547	6,793	25
Ellsworth	29,349	2,140	6
Finney	57,232	1,740	4
Ford	49,329	1,966	9
Franklin	8,742	0	0
Geary	2,933	160	1
Gove	18,415	2,240	4
Graham	67,602	6,150	23
Grant	29,849	320	1
Gray	37,886	2,800	10
Greeley	84,774	5,703	16
Greenwood	4,862	0	0
Hamilton	126,047	8,282	14
Harper	30,864	1,599	8
Harvey	5,950	160	2
Haskell	19,164	0	0

County	CRP Acres	WIHA Acres	No. of Landowners in WIHA program
Hodgeman	27,755	3,070	17
Jackson	19,633	1,189	9
Jefferson	14,226	590	2
Jewell	26,320	1,160	5
Johnson	1,869	0	0
Kearny	70,306	2,160	5
Kingman	45,618	1,610	12
Kiowa	54,835	7,133	20
Labette	6,724	2,630	7
Lane	24,852	2,740	9
Leavenworth	5,284	0	0
Lincoln	18,829	2,240	11
Linn	25,608	960	6
Logan	32,396	6	
Lyon	21,478	670	1
McPherson	15,374	903	7
Marion	18,105	2,597	14
Marshall	22,336	5,352	18
Meade	34,804	4,120	11
Miami	10,271	0	0
Mitchell	20,905	800	5
Montgomery	3,137	0	0
Morris	6,090	2,205	8
Morton	85,964	12,720	29
Nemaha	31,932	8,139	37
Neosho	16,259	4,184	6
Ness	39,200	7,933	25
Norton	42,589	17,428	50
Osage	15,064	1,292	7
Osborne	22,145	6,408	25
Ottawa	17,399	320	1
Pawnee	58,575	14,332	51
Phillips	26,766	5,724	18
Pottawatomie	14,908	0	0
Pratt	47,381	960	6
Rawlins	12,696	1,200	6
Reno	94,055	5,364	25
Republic	14,237	3,260	11
Rice	16,591	2,801	15
Riley	4,539	760	2
Rooks	43,371	6,358	25

County	CRP Acres	WIHA Acres	No. of Landowners in WIHA program
Rush	36,899	9,580	45
Russell	52,289	6,646	33
Saline	21,868	320	2
Scott	21,791	1,788	8
Sedgwick	7,533	563	4
Seward	42,608	880	4
Shawnee	6,495	148	1
Sheridan	8,602	8,172	10
Sherman	39,047	4,720	15
Smith	21,506	6,470	18
Stafford	38,546	1,440	8
Stanton	98,842	320	2
Stevens	65,177	1,280	6
Sumner	8,040	2,600	8
Thomas	15,986	3,600	6
Trego	32,043	6,500	26
Wabaunsee	13,633	3,428	7
Wallace	67,260	8,244	22
Washington	29,870	7,265	27
Wichita	46,498	3,480	13
Wilson	10,570	0	0
Woodson	4,047	480	2
Wyandotte	170	0	0

Private Land Access

An Explanation of Kansas's Trespassing Laws

Kansas is 98-percent private land. The small percentage of public lands open to public hunting are found only after some serious map study sessions.

Kansas's 3 trespass laws are very specific. The first is a Department of Wildlife and Parks statute that applies to those trespassing illegally on lands posted with signs that specify "Written Permission Only." Land posted with such signs require 1 person within the hunting party to carry written trespass authorization from the landowner or the person managing the farming activities.

The second, more serious, violation is of the *Criminal Hunting Statute*. This pertains to property posted "No trespassing and or hunting", "No trespassing and/or hunting without permission", or lands not posted in any manner. With this statute, a law enforcement officer may accept an admission of verbal permission but will then, at the officer's discretion, verify the hunter's permission with the landowner or their agent. The minimum requirement is still verbal permission. Those individuals accessing lands without first obtaining verbal consent of the landowner or operator are in violation and subject to a more serious citation.

Third, the *Criminal Trespass Statute* is the most severe. This statute applies when a person or persons are approached in the field by a landowner or his agent and informed that they are illegally trespassing. If those individuals refuse to leave, or get argumentative, they may then be cited for criminal trespass.

In Kansas, any law enforcement officer can respond to and enforce Department of Wildlife and Parks statutes, including sheriff's deputies and personnel of the Kansas Highway Patrol or State Troopers.

The short of all this is that before entering any land, a person must either be certain that the land is public ground or speak to the landowner/operator and, depending on how the land is posted, receive verbal or written permission.

The hardest part of obtaining permission is finding the correct person to ask. Often, it may take two or three farmhouses before you find the right door to knock on. There isn't an easy answer for locating landowners. Many of the lands no longer have anyone living on them, and may be worked by adjacent farmers on a lease basis. In the case of rangelands, the owner may literally live in Topeka.

County plot maps that show land ownership are available. Although these maps are a good place to start in finding the owner of a piece of property, they will be most useful to those who live in the area and are familiar with the names of local residents. These are available through the Kansas Blue Print Company:

Kansas Blue Print Co. Inc.
1650 South Broadway/P.O. Box 793
Wichita, KS 67201-0793
316-264-9344

Asking permission.

Appendix I
The Hunting Rig

The choice of a hunting vehicle is as much a matter of personal taste as the type of shotgun a person shoots. A host of factors influence the decision and two people, given the same set of variables, will probably make radically different final choices. That being the case, I won't tell you what I think would work for another hunter, but I will tell you some of the things I found of value for myself while traveling in Kansas.

All my trips were with a 2WD truck. There were a few times when 4wd would have been nice, but with a few rare exceptions the 2WD was sufficient. The road system in Kansas is extensive and in good repair. Most of the state is divided by roads into square sections, and there was always at least one passable dirt road to get a person within walking distance of anywhere a bird might be hiding. One of my personal concerns was the large amount of freeway miles I had to drive just to get to Kansas. I needed a vehicle that could tow a dog trailer comfortably, at freeway speeds, for long distances and not cost a fortune in gasoline. I traded 4WD capability for 2WD ease of travel.

It goes without saying that the chosen vehicle should be in top mechanical condition. Things like jumper cables, a tire pressure gauge, and a basic tool kit should be standard equipment on the vehicle. I traveled with a citizen band radio for road information, for communication in case of an emergency, and to keep me awake while driving at night. Before leaving for each trip, I went to our public library and checked out a bag of books on tape. Listening to a good book can make the long miles fly past.

I also traveled with a cellular phone and was able to get reception throughout most of the state. In the western portion of Kansas, where the towns are fewer and further between, reception was sometimes limited to the areas surrounding the towns. My wife and I had an appointed time each evening when I would have the phone turned on and she could reach me. Even in some of the more remote parts of the state, she was usually able to get through.

For ease of packing and to maintain organization in the back of the truck, I used some stacking storage boxes that have two piece hinged lids. I labeled them according to content and was able to keep the right stuff in the right box. I found they stacked in the back of the campershell well, didn't slide around, and left room for other gear. When the food supply thinned down, I was able to consolidate the contents and stack one box inside of another in order to generate more room in the back of the truck.

Weather was a constant concern during the months that I visited Kansas, doubly so when I was towing a trailer. I kept a watch on the weather reports so that I didn't get into trouble. There were a few days when I had to lay low and let a storm blow over. When road conditions get bad, they can be real bad.

Vehicle Emergency Gear Checklist

_____ Communication device (C.B. radio or Cellular Phone)

_____ Flash light

_____ Road maps

_____ First aid kit

_____ Five gallons of drinkable water

_____ Food

_____ Spare tire/s

_____ Hi-lift jack

_____ Snow chains or cables

_____ Tow rope or strap

_____ Shovel

_____ Axe

_____ Leather work gloves

_____ Tools/spare parts/emergency kit

_____ Air compressor/compressed air cylinder

_____ Sleeping bag/s

_____ Matches/lighter

Appendix II
Hunting Dog Conditioning

I have seen people go to extremes in an attempt to get their dogs conditioned for the beginning of the season. Despite my best efforts, my dogs still come up short. My dogs are kenneled on gravel and run daily, yet they still go through their pads in the first month of heavy hunting.

I think the most productive method a person can use is to run his dogs as often as possible, starting in earnest two to three months before the hunting season begins. Gradually extend the dog's runs up to two hours, and use rocky ground if available. Check their feet daily, and give them a few days off if you observe any damage. My dogs wear holes through their pads when they begin hunting heavy. If their conditioning is maintained, their feet should hold up for the rest of the season. Dogs need to be in excellent condition to stand up to extended periods of hunting. They are further stressed by a long drive to Kansas, days of travel spent living in a dog crate or trailer. The most that can be expected from a soft dog is one or two days in the field.

Watch your dogs closely while hunting. Dogs can tolerate cold very well, but don't take overheating at all. If the temperature is warm, you may only want to run them an hour or two at a time, keeping them well watered. A dog can die quickly from overheating. If your dog is staggering and incoherent, you have an emergency on your hands. Don't let it get that far. If a dog gets warm, wet his belly to cool him down. Make him rest. If possible, find some water and get the dog soaking in it.

Traveling with a Dog Checklist

_____ Kennel crates

_____ Dog first aid kit

_____ Water container (five gallon with spigot)

_____ Bucket for watering dogs

_____ Dog food/bucket for feeding

_____ Tie-out cables/chain gang

_____ Leashes

_____ Record of vaccinations

_____ Certificate of good health

_____ Bells/beeper collars

_____ Pump sprayer (type used for insecticides) For use with water only, to wet down dogs, clean up after finding cowpies, and spraying out after kennel crate accidents (also good for hunters as a portable shower).

Appendix III
Hunter Conditioning
and Equipment

Just like their hunting dogs, hunters need to be in good condition to enjoy and get the most out of their Kansas bird hunt. As a hunting guide, I have seen the resulting wreckage of an ill-prepared hunter on the second morning of a three-day hunt. Often, physical pre-conditions such as bad backs, bad knees, or bad whatevers will rear their ugly heads and rob pleasure from the hunt or downright derail it.

The feet are generally the first part of the body to go: blisters, strains, and the like. Often, new or ill-fitting boots are the problem, and the hunter is left hobbled and in pain. Be sure that new boots are broken in and no longer new before leaving for the hunt. Bring along moleskin and use it to prevent blisters from occuring, or to keep them from getting worse when a blister hot spot starts.

Be realistic! If a hunter can admit that he is not quite where he wants to be conditioning-wise and starts slow, he can ease into the hunt and not destroy himself in the first hurrah. Often, with a couple of easy days in the beginning, a hunter can work into a more strenuous last half of the hunt.

I am not an authority on physical conditioning and, rather than pretend to be something I'm not, I would advise you to consult someone who is. Consult this expert months before the date of the hunt and follow his or her advice.

Appendix IV
Equipment Checklist

Upland Bird Hunting Equipment Checklist

_____ Shoulder strap style hunting vest

_____ Upland shooting coat

_____ Dog whistle

_____ Swiss army knife in belt sheath

_____ Hat

_____ Shooting gloves

_____ Short dog lead with belt clip (one lead per dog)

_____ Upland shooting boots

_____ Waterproof pullover shell/lightweight poncho

_____ Handkerchief

_____ Sunglasses/shooting glasses/ear protection

_____ Lip balm/sunscreen

_____ Small AA Mag-lite

_____ Bird knife with gut hook

_____ Cactus spine pulling kit (needle-nosed pliers & forceps)

_____ Removable shotgun sling

_____ Canteen belt

_____ Additional water containers (optional)

_____ Small white margarine cup for watering dogs

_____ *Powerbars* (athletic energy bars)

_____ Short check-cord (optional)

_____ One roll Vet-rap (dog first aid)

_____ Small pair of binoculars (optional)

_____ Bird mounting kit (optional)

_____ Small camera (optional)

_____ Compass (optional)

Waterfowl Hunting Equipment Checklist

_____ Shotgun

_____ Spare choke tubes and wrench

_____ Shells (nontoxic)

_____ Possibles bag

_____ Camouflage parka, hat, gloves, face mask

_____ Flashlight

_____ Hot thermos/lunch

_____ Binoculars

_____ Waders

_____ Decoys

_____ Calls

Dove Hunting Equipment Checklist

_____ Bird bucket (for birds and empty shells)

_____ Shooting stool (optional)

_____ Hat

_____ Sunglasses/shooting glasses/ear protection

_____ Water bucket for dog/s

_____ Drinking water for hunter

_____ Lip balm/sunscreen

_____ Handkerchief

_____ Swiss army knife in belt sheath

_____ Short dog lead with belt clip

_____ Jaegar dog lead (tie-out cable)

_____ Dog whistle

_____ Cactus spine pulling kit (needle-nosed pliers & forceps)

_____ Shooting gloves

_____ Snake chaps/gaiters/boots

_____ One roll vet-rap

_____ Plastic trash bag (for policing shooting area, cleaning birds, empty shells)

_____ Small binoculars (optional)

_____ Bird mounting kit (optional)

_____ Small camera (optional)

Hunting Supplies Checklist

_____ License and hunt proclamation

_____ Maps

_____ Guns

_____ Spare choke tubes

_____ Gun cleaning kit

_____ Shotgun shells

_____ Binoculars

_____ Game shears

_____ Ice chest/s

_____ Cook gear/stove/matches

_____ Flash lights

_____ Compass

_____ Knife

_____ Sleeping bag/s

Hunting Clothes Checklist

_____ Underwear

_____ Inner socks

_____ Outer socks

_____ T-shirts

_____ Long-sleeved canvas/chamois shirt

_____ Brush pants

_____ Hi-top leather boots

_____ Hat

_____ Bandana

_____ Shooting gloves

_____ Sunglasses/shooting glasses, ear protection

_____ Polarfleece

_____ Shell jacket

_____ Snake gear/chaps/gators/boots

_____ Rain gear

_____ Chest waders/hip waders/rubber boots

Dog First Aid Kit List

_____ Vetrap bandaging tape in assorted widths

_____ Gauze

_____ Johnson and Johnson waterproof tape

_____ 12 fl. oz. aerosol can of saline (for contact lens) to clean debris from wounds

_____ Panolog ointment

_____ Benadryl (for insect and snake bite)

_____ Aspirin

_____ Nolvasan Otic cleansing solution (for cleaning ears)

_____ Opticlear (eyewash)

_____ Wound-kote spray wound dressing

_____ Cut-Heal medication

_____ Hydrocortisone cream

_____ Wound powder

_____ Styptic pencils

_____ Ear, nose, throat med-check light

_____ Thermometer

_____ 3-inch and 6-inch tweezers

_____ Canine nail cutter

_____ Disposable razors

_____ Assorted scissors

_____ Rubber tubing (for tourniquet)

_____ Several cotton socks

_____ Tarp or sheet plastic (For carrying a bleeding dog in a vehicle)

_____ Wood dowel (for holding a dog's mouth open while pulling cactus or quills)

_____ Wire muzzle

_____ Book: _A Field Guide: Dog First Aid_ by Randy Acker, D.V.M. and Jim Fergus

_____ Notepad and pencil

Appendix V
Preparing a Bird
for Mounting in the Field

The art of taxidermy has made considerable advances in recent years. This is especially true in the realm of bird taxidermy. How you take care of your birds in the field determines the finished quality of your mounts. This crucial step is out of the control of the taxidermist. However, with a modicum of preparation, you can proceed confidently when you are holding a freshly taken bird destined for the book shelf.

Start by putting together a small kit to be carried with you in the field. Use a small plastic container, such as a plastic traveler's soap box. Throw in some cotton balls, a few wooden tooth picks, a dozen or so folded sheets of toilet paper, and a pair of panty hose.

After shooting a bird, examine it closely. First, look for pin feathers. If there are any present, you will notice them on the head directly behind the beak or bill and on the main side coverts below the bird's wing. If there are even a few pinfeathers, the specimen may not be worth mounting. By all means, save it and let your taxidermist make the decision. However, it wouldn't hurt to examine additional birds to find one with better plumage. The taxidermist can always use extra birds for spare parts.

The next step is to check for any bleeding wounds in order to prevent the taxidermist from having to wash the bird before mounting. Plug any visible wounds with cotton. Use a tooth pick as a probe to push the cotton into the holes. Now, pack the mouth and nostrils, remembering that the body is a reservoir of fluids that can drain down the neck. Make a note or take a photo of any brightly colored soft tissue parts (unfeathered areas) for the taxidermist's reference later. Fold several sheets of toilet paper and lay them between the wings and the body. Should the body bleed, this will protect the undersides of the wing from being soiled. Slide the bird head-first into the nylon stocking. Remember that feathers lay like shingles: they slide forward in the stocking smoothly, but will ruffle if you pull the bird back out the same end. The taxidermist will remove it by cutting a hole in the material at the toe and sliding the bird forward. When the specimen is all the way down, knot the nylon behind its tail. Now you are ready to slide the next one in behind it.

Place the wrapped bird in an empty game vest pocket, allow it to cool and protect it from getting wet. When you return to your vehicle, place the bird in a cool spot. At home, put it in a plastic bag to prevent freezer burn, and freeze it solid. You can safely wait several months before dropping it off at the taxidermist.

For the traveling hunter, there is the option of next-day air shipping. Provided that you can find a place to freeze the birds overnight, even a hunter on the other side of the nation can get birds to his taxidermist in good shape. Wrap the frozen birds, nylons and all, in disposable diapers. Line a shipping box with wadded newspapers. Place the birds in the middle with dry ice. Dry ice is available in some major supermarkets. Call your taxidermist to be sure someone will be there, and then ship the parcel next-day air. Be sure to contact them the next day so that a search can be instituted in the event that the parcel did not arrive.

Mounted birds are a beautiful memory of your days in the field. With just a little bit of advance preparation, you can be assured of a top-quality mount.

Appendix VI
Field Preparation
of Game Birds for the Table

Game birds make excellent table fare. They can be taken care of quickly, on the back of the tailgate at the end of the hunt, by skinning or breasting out. When time or personal preference permits, birds can be plucked for a more formal presentation.

Breasting involves taking off both wings. A pair of game shears may be necessary depending on the size of the bird. For the smaller species, the procedure can be done unaided with just a pair of bare hands. Twist the wings and pull them out at the shoulder joint. Pull the neck and head back over the bird's spine and cut or pull them off. Rip and peel the skin down over the front of the bird's breast, until a thumbnail can be worked up under the bird's breast at the point of the sternum. Lever the breast up and away from the rest of the body. Be careful not to be cut by the broken wing bones. Shears may be necessary to cut the breast free. A person can save the legs at this point and discard the rest. No gutting is necessary: everything stays intact in the body cavity.

Skinning is a similar process with the exception that once the wings and neck are removed from the body, a pair of game shears are used to make a cut straight up the back of the bird. The cut should start at the base of the neck and travel to the bird's tail button. The point of the shears can then be used to cut around the bird's rectum. With the shears, detach both legs where the feathers stop and then peel the bird's skin completely off. Spread the bird's body at the back as if opening a clam. Use the shears to scoop out the offal and the meat is ready to be rinsed and stored. Zip lock bags do a fine job of keeping the meat clean while a hunter is in transit home and the bagged meat can go straight into the freezer for prolonged storage.

It is a lot of work, but plucked birds make the prettiest presentation. If convenient, the majority of a bird's feathers can be plucked, in the field, immediately after being taken. Once the body is allowed to cool, the skin tears much more readily and makes the process more tedious than it has to be. In the field, I remove all the feathers, with the exception of the wing and tail feathers, unless the shooting is slow and I don't expect another shooting opportunity any time soon. Of course, it seems that the surest way to generate a shooting opportunity is to not be ready to take it. Get the body feathers off and use a knife with a gut hook to pull the offal. Leave the bird to cool in your game bag or on a carrying strap and finish the job after returning from the field.

When time permits, after the completion of the hunt, remove all remaining feathers. Once a bird is completely plucked, I flash singe the surface of the skin with a propane touch to remove any remnants of feathers. The meat is then ready to be washed, patted dry with a paper towel, and wrapped for storage.

Appendix VII
Kansas Information Sources

Map Sources

Kansas Blue Print Co. Inc.
1650 South Broadway/P.O. Box 793
Wichita, KS 67200-0793
316-264-9344
• This company offers county land ownership maps.

Kansas Geological Survey
University of Kansas
1930 Constant Ave
Lawrence, KS 66047-3726
785-864-3965
FAX: 785-864-5317
http://www.kgs.ukans.edu/

Kansas Department of Wildlife and Parks
512 SE 25th Ave.
Pratt, KS 67124
316-672-5911
• Public hunting area maps

U.S. Army Corps of Engineers
700 Federal Building
601 East 12th St.
Kansas City, MO 64106-2896
816-426-6816
http://www.usace.army.mil
• U.S.A.C.E. lake project maps

U.S. Fish and Wildlife Service
P.O.Box 25486
Denver Federal Center
Denver, CO 80225
303-236-8155
http://www.fws.gov
• National wildlife refuge maps

More Information Sources

Kansas Department of Wildlife and Parks
900 SW Jackson St., Suite 502
Topeka, KS 66612-1233
913-296-2281
• The Kansas Department of Wildlife and Parks mantians a web site with information relating to hunting. The address of the site is:
  http://www.ink.org/public/kdwp/Hunting/hunt.html
• The Kansas Department of Wildlife and Parks mantians a web site with information relating to state parks. The address of the site is: http://www.ink.org/public/kdwp/Parks/Parks.html

Kansas State Historical Society
6425 SW 6th Avenue
Topeka, KS 66615-1099
913-272-8681
http://history.cc.ukans.edu/heritage/kshs/kshs1.html

Kansas Outdoor Store
Kansas Department of Wildlife and Parks
512 SE 25th Ave.
Pratt, KS 67124
316-672-5911
- The Outdoor Store is run by the Department of Wildlife and Parks and offers a selection of books and merchandise that relate to the flora and fauna of the state. A brochure of products and merchandise is available upon request.

Kansas Travel and Tourism
700 SW Harrison St., Suite 1300
Topeka, KS 66603-3712
800-252-6727
http://kicin.cecase.ukans.edu/kdoch/html/tour1.html

U.S. Army Corps of Engineers
700 Federal Building
601 East 12th St.
Kansas City, MO 64106-2896
816-426-6816
http://www.usace.army.mil

U.S. Fish and Wildlife Service
P.O.Box 25486
Denver Federal Center
Denver, CO 80225
303-236-8155
http://www.fws.gov

Federal Lands and Refuges

Cimarron National Grasslands
U.S. Forest Service
242 Highway 56 East, P.O.Box 300
Elkhart, KS 67950
316-697-4621
http://www.fs.fed.us

Flint Hills National Wildlife Refuge
P.O.Box 128
Hartford, KS 66854
316-392-5553

Kanopolis Reservoir
U.S. Army Corps of Engineers
Kanopolis Project Office
105 Riverside Dr.
Marquette, KS 67464
913-546-2294

Kirwin National Wildlife Refuge
R.R. 1, Box 103
Kirwin, KS 67644
913-543-6673

Pomona Reservoir
U.S. Army Corps of Engineers
Pomona Project Office
5260 Pomona Dam Rd.
Vassar, KS 66543
913-453-2202

Quivira National Wildlife Refuge
R.R. 3, Box 48A
Stafford, KS 67578
316-486-2393

Wildlife Area Offices

Cedar Bluff State Park: 913-726-3212
Cheney State Park: 316-542-3664
Cheyenne Bottoms: 316-793-7730
Clinton State Park: 913-842-8562
Council Grove WA: 316-767-5900
Crawford State Park: 316-362-3671
Eisenhower State Park: 913-528-4102
El Dorado State Park: 316-327180
Elk City State Park: 316-336295
Glen Elder State Park: 913-545-3345
Hillsdale State Park: 913-783-4507
Kanopolis State Park: 913-546-2565
Lovewell State Park: 913-753-4971
Marais des Cygnes WA: 913-352-8941
Meade State Park: 316-873-2572
Milford State Park: 913-283-3014
Mined Land WA: 316-233173
Perry State Park: 913-246-3449
Scott State Park: 316-872-2061
Toronto/Fall River: 316-637-2213
Tuttle Creek State Park: 913-539-7941

Pomona State Park: 913-828-4933
Prairie Dog State Park: 913-877-2953
Webster State Park: 913-425-6775
Wilson State Park: 913-658-2465

Kansas Department of Wildlife and Parks Offices

Office of the Secretary
900 Southwest Jackson Suite 502
Topeka, Kansas 66612-1233
913-296-2281

Operations Office
512 Southeast 25th Avenue
Pratt, Kansas 67124-8174
316-672-5911

Kansas City Office
14639 West 95th
Lenexa, Kansas 66215-1164
913-894-9113

Emporia Investigations Office
1830 Merchant
Emporia, Kansas 66801525
316-342-0658

Region One
PO Box 338
U.S. 183 Bypass
Hays, Kansas 67600338
913-628-8614

Region Two
3300 Southwest 29th
Topeka, Kansas 66614-2053
913-273-6740

Region Three
808 McArtor Rd.
Dodge City, Kansas 67806024
316-227-8609

Region Four
6232 East 29th North
Wichita, Kansas 67202
316-683-8069

Region Five
1500 West 7th
PO Box 777
Chanute, Kansas 66720-0777
316-430380

For state-wide information and a list of hunting guides contact:
The Kansas Outfitters Association
1548 17th Road
Washington, KS 66968
785-325-2747

Operations Office of the Kansas Wildlife and Parks Department
512 SE 25th Ave.
Pratt, KS 67124-8174
316-672-5911

For state wide information on shooting preserves contact:
The Kansas Sport Hunting Association
P.O. Box 174
Tipton, KS 67485
913-373-4965

Appendix VIII
Recommended
Product Sources

Clothing & Equipment

Orvis Patagonia
Historic Route 7A
Manchester, VT 05254
800-548-9548

Orvis Patagonia
8550 White Fir Street
Reno, Nevada 89533
800-638-6464

Simms
101 Evergreen Drive
Bozeman, MT 59772
406-585-3557

Cabela's
One Cabela Drive
Sidney, Nebraska 69160
800-237-4444

Redhead
1935 South Campbell
Springfield, Missouri 65898-0300
888-733-4323
http://www.basspro.com

Filson
C.C. Filson Company
PO Box 34020
Seattle, Washington 98124
800-624-0201
206-624-4437
FAX: 206-624-4539

L.L. Bean, Inc.
Freeport, Maine 04033
800-224221

Stafford's
808 Smith Ave.
PO Box 2055
Thomasville, Georgia 31799-2055
800-826-0948

Waterfowler's Supplies

Herter's
PO Box 1819
Burnsville, MN 55337-0499
800-654-3825
FAX: 612-894-0083
http://www.herters.com

Outlaw Companies
624 North Fancher Rd.
Spokane, Washington 99219
800-OUTLAWS or 800-653-3269

Tidewater Specialities
PO Box 158
Wye Mills, Maryland 21679
800-535-1314
FAX: 410-364-5215

Knutson's
164 Wamplers Lake Road
PO Box 457
Brooklyn, Michigan 49230-0457
800-248-9318
FAX: 517-592-3249

Woods Calls, Inc.
PO Box 29434
Lincoln, Nebraska 68529
402-466-8688
800-336-5197

Dog Supplies

Foster & Smith
2253 Airpark Rd.
PO Box 100
Rhinelander, Wisconsin 54500-0100
800-826-7203

Dunn's
PO Box 509
Grand Junction, Tennessee 38039-0509
800-353-8621
FAX: 612-894-0083

Happy Jack
PO Box 475
Highway 258
Snow Hill, North Carolina 28580
800-326-JACK

Timothy's
PO Box 8300
Little Rock, Arkansas 72222
800-762-7049

R. C. Steele
1989 Transit Way
PO Box 190
Brockport, New York 14420-0910
800-872-3773

Veterinary Supplies

Foster & Smith
2253 Airpark Rd.
PO Box 100
Rhinelander, Wisconsin 54500-0100
800-826-7203

KV Vet Supply Company
3190 North Road
PO Box 245
David City, Nebraska 68632
800-423-8211

Jeffers Pet Catalog
PO Box 948
West Plains, Missouri 65775-0948
800-533-3377

Recommended Reading

General Information

• *Kansas Atlas & Gazetteer.* DeLorme Mapping. Freeport, ME: DeLorme Mapping, 1997.

An Illustrated Guide to Endangered or Threatened Species in Kansas. Joseph T. Collins, et al. Lawrence, KS: University Press of Kansas, 1995.

The Audubon Society Field Guide to North American Birds (Western Region). Miklos D. F. Udvardy. New York: Knopf, 1977.

Birds of Cimarron National Grassland. Ted T. Cable. USDA Forest Service, General Technical Report RM-GTR-281, 1996.

Birds in Kansas: Volume 1. Max C. Thompson & Charles Ely. Lawrence, KS: University of Kansas Museum of Natural History, 1989.

• *Fool Hen Blues.* E. Donnall Thomas. Gallatin Gateway, MT: Wilderness Adventures Press, 1994.

• *Good Guns Again.* Stephen Bodio. Gallatin Gateway, MT: Wilderness Adventures Press, 1994.

• *A Hunter's Road.* Jim Fergus. New York: Henry Holt and Company, 1992.

• *Meditations on Hunting.* José Ortega y Gasset, trans. Howard B. Wescott. Gallatin Gateway, MT: Wilderness Adventures Press, 1995.

North American Game Birds of Upland and Shoreline. Paul A. Johnsgard. Lincoln, NE: University of Nebraska Press, 1975.

Watching Kansas Wildlife: A Guide to 101 Sites. Bob Gress and George Potts. Lawrence, KS: University Press of Kansas, 1993.

Upland Bird Hunting

• *Pheasants of the Mind: A Hunter's Search for a Mythic Bird.* Datus C. Proper. New York: Prentice Hall Press, 1990.

Upland Game Birds. Dick Sternberg. Minnetonka, MN: Cy DeCosse Inc., 1995.

• *Western Wings: Hunting Upland Birds on the Northern Plains.* Ben O. Williams. Gallatin Gateway, MT: Wilderness Adventures Press, 1998.

• *Wingshooter's Guide to Arizona: Upland Birds and Waterfowl.* William "Web" Parton, Gallatin Gateway, MT: Wilderness Adventures Press, 1996.

• *Wingshooter's Guide to Iowa: Upland Birds and Waterfowl.* Larry Brown. Gallatin Gateway, MT: Wilderness Adventures Press, 1998.

• *Wingshooter's Guide to Idaho: Upland Birds and Waterfowl.* Ken Retallic and Rocky Barker. Gallatin Gateway, MT: Wilderness Adventures Press, 1997.

• *Wingshooter's Guide to Montana: Upland Birds and Waterfowl.* Chuck Johnson and Ben O. Williams. Gallatin Gateway, MT: Wilderness Adventures Press, 1995.

• *Wingshooter's Guide to North Dakota: Upland Birds and Waterfowl.* Chuck Johnson. Gallatin Gateway, MT: Wilderness Adventures Press, 1997.

• *Wingshooter's Guide to South Dakota: Upland Birds and Waterfowl.* Ben O. Williams and Chuck Johnson. Gallatin Gateway, MT: Wilderness Adventures Press, 1996.

Waterfowling Books

American Duck, Goose & Brant Shooting. Dr. William Bruette. New York City: G. Howard Watt, 1929.

• *American Duck Shooting.* George Bird Grinnell. Harrisburg, PA: Stackpole Books, 1991.

• *Duck Decoys and How to Rig Them.* Ralf Coykendall. New York: Lyons & Burford, 1983. *Duck Shooting along the Atlantic Tidewater.* Eugene V. Connett. New York City: Bonanza Books, 1947.

• *Waterfowling Horizons: Shooting Ducks and Geese in the Twenty-first Century.* Christopher S. Smith and Jason A. Smith. Gallatin Gateway, MT: Wilderness Adventures Press, 1997.

Gun Dogs

• *Best Way to Train your Gun Dog.* Bill Tarrant. New York: David McKay Company, Inc., 1977.

• *Gun Dogs and Bird Dogs: A Charley Waterman Reader.* Charles F. Waterman. South Hamilton, MA: GSJ Press, 1986.

• *Hey Pup, Fetch It Up! The Complete Retriever Training Book.* Bill Tarrant. Sedona, AZ: Sedona Publishing Company, 1979.

• *Tarrant Trains Gun Dogs: Humane Way to Get Top Results.* Bill Tarrant. Harrisburg, PA: Stackpole Books, 1989.

• *Training the Versatile Retriever to Hunt Upland Birds.* Bill Tarrant. Gallatin Gateway, MT: Wilderness Adventures Press, 1996.

• *A Field Guide: Dog First Aid.* Randy Acker, D.V.M., and Jim Fergus. Gallatin Gateway, MT: Wilderness Adventures Press, 1994.

• Denotes titles available from Wilderness Adventures

Index

WILDERNESS ADVENTURES
GUIDE SERIES

If you would like to order additional copies of this book or our other Wilderness Adventures Press guidebooks, please fill out the order form below or call **800-925-3339** or **fax 800-390-7558.** Visit our website for a listing of over 2500 sporting books—the largest online: **www.wildadv.com**

Mail to: Wilderness Adventures Press, P.O. Box 627, Gallatin Gateway, MT 59730

☐ **Please send me your quarterly catalog on hunting and fishing books.**

Ship to:

Name _____

Address _____

City _____ State_____ Zip_____

Home Phone_____ Work Phone_____

Payment: ☐ Check ☐ Visa ☐ Mastercard ☐ Discover ☐ American Express

Card Number _____ Expiration Date_____

Qty	Title of Book and Author	Price	Total
	Wingshooter's Guide to Iowa	$26.95	
	Wingshooter's Guide to Montana	$26.00	
	Wingshooter's Guide to South Dakota	$26.95	
	Wingshooter's Guide to North Dakota	$26.95	
	Wingshooter's Guide to Arizona	$26.95	
	Wingshooter's Guide to Idaho	$26.95	
	Flyfisher's Guide to Colorado	$26.95	
	Flyfisher's Guide to Idaho	$26.95	
	Flyfisher's Guide to Montana	$26.95	
	Flyfisher's Guide to Northern California	$26.95	
	Flyfisher's Guide to Wyoming	$26.95	
	Total Order + shipping & handling		

**Shipping and handling: $4.00 for first book,
$2.50 per additional book, up to $11.50 maximum**

NOTES